[*Praise*]

"Products today aren't designed like they were even ⌐
ago. This breezy, easy-to-read guide walks you throu First edition.
product design as it's practiced in the field by some of today's best
designers. Both an overview of the field and a handy how-to guide,
this book has something for everyone working to make products
people love."

DAN SAFFER, AUTHOR OF *MICROINTERACTIONS*

"In a quickly changing space, Scott Hurff shares an informed,
actionable perspective."

RANDY J. HUNT, VP DESIGN, ETSY

"Scott's new book connects the world of fast, startup-driven,
design-for-mobile thinking with the traditional world of comparatively
slower, "do-it-the-right-way" design and brand thinking. The new
world of digital product design is interminably evolving, so this book
is a great 2015 snapshot of the way modern digital designers needs
to act and behave as more like explorers rather than conservators.
Keep in mind that in 2016, 2017, and beyond, however, we should
expect even more change to the field of digital product design—so
I look forward to the future editions of Scott's work as a historian
of sorts in a rapidly evolving present-tense that gets old the very
moment it ships."

**JOHN MAEDA, DESIGN PARTNER AT KLEINER PERKINS
CAUFIELD & BYERS**

"A thoughtful and charming guidebook for making great things."

SCOTT BERKUN, AUTHOR OF *THE MYTHS OF INNOVATION*

Designing Products People Love

How Great Designers Create Successful Products

Scott Hurff

 Beijing · Boston · Farnham · Sebastopol · Tokyo

Designing Products People Love
by Scott Hurff

Published by O'Reilly Media, Inc., 1005 Gravenstein Highway North, Sebastopol, CA 95472.

O'Reilly books may be purchased for educational, business, or sales promotional use. Online editions are also available for most titles (*safaribooksonline.com*). For more information, contact our corporate/institutional sales department: (800) 998-9938 or *corporate@oreilly.com*.

Acquisitions Editor: Mary Treseler
Editor: Angela Rufino
Production Editor: Kristen Brown
Proofreader: Rachel Monaghan
Indexer: Bob Pfahler

Cover Designer: Randy Comer
Interior Designers: Ron Bilodeau and Monica Kamsvaag
Illustrator: Rebecca Demarest
Compositor: Kristen Brown

December 2015: First Edition.

Revision History for the First Edition:

2015-12-08   First release

See *http://oreilly.com/catalog/errata.csp?isbn=0636920038917* for release details.

[Contents]

Acknowledgments

This book is almost two years in the making and was made possible by a countless number of people.

My heartfelt gratitude to Mary and Angela for introducing me into the O'Reilly family and for keeping me on deadline. Instrumental in both the early days and the daily grind of writing was Cynthia. Many thanks to Jeff, Mike (x2), Chris, Dan G., Brian, Jason C., Noah, Anton, Amy, Alex, Andrew, Dan S., John, Hannah, and Jason, who read early drafts. You each got me into the mindset and across the finish line. I'm also grateful for every person who agreed to be interviewed for the book—your knowledge will echo for a long while. And, finally, a huge thanks to Mom and Dad for hammering home the importance of writing from my youngest days.

Products Are for Customers

PRODUCT DESIGN IS NOT JUST ABOUT *shipping.*

It's not just about being original.

It's not just about making things beautiful or stylish.

And it's not just about making something easy to use.

Product design is about creating something that's right for your customer by completely understanding what they feel, what they think, and what they want.

But, ultimately, designing a product means *designing something that sells.*

Because that's why a product exists in the first place.

This isn't a new notion. "The purpose of the enterprise is to create a customer," wrote legendary organizational expert Peter Drucker in *The Practice of Management.** And he wrote that almost 50 years ago.

Maybe you're reading this book because you or your team have been stuck in the ship-pivot-ship loop of death, and can't figure out how to get out of it.

Perhaps you're reading this book because your team wants more "design-minded solutions," and you're in an ancillary design role.

Or you might've been intrigued by the money. It's hard not to be. The number of designer-led companies that have raised money or have been acquired in the past few years is only rising.†

---

* Peter Drucker, *The Practice of Management* (New York: Harper Business, 1993), 317.

† *http://www.kpcb.com/blog/design-in-tech-report-2015*

Whether it's for survival, adaptation, or vanity—or none of the above—I'm glad you're here.

You're going to learn how to ignore all of the noise.

You're going to learn how to create products that *sell*.

Creating a successful digital product is the ultimate realization of creativity, hard work, and leadership. We too easily forget that products are made *by* people, *for* people.

The result is that the *how* of building a product has become mystified, detached from the *what* of a product.

That's because the way that successful products are built is a competitive advantage for all companies, from the largest—like Facebook and LinkedIn—to the smallest up-and-coming startups you haven't even heard of yet.

Overnight successes are rare. Successful products aren't happy accidents, as we're led to believe. And most of them are too often made sloppily and without good practices.

So how do you create a product that sells?

I'll promise you that it doesn't begin with devouring biographies of mythologized figures, repeating the phrase "if you build it, they will come," or thinking that *if we just get it out there, we'll know what to build next.*

Let's talk about why this is the book for you.

Why This Book Is for You

The dopamine rush is as clear as yesterday.

I was a founding team member of a Kleiner Perkins–backed online video startup, leading product.

And we were adding one million users a day.

These stats seemed to validate that people loved the product I helped to create.

But the party didn't last. We rode a wave of hope to over 20 million registrations until traffic died, interest waned, and the product was shut down in November 2013.

I wondered why it happened. How over 20 million people were convinced to sign up for something they didn't want. And what led us to believe that this was real success.

The experience left me hungry to know how the best products are made. It led me to examine how product designers work, how they create products people want, crave, can't live without—and how they do it over and over again.

One might chalk up this anecdote to not achieving the exalted "product/market fit," after which one might encourage me to "fail faster" by "pivoting" into a new idea. After that, we'd then turn around and "validate" the idea and tweak accordingly.

But this process also led me to wonder—what if this framework was flawed? What if we didn't have to launch products with prayer and carefully planned viral loops, only to keep praying as we dove into the next pivot?

This Book Is For You

This book is written for anyone who wants to be better at creating digital products. Because when we learn to improve the *how* of doing things, everybody benefits when we put it into practice.

My goal is to show you how to create successful digital products, regardless of the industry in which you operate. I've interviewed more than 30 product leaders, studied the history of how products came to be made, and pulled out the repeatable processes and strategies they used to win.

You'll find my interviews with these experienced product designers at the end of each chapter. All, however, have been truncated for brevity. You'll be able to read all interviews in their entirety at *http://scotthurff. com/dppl/interviews*.

In these Q&A sessions, you'll learn about how these accomplished product designers work. How they grind through creative dry spells. Where they seek inspiration, and how they work through product challenges with their teams. And better yet, you'll learn the repeatable processes they use to churn out products that people use again and again.

At the end, you'll see how products like Medium, Twitter, and Squarespace—along with *many* others—are created and improved. Their workflows and processes are here for you to dissect, and to apply immediately.

We'll see how they come up with early gems of product ideas, the methods they use to gut-check those gems, and how this research affects the actual product design.

Then, we'll step into their heads as they design, prototype, iterate, and test the actual product. We'll hear about how they gather customer feedback and use it to stack the odds in their favor when they finally launch.

That being said, the techniques in this book are useful for anyone, whether you're a solo entrepreneur, startup worker, or a member of a larger organization experiencing any of the following challenges:

- Products built with a head-in-the-clouds mentality that results in a launch that finds no customers.

- Projects that are plagued by last-minute changes, not-fully-considered flows, or technology that can't deliver on the product's promise.

- Customers who are confused about how to use a product that was just launched, despite it seeming "obvious" to the team.

- Fear that you're falling behind, not learning fast enough, and not offering enough creative ideas.

- An ability to recognize "good design," but a tendency to get caught up in the details, second-guessing design decisions and forgetting the entire purpose of the product: putting the customer first, not second to the user interface convention of the moment.

When you're finished with this book, my goal is for you to take away the following:

- Understand how the products you use on a daily basis came to life. Jump inside the minds of highly effective product designers in top companies to learn how great products get made. Apply these workflows immediately to your own.

- Learn simpler ways of discovering and interpreting customer pain or joy, and how you can use this as a vision to guide your team through the messy product creation process.

- Take away the pain of designing interfaces across different form factors—mobile, desktop, tablet, web, TV, cars—by learning about user flow, epicenter design, state awareness, and primary actions.

- Discover the latest psychological research being used by product designers to create habit-forming and emotionally engaging experiences.

I'm not going to pretend that everything in this book is novel, original, or has never been done before. That's, in fact, the point. The reason this book exists is because I wanted to find product designers actually doing the work. They're the ones who've taken the various popular models and methods and actually turned them into something real. Here, you'll read about how the *real* work is done.

What's in the Book

Creating a new product is like taking a photo.

The picture you want to capture is right in front of you, but you're not sure which zoom setting will bring your subject's crisp lines, sharp angles, and stark detail into the frame. So you turn the lens back and forth, gradually settling on the zoom that's right for the lens and for the photo.

Of course, the subject in front of you could be moving—smiles and facial expressions, leaves blowing in the wind, wildlife running out of frame. So you do your best to capture the best possible story in one frame, adapting to the realities on the ground.

Building a product has similar challenges. This is a process that starts out with a clear goal and stated target, but will probably be forced to adapt its angle and scope along the way. Even so, you try to find the best possible solution to meet your goals and satisfy a customer.

But we're not the first ones to face the challenges of creating products for other human beings. That's why we're going to examine the past so we can design the future.

THE PRODUCT CREATION MODEL

The process of creating a product is messy. But I've tried to break this complex creation process down into four basic steps. These steps provide the framework for the chapters in this book (Figure P-1):

1. Hunt and synthesize

2. Build

3. Test and level up

4. Launch, monitor, and start over

FIGURE P-1

The product creation model captures the four basic steps of creating a product, despite it being a messy process.

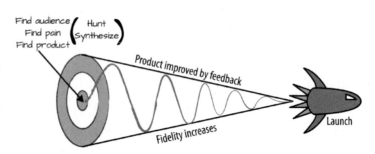

You'll be seeing this a lot throughout the book, so let's explore what it means for a second.

Hunt and synthesize

Products begin and end with the pain and joy of your customers. Coming up with product ideas that'll work is really the search for these two traits in your target audience. Doing the hard, laborious, unforgiving work of searching for pain and joy among your target audience guarantees you'll discover a need that is being underfulfilled or overlooked by your competitors.

In **Chapter 1**, you'll trace the origins of modern digital product design to the 20th century's earliest pioneers of product creation: Lillian Gilbreth, Henry Dreyfuss, and Neil McElroy. Each conducted painstaking, extensive customer research in the field and used it to shape the products they made.

In **Chapter 2**, you'll learn why the act of uncovering people's pain is at the source of product success. You'll discover how to analyze customers in their natural habitats, and learn about the Pain Matrix, which helps you understand how different types of products create a variety of emotional responses in their customers.

The next step is to take this research and to make it consumable by your team. You'll need to convince them of the right path, so in **Chapter 3**, you'll discover how to rally people around your cause while deciding what product to build. Who's in the room together? How much do they know about the pains you've found? What evidence should you bring to the table? And how do you frame the discussion? Here, you'll learn how to home in on the customer's need as a foundation, and guide the process by which a product is built upon this foundation. You'll see how the findings of your customer research should be vetted with your team, learn meeting techniques that get results, and discover how to keep people on task and engaged after the first meeting is over.

Build

Don't design the logo first. Don't design the marketing site first. Design the product's interface first.

Designing the product's interface starts with actually writing the interface, creating and analyzing user flows, building prototypes to externalize your ideas, and evolving the interface on top of the prototype. As you approach product launch, this phase will bring your product more into focus as fidelity increases from testing feedback.

Mapping out every screen with the prewritten copy helps identify the major problems of user flows early on. It also requires you to think ahead about what types of data are required and when, forcing you to build data collection steps into these flows. This is what we'll examine in **Chapter 4**, where we'll also explore the various techniques product designers use for creating user flows. Sketching? Wireframing? How do you express each possible state? The takeaway is that there's no one perfect way to do this. The goal is, as a famous stormtrooper once said, to "move along now," and get something working as quickly as possible without having to juggle all of the product's variables in your head. Clarity and communication are paramount.

Product design thrives on the power of prototyping and externalizing the ideas in your head to visuals for your team, clients, and potential customers. You'll learn about this in **Chapter 5**. The importance of this early lower-fidelity work increases as we enter this next phase of the design process. Your earlier investment in this foundation serves as a guide for what you'll be doing next. Once the copywriting has been roughed out and the user flows mapped, the goal in this phase should be to get something working as quickly as possible—*working* being the operative word.

Chapter 6 examines the mechanics of interface design. You'll learn about the five base states of every product's screen and how to design for them, while incorporating essential user interface principles. Here, you'll also come to understand the delicate transition that occurs when moving from a rough prototype and into more high-fidelity screens. Next, you'll see what it takes to design across different form factors—mobile, web, desktop, TV, watch—and how to optimize for human hands.

But simulated prototypes and static mock-ups aren't the only things that make up a user interface and create memorable product experiences. **Chapter 7** will help you tap into the psychology of the experience. We're all human and we're not immune to emotion. How can products tap into that emotion? How can emotion be used to create powerful feedback loops that draw your customers into the experience, and keep them coming back for more?

You'll also learn why transitions, animations, personality, and positive reinforcement are essential to the psychological impact of your product. And you'll see the power of infusing your product with personality and the various ways that this personality can shine through (copywriting, characters, art, inside jokes). You'll also learn how to design transitions and animations that match the personality of your product. Finally, you'll see why it's essential to examine your product's flows to create powerful feedback and engagement loops. Beyond alleviating your customer's pain, how do you make people want to use your product? What psychological underpinnings should you keep in mind?

Test and level up

Creating a product is a long road of refinement before each release. And refinement comes from real feedback and critiques of prototypes of various levels of fidelity—from your team, friends, family, outside beta testers, or even customers. You'll learn in **Chapter 8** how to take this feedback—good and bad—in the gut and soldier on. This is where we examine the practical aspects of gathering this feedback and how to interpret it. You'll also learn the early warning signs that you're building the wrong product, and understand the role of feedback in "leveling up" your product.

Launch, monitor, and start over

How do you know when to ship? How do you prepare for launch? **Chapter 9** shows you why it's essential now that you take special care of every aspect of your product at this stage. You're the "COE" (chief of everything) of your product. You need to know how it works, what stage it's in, what issues are open, and what's next at all times. And your responsibility doesn't end once the product has shipped.

Here you'll see how to combat the cult of "minimum viable product" and how quickly you've built something versus the quality and efficiency of the product. We'll contrast this with the notion of "minimum lovable products"—the point where a product is capable of being accepted by your customers either as a problem solver or bringer of joy—but with the understanding that it's not without flaws.

Finally, you'll learn what things to monitor after launch, and how to stay both sane and creative in the trough of despair.

I can't give you a recipe for how to make a successful product or satisfy a customer, because building a product depends on a multitude of factors—the market you're in, the people with whom you work, and the inherent biases you or your team might have.

What we can do together, though, is explore examples of successful work being done, while providing both frameworks and principles you can bring into your own work life.

Rather than be a simple series of do's and don'ts, I want to take you on a journey through the creation of a product through the eyes of experienced product designers.

How to Use This Book

A short note before we begin: at the end of each chapter, you'll find three items.

First, I'll recap what you just read in bite-sized bits. Copying and pasting these into a document, writing them down in a Moleskine, or posting them on your social network of choice will help you to remember what you just read and help you return to your favorite passages at a future date.

Second, the "Do This Now" sections will help you to implement what you read into your own process.

Third, each chapter concludes with a transcript of interviews I conducted with experienced product designers (you're reading a preface, so they'll start with the next chapter). Each interview fits within the theme of the chapter. My hope is that you'll be able to understand the background, motivations, and techniques of the individual product designers who've helped form the thinking behind this book.

So, what's next?

We'll examine why successful products start with observing what real people do—*not* what you *think* they do. We'll then explore time-tested techniques for figuring out what your potential customers really want.

Let's begin.

Shareable Notes

- *How* products get made is a competitive advantage for all companies.

- Most products, both successful and unsuccessful, are too often made sloppily and without good practices. The biggest offender? Believing that technology is special, and that we can ignore time-tested product-building practices simply because distribution and creation are cheaper.

- The proliferation of connectivity, mobile devices, and cheap technology is making design more valuable than ever.

- The product creation process has four phases: hunt and synthesize; build; test and level up; launch, monitor, and start over.

Do This Now

Read the next chapter!

Why Products Exist

What's Product Design?

"WHAT IS PRODUCT DESIGN?"

"What does a product designer do?"

"What's the difference between a product designer and a product manager?"

The interest in what product design is and what it does has surged in recent years. Now, more than ever, those of us working in—or wanting to work in—technology have become more curious about what product design is capable of and what it even is.

That's because we need something bigger to describe the responsibilities placed on product teams. As technology continues to force its way into the lives of the global population, the implications of how a product is designed can put not only entire businesses at stake, but the lives of our customers as well.

But product design remains a difficult concept to grasp, even by people who are actually doing the work.

It's fascinating to see the wide range of responses among the product designers I interviewed. Here's how they describe what they do.

Josh Brewer, former principal designer at Twitter:

Product designers are people who have a set of knowledge that's broader. They may be very deep in one or two areas, but they have an understanding of the entire process of bringing a product to life. You have to have a pretty decent domain expertise across things.

Nathan Kontny, CEO of Highrise:

I think product design is becoming more and more this search for friction people have getting [a] task done. As a product designer, I'm trying to really understand a task people have and look at the steps people have doing that task. Then, trying to figure out where I can start removing some of those steps. Is it combining some of those steps? Is it removing some of the steps? Often, I'm finding just removing one step can make a big difference in making a product save people time.

Ryan Hoover, founder of Product Hunt:

[Product design] is a more comprehensive view of what the product is that you're trying to achieve or solve, and how do we solve that as efficiently and easily as possible for the user. It's more of a comprehensive view of "how do we craft an experience and solution to meet that particular need?" It involves, I believe, more user psychology and understanding of how to build an interface that's useful. And how you communicate from a marketing perspective what that value proposition is.

Keenan Cummings, product designer at Airbnb, Yahoo!, and Days:

Product design is about understanding people. We have to get outside our own heads and that means tearing down a fortress of assumptions that keep us feeling comfortable in the world. You have to constantly challenge how the world looks from your cozy spot in it. People will always surprise you. The only assumption I allow myself to entertain freely was something I read in The Internet and Everyone *by John Chris Jones: "Design everything on the assumption that people are not heartless or stupid but marvelously capable, given the chance."*

But that is merely the observation part. Discovering and understanding motivations is a process of empathy. This is what I was referring to when I said designers have a leg up in learning product design. Design really is just a practice of empathy. It is about synthesizing culture and movements of ideas and distilling that into something interesting. Designers do this without thinking. They work with the intent to spread ideas. And they are good at making things that are spreadable. That comes from empathy. They get outside their own frame of reference so they can make something that touches the masses.

And "taste" kills empathy. Taste is when you've amassed enough of those cultural influences that you start to believe the ideas and the cultural synthesis come from within. The moment that happens you stop observing. You stop absorbing the influences because you see yourself as the source. It's subtle, easy to miss. But slowly your source material narrows, your resources diminish, and you are left to repeat yourself. Culture goes on, dynamic and ever changing, and you are left with the same material to chew on. This is where "taste" leads you.

Ryan Scherf, product designer at Quirky:

It's creating something that people want to use. As product designers, part of our job is to create something that's simple, something that can be motivational at times. Something that's emotional. It evokes emotion for us. And, ultimately, it has to meet expectations. [Without this], you're not going to make it.

Sahil Lavingia, founder and CEO of Gumroad, former product designer at Pinterest:

Product design is less about building a company, or raising money, or revenue or profit. It's really just about identifying the problem and how to solve it. If these are the thirty things we could do that could solve this problem, which one solves it the best way?

I like the phrase "product design" because it's very physical. I always use the example of a cup. A well-designed cup is not a cup that you look at and say, "wow, that's a sexy cup." A good cup is something that does its job. It holds coffee well or whatever. That means maybe the material it's using prevents the cup from transferring heat to burn your hand, or there's no hole in the bottom so the coffee doesn't fall out. Typically, those are the attributes of a well-designed product, or a well-designed cup.

Applying that to software means, "what is this thing trying to do?" What is its equivalent of holding liquid, and how do we design it? How do we choose the proper attributes of this product to do that, within whatever constraints we have? The best coffee cup might cost $8,000 to make because it's made of this crazy material that's only mined on the moon, [but that's not feasible]. That's what I think product design is.

It's clear that the definition of product design shifts slightly with every new company and challenge. In some places, product designers might need to learn to write code to bring a product to life. In others, a deep understanding of a customer's psychology is a critical ingredient.

This just shows that product design is the synthesis of different methodologies being pulled together, piece by piece. There's not just one job involved. And the demand for this type of person is only getting stronger.

But this isn't the first time that such demands have been placed on those designing products. Digital products aren't special, and they don't have any special properties that imply designers can break the basic rules of designing for humans.

We learn not only from new experiences, but by studying the past. Let's learn more about product design by understanding the work of those who came before us.

Product Design's Heritage

Five years. Three products. $10 million.

During my ~60 months at a venture-backed startup, my team and I built a new product concept every eight months, on average. And with those eight months came a new target audience, a complete rebranding, and a "burn the ships" focus on moving ahead.

I thought that's how life at a startup just *was*. Immense uncertainty. Gut calls after asking customers what they wanted. Full faith in the Lean Startup model. Rushing to get our "minimum viable product" out the door, only to "pivot" when we couldn't find an audience.

And pivot we did.

What weren't we getting right?

I was getting beaten down and burned out. The data didn't make any sense. People were signing up and saying they loved our products...but weren't coming back. We had no idea why.

Looking for answers, I began to see the same patterns around me: slews of web and mobile apps "failing fast" while venture and angel money burned brightly. And nobody seemed to understand why, either.

As an industry, we tend to fawn over successes at the expense of learning from the failures. There's a dearth of data out there about startup deaths as compared to what we hear about the rare, unicorn-like successes. Business advice and blogs in the startup and technology realms are plagued with survivorship bias.[*]

And that's startling. Because from what we *can* gather from the past 20 years, 62 out of 100 venture capital funds failed to beat returns available from public markets.[†] Even worse, only 20 of 100 funds generated returns that beat public markets by 3 percent annually. Half of these funds began investing—prior to 1995!

You could argue that these companies just ran out of money. Or had bad timing. Or that their technology was too expensive to build.

This may be so. But every one of these scenarios has a common thread: they each failed to find enough customers to keep them alive.

So I decided to study how successful products get made. And in doing so, I realized that our ability as designers to create beautiful, obvious, and, heck, even "viral" apps that, on the surface, seemed immensely popular had no bearing on whether a product actually worked. What did the creators of Facebook know that we didn't? Why did Dropbox initially succeed despite being launched into a slew of competitors? How has Basecamp survived since 1999 as a simple project management business?

Technology isn't special, but we think it is. After all, the computer, the mobile phone, and the Internet are among the fastest-adopted technologies in history. The hopeful specter of instant distribution lingers over our heads, because, after all, it's just so *cheap* to create something these days (see Figure 1-1).

---

[*] http://blog.asmartbear.com/business-advice-plagued-by-survivor-bias.html

[†] http://www.kauffman.org/what-we-do/research/2012/05/we-have-met-the-enemy-and-he-is-us

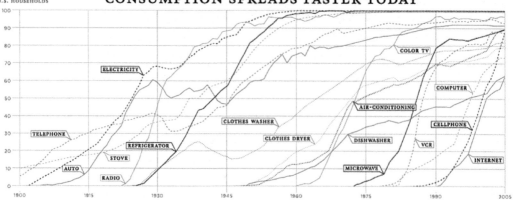

FIGURE 1-1

Historically speaking, the adoption of mobile phones is faster than even air conditioning. (Source: New York Times.*)

Why not just throw something out there and see if it works? And if it doesn't work, why not just ask people what they'd like instead?

But the rules of creating something that people want haven't changed, even if we are creating products for an industry that barely existed 20 years ago. Our judgment's been clouded. Easy distribution and a blind dedication to "customer validation" has turned the lot of us lazy or, at worst, into newly spiritual people with prayerful intent.

The practice of creating products that people want didn't just beam in like an away team in a *Star Trek* episode. It's been around for hundreds of years, a heritage enriched by many people alongside the path of an ever-maturing society.

You want to design the product of the future? You'd better know your design history.

So, what if I told you that we can trace how to create innovative, human-centered products to the 1920s, when a woman who couldn't cook reinvented the modern kitchen?

Unless there's a DeLorean and a crazy, wide-eyed scientist involved, you probably wouldn't believe me. But let me take you back.

---

* *http://nyti.ms/1GJQTfm*

Lillian and Frank Gilbreth: Revolutionizing Industries Through Observation

It's 1924. Lillian Gilbreth's husband, Frank, has just died. Together, they'd completely revolutionized the study of how people worked.

Picture this: you're a factory worker and two strangers ask you to attach mini lights to your fingers. Not only do they make you look like some perverted character from *Edward Scissorhands*, but they want to *film* you, with said fingerlights, with some newfangled, expensive camera. There's no catch. You just do what you do every day at work.

This was the Gilbreths' pioneering creation: using what they called "motion studies" to analyze workers' movements in slow motion.[†] With lights attached to their subjects' fingers, the Gilbreths were able to capture the exact motions workers took to perform their jobs while recording them with a motion picture camera (Figure 1-2).[‡, §]

FIGURE 1-2

An example of the Gilbreths' pioneering research. Called motion studies, they were used to research how workers performed their jobs to improve efficiency.

---

† http://www.moma.org/interactives/exhibitions/2010/counter_space/the_new_kitchen

‡ http://americanhistory.si.edu/ontime/saving/kitchen.html

§ http://blog.abegong.com/2014/03/therbligs-for-data-science.html

The point? To improve the effectiveness and efficiency of how people worked. Each observed movement was broken down into what the Gilbreths called "therbligs" (the reverse of *Gilbreth*)—hieroglyphic-like symbols that they used to document a workflow—to determine the best way to get a job done (Figure 1-3).* The end result? Making something happen with the least amount of effort in the least amount of time.

⊂⊃	**SEARCH**	0	**INSPECT**
⊂⊙⊃	**FIND**	ⵁ	**PRE-POSITION**
→	**SELECT**	⌒	**RELEASE LOAD**
∩	**GRASP**	⌣	**TRANSPORT EMPTY**
⌣	**TRANSPORT LOADED**	⫯	**REST FOR OVER COMING FATIGUE**
9	**POSITION**	⌒o	**UNAVOIDABLE DELAY**
#	**ASSEMBLE**	⌐o	**AVOIDABLE DELAY**
U	**USE**	⫯	**PLAN**
⫯⫯	**DISASSEMBLE**		

But as it turned out, all this was just buildup to a bigger plot. After Frank's death, Lillian turned her attention to the kitchen—an under-appreciated area of the home at the time—viewing kitchen work as "unpaid labor" that could be optimized like any other factory.

Lillian would become the first engineer to observe the home and bring efficiencies to it, using motion studies to analyze how women moved while they prepared food, cooked, and did the dishes.

---

* Ibid.

It didn't matter that Lillian couldn't cook. By studying how women actually worked in their kitchens, she was able to observe the inefficiencies of food preparation and devise her own alternatives. One early test put on by the *Herald Tribune* showed that using Lillian's kitchen layout reduced the number of steps from 281 to 45.[†]

The kitchen you're now used to cooking and eating in is based entirely on Lillian Gilbreth's ethnographic research, which revolutionized kitchen design forever. By treating kitchens as something that could be optimized for humans, she invented concepts like the "work triangle"—a concept that designers use to determine efficient kitchen and work layouts to this day.[‡]

Henry Dreyfuss: The Founding of Human-Centered Design

In parallel to the Gilbreths' work, the self-taught founding father of human-centered design was making a name for himself in the 1930s: Henry Dreyfuss.

For all intents and purposes, Dreyfuss could be considered the Steve Jobs of the early-to-mid 20th century, transitioning from a career in set design to industrial designer.

He defined the role as one that must embody many people: a researcher, guinea pig, engineer, artist, politician, and builder.[§]

> We begin with men and women and we end with them. We consider the potential users' habits, physical dimensions, and psychological impulses...for we must conceive not only a satisfactory design, but also one that incorporates that indefinable appeal to assure purchase.[¶]

It's this mentality that makes him responsible for many of the most common, long-lasting products of the 20th century. The Bell Model 302 telephone. The Honeywell T87 circular thermostat. The Polaroid Model 100.[**]

---

† *http://www.slate.com/articles/life/design/2012/10/lillian_gilbreth_s_kitchen_practical_how_it_reinvented_the_modern_kitchen.html*

‡ *http://www.kitchens.com/design/layouts/the-work-triangle/the-work-triangle*

§ Henry Dreyfuss, *Designing for People* (New York: Simon & Schuster, 1955)

¶ *Designing for People*, 219.

** *http://www.podwits.com/2013/03/20/podwits-profile-henry-dreyfuss-industrial-designer/*

When the Bell Model 302 telephone was released in 1937, for example, it was a startlingly innovative design—taking into careful account how people used and held telephones. It's one of the most iconic designs of the early 1900s, and gained ultimate fame with its frequent use on the set of *I Love Lucy* (Figure 1-4).[*]

Dreyfuss believed that good design could improve a company's profits. He was one of the first to market his services to potential clients as such—promoting "his ability to give insider knowledge—thinking about an object from the user end—and not just [to] create prettier objects, but better objects."[†]

FIGURE 1-4
Henry Dreyfuss invented the famous "Lucy" phone, as well as countless other products that were researched through meticulous observation.

This was a huge shift in thinking at the time. Dreyfuss considered the role of a designer to be more than simply removing unnecessary ornamentation from a product after the fact. Instead, an industrial designer now had to understand how a product contributed to a customer's well-being to be successful.

He used Lillian Gilbreth's transformative work in motion studies and observation to define how his clients' products should be made—observing a vast array of activities such as how trains were driven,

---

[*] *https://www.yalealumnimagazine.com/articles/3372/the-making-of-modern*
[†] *http://news.yale.edu/2015/01/23/candlestick-lucy-telephone-tells-national-story*

how manure was spread, and how phone companies conducted service calls. "There is no substitute for first-hand research in the matter of keeping up to the minute on the sales moods of the public," he wrote.[‡]

Why this obsession with research? Because a company couldn't afford to risk releasing a product that they didn't know people wanted. Pretty products didn't cut it.

The penultimate example at the time was the 1936 Chrysler Airflow, a car that had millions of dollars sunk into its production and advertising. Yet it was a major failure for the company, because "the public's taste and acceptance had not been accurately assessed."[§]

Ultimately, Dreyfuss believed that his painstaking study and research would create products where "people are made safer, more comfortable, more eager to purchase, more efficient—or just plain happier."[¶]

Neil McElroy: Inventing the "Brand Man"

We can continue to trace the origins of the product designer in business to a typewritten memo from 1931, written by a manager at Proctor & Gamble—who would later become Secretary of Defense under President Eisenhower and create NASA.

It's May 1931. Cincinnati, Ohio. Neil McElroy is responsible for growing sales for the Camay soap brand. It wasn't going well, and he was being overshadowed by P&G's Ivory soap.

McElroy realizes that the way his organization is structured is limiting his ability to make Camay successful. He's unable to get the resources he needs to really understand *who* Camay is supposed to be serving.

So he types a fateful memo on his Royal Typewriter and proposes a concept that would have a significant ripple effect—even on industries that didn't even exist yet. He calls this the concept of the *brand man* (Figure 1-5).[**]

[‡] *Designing for People*, 67
[§] Ibid., 68
[¶] Ibid., 24
[**] http://www.innovationinpractice.com/Neil%20McElroy%20Memo%201931.pdf

COPY

MARKETING
- Brand Teams, 1931

cc: Mr. W. G. Werner

Mr. N. H. McElroy   May 13, 1931

Mr. R. F. Rogan

ADV**N. H. MCELROY

Because I think it may be of some help to you in putting through our recommendation for additional men for the Promotion Department, I am outlining briefly below the duties and responsibilities of the brand men.

This outline does not represent the situation as it is but as we will have it when we have sufficient man power. In past years the brand men have been forced to do work that should have been passed on to assistant brand men, if they had been available and equal to the job.

Brand Man

(1) Study carefully shipments of his brands by units:

(2) Where brand development is heavy and where it is progressing, examine carefully the combination of effort that seems to be clicking and try to apply this same treatment to other territories that are comparable.

(3) Where brand development is light

   (a) Study the past advertising and promotional history of the brand; study the territory personally at first hand - both dealers and consumers - in order to find out the trouble.
   (b) After uncovering our weakness, develop a plan that can be applied to this local sore spot. It is necessary, of course, not simply to work out the plan but also to be sure that the amount of money proposed can be expected to produce results at a reasonable cost per case.
   (c) Outline this plan in detail to the Division Manager under whose jurisdiction the weak territory is, obtain his authority and support for the corrective action.

The brand man was a novel idea at the time. At companies like P&G, people were hired for specific business functions such as, say, sales or research or administration.*

So what was different? The brand man—later, *brand manager*—was defined as the person responsible for guiding a product to success. This person would seek to understand the processes that worked and those that didn't, examining "carefully the combination of effort that seems to be clicking and [trying] to apply this same treatment to other

---

* *http://www.innovationinpractice.com/innovation_in_practice/2010/06/brand-man.html*

territories that are comparable." And this person would go *into the field* to measure the results of these plans, reporting back with data to tweak the group's approach.[†]

"Where brand development is light...study the territory personally at first hand," he wrote. "Find out the trouble...develop a plan...outline this plan...prepare...all other necessary material for carrying out the plan...keep whatever records are necessary."

Soon, P&G reorganized their company around this newly invented role, and McElroy went on to lead the company. Their competitors around the world copied them.

Just like the work of Lillian Gilbreth and Henry Dreyfuss, McElroy's "brand man" memo would have vast ramifications for product design as we know it. He couldn't have foreseen that he would set the template for product management in software.

In fact, it was a former P&G brand manager that would introduce McElroy's concepts to software in 1981: Scott Cook, founder of Intuit. Their first product was Quicken. You may have heard of it.

Scott Cook: Bringing the Brand Manager to Technology

Software companies were on the rise in the early 1980s. As the development of new products got more complicated and engineers stretched too thin, usability tended to suffer. On top of that, products were becoming more and more consumer-oriented.

Scott Cook was one of the first people to implement brand manager-like principles at a tech company. From day one, he sought out to observe customer needs and solve them with a product.

At P&G, Cook learned that researching customer needs throughout a product's lifecycle was the key to satisfying them. The research even brought him understanding beyond the development of the product to its pitch.[‡]

Breaking into software with this mentality brought Cook an advantage at the perfect time. He believed that understanding their customers couldn't come thirdhand or from management presentations. To

---

† *http://onproductmanagement.net/2010/03/08/the-origins-of-product-management-part-1/*

‡ Suzanne Taylor and Kathy Shroeder, *Inside Intuit: How the Makers of Quicken Beat Microsoft and Revolutionized an Entire Industry* (Boston: Harvard Business Review Press, 2003), 6.

combat this, Cook conducted regular user studies and implemented a "Follow Me Home" program where Intuit staff would follow willing, first-time customers home. There, they'd observe how new customers installed and used Quicken.

Cook combined these studies with the dissemination of mailed-in customer complaint cards that were included in every box of Quicken. He also required everybody to answer customer service and support calls for "four hours each month, increasing to twelve hours a month when the company launched new products."[*]

Finally, he made product managers also oversee the product's income statement and "all aspects of building the business…acting as champions for their products, embodying the voice of the customer not just for product development and marketing communications for also for technical support."[†]

Why the History Matters

All of this traveling around in the DeLorean time machine has had a purpose: to show that the idea of designing a product with a *human* at the center isn't new—and that the most iconic, long-lasting products in human history were built with the same easily identifiable methods.

The other purpose was to illustrate how difficult this process can be. It requires hundreds of hours of observation to understand what people really do.

And almost 30 years later, we're now witnessing the rise of product design in software, much in the same tradition of those who came before us—the industrial designer, the brand manager, and those who pioneered their techniques.

It's not coincidental. Products are failing at more rapid rates than ever. We realize that a more human-centered worldview is required if digital products are going to be successful.

That's because the rapid adoption of the Internet and mobile technology—and with it the possibility of instant distribution—has turned many of us over to bad habits. Making matters worse, our customers' attention spans are fracturing. People are becoming lazier. New products need to work harder than ever to stand out and get attention.

---

[*] Ibid., 73.

[†] Ibid., 67.

That means that digital products need people who understand their customers. The problems they face. And how to improve the product on an ongoing basis to help them be better at what they do. And, if you're really good, to help them live better lives.

Digital products need people who can then visualize and design the solution. Infuse the product with soul and personality. And steer its existence into reality by guiding the engineers, marketers, and other essential talents required to realize anything substantial.

What the History Tells Us

"Facts are better than dreams," goes a famous phrase by Winston Churchill.

This was the rationale by which he operated during World War II, even though he was publicly known for his grand, bold visions about how Britain would win the war.

Anybody with an inkling of knowledge about Churchill and WWII would know that he was armed with an incredibly strong personality that, at times, intimidated those who worked for him.

Churchill became so concerned that this would prevent his staff from delivering bad news during the war that he created an office separate from the normal chain of command. Its job? To deliver uncompromising, unfiltered news and facts about the war effort.

Churchill relied on this Central Statistical Office to make every important decision during the war. It was headed by a civilian and tracked essential areas like aircraft production and losses, munitions production, and import/export balances.

Churchill didn't dream his way into helping the Allies win the war. He relied on observations of his staff to make decisions, using these facts to create a scenario for victory.

That's a common thread among people like the Gilbreths, Fords, McElroys, and Cooks of our product heritage. They painstakingly conducted firsthand observations of their audience, and understood the context in which they existed even *better* than their customers did.

Listening, studying, organizing—this common thread has its roots in a form of study called ethnography.

Upgrading Ethnography for a Digital Era

Ethnography's central premise is that you can learn what people actually do when nobody's looking. You can tell how people live their lives by observing what they do and listening to what they say. By doing so, you'll understand how people behave on their terms and not on yours. Ethnography enlightens us about the contexts in which customers might use a product, and how that affects the relative value of your product in their daily lives.

My journey to understand this practice took me to an unlikely place, leading me to the work of two individuals I'd never met: Amy Hoy and Alex Hillman. Their ideas helped me to see the patterns that the most successful products used to find customers.

Hoy and Hillman invented a new approach—based purposefully on ethnography—to creating products people want: observing intently, listening without bias, and analyzing the patterns to invent an endless stream of product ideas.

The lessons are based upon the same ethnographic techniques that researchers have used for at least a hundred years to understand isolated and insular cultures (a concept that oddly resembles many of our customer bases).

But this modern take on the ethnographic process takes advantage of the tools we now have at our fingertips: access to practically any audience we want and the ability to just sit back and listen. Hoy and Hillman taught me that if you observe and analyze without bias, customers will tell you exactly what they wish they could buy.

Hoy and Hillman also taught me that if you look closely enough between the lines, you can observe the principles of listening, studying, and organizing in a slew of successful products—modern, digital products like Dropbox, many of Apple's offerings, and Product Hunt.

Time-Tested Techniques in Modern Products

DROPBOX

Drew Houston's creation of Dropbox has been labeled for years as the quintessential example of the "minimum viable product." The story goes that Drew couldn't get funding for his idea of a seamlessly syncing file service. So he did what any aspiring entrepreneur did in 2008: he made a video and submitted it to the online communities he frequented.

It was an instant hit, driving 70,000 new email subscribers through a simple landing page (Figure 1-6*).[†]

FIGURE 1-6
Dropbox's original landing page.

Dropbox synchronizes files across your computers and your team's computers. It's better than email, uploading, or a Windows file share. It just works.

It's seamlessly integrated into Windows, but there's also a web interface. It also stores past versions of documents, handles huge

Simple landing page: capture interest/email address

people into the beta. We'd be happy to keep you posted about the beta program and launch (your email won't be used for anything else.)

E-mail address: you@example.com   Submit

But the lore surrounding this launch masks what really happened. Drew didn't just *get lucky*. This was the embodiment of somebody who did the work to understand an audience, weaving that knowledge into his product and his pitch.

As an example, he got his audience's attention by riddling the video with inside jokes and references only somebody who spent time in these online watering holes would recognize.

But even more powerfully, he spoke directly to them, in their language, about the problem his product solved:

> The point is that if you've ever worked with multiple computers or carried around a USB drive or emailed yourself files from work, you can see that this is a much easier way of managing your stuff.

> Normally, if I want to send something, I have to send an email attachment or something like that. But Dropbox has this special public folder where every file you put in here has a URL associated with it.

---

*   http://www.slideshare.net/adamsmith1/from-zero-to-a-million-users-dropbox-and-xobni-lessons-learned

†   http://techcrunch.com/2011/10/19/dropbox-minimal-viable-product/

Luckily for us, the Reddit thread created in response to Drew's video still lives. The responses are testament to the fact that both the pitch and the product got their attention.

"Apple? You listening? This is how iDisk should work. Your dismal effort is a total embarrassment."

"So many more references to /b/ and teh interwebz i cant even count them all... :O"

"My Grandma is the sultan of stubborn! She just images partitions into a file using 'dd' and uses 'strings' to find things that she wants. Still has to use 'grep' though! Crazy lady."

Drew's takeaways? The biggest risk of creating a product is "making something no one wants" (Figure 1-7).* Find customers by knowing "where [your] target audience hangs out & speak to them in an authentic way."

What we learned

- **Biggest risk: making something no one wants**
- **Not launching → painful, but not learning → fatal**
- **Put something in users hands (doesn't have to be code) and get real feedback ASAP**
- **Know where your target audience hangs out & speak to them in an authentic way**

APPLE

Mentioning Apple here might come as a shock to you. Can't they get away without talking to customers because they're special? Don't they have a cult-like following that will buy absolutely anything?

---

* *http://techcrunch.com/2011/10/19/dropbox-minimal-viable-product*

Of course, Apple has a massive following that's only expanded in the past few years. But while the company may have zealots, its ambitions aren't to cater just to this crowd. To remain in business, Apple has to listen to its customers and immerse itself in their worlds.

When it comes to Apple, we can easily get swept away by anecdotes of perfectionist tantrums or demonstrations of borderline obsessive-compulsive disorder (Steve Jobs, according to one account, had the marble for the New York Apple Store floor shipped to his office in California to inspect the veining[†]). This makes it hard to analyze what's staring us in the face: Apple builds products not by asking what people want, but by observing how they behave and imagining what could change their lives.

"We do no market research," Jobs famously once said. "You can't go out and ask people what the next big thing is."[‡] We frequently misinterpret this quote to mean that Apple simply trusted completely in their own sense of taste and refinement to choose what products to build. Instead, Jobs was saying that you can't understand how to serve a customer by asking him—you understand how to serve him by watching.

Jobs's "own research and intuition, not focus groups, were his guide."[§] None of us are or ever will be Steve Jobs—but we can learn from actions here. Jobs didn't give away Starbucks gift cards or take people to lunch to get their opinions and feedback. He didn't send out email surveys to figure out what product to build next. He analyzed how people used technology, learned what brought them joy, and understood especially well what pissed them off.

We see parallels to this approach from other Apple members. Mitch Stein, who was the director of human interface technologies for Apple in the 1990s and coined the phrase "user experience," explained a very similar process[¶]

> This is key. First, assimilate: You don't ask the user what they want—you go out and live with them and literally become the user. You do it with a wide-angle lens. You do it not just to tackle

---

† https://books.google.com/books?id=87ab4H3hJRwC&pg=PA179&lpg

‡ http://archive.fortune.com/galleries/2008/fortune/0803/gallery.jobsqna.fortune/2.html

§ http://www.nytimes.com/2011/10/06/business/steve-jobs-of-apple-dies-at-56.html?pagewanted=all&_r=0

¶ http://www.geekwire.com/2013/mitch-stein-user-experience/

the problem you think you're solving—you need to understand the culture they live in, what motivates them, that sort of stuff. I know that sounds touchy feel-y, but it really works.

Time Machine, the original iPhone, and iPhone 6 are three strong examples from Apple of observational research in action.

Time Machine

Apple's Time Machine is one of those easily overlooked products from the hardware and software giant. It's not flashy, it's embedded within the desktop operating system, and it's only important when you really need it.

But that's the beauty of the product. It solves a searing pain that we all face using digital storage: what happens when your hard drive goes bad?

Steve Jobs introduced Time Machine in 2008 with OS X Leopard.* Here was his pitch (Figure 1-8):

> *We're using our computers not just to store our work documents but really our digital lives. We've got things on our computers now that used to be in our precious shoeboxes that would never get lost. But if you just lose one precious photograph you'd be really bummed. Imagine if you lost your whole library of photographs... and yet almost no one backs up their computer automatically. Almost all of us do not.*

FIGURE 1-8
Steve Jobs making the case for Apple's Time Machine product in 2008.

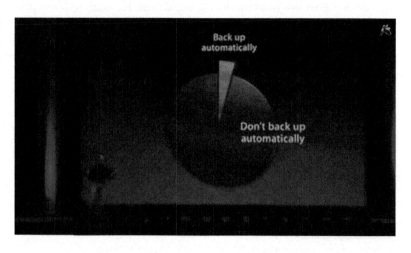

* *http://youtu.be/STuhwRwRqD4?t=45m5s*

We are just walking time bombs waiting to happen in terms of having something go wrong and misplacing some information. Mistakenly deleting it. Or worse.

This is what Time Machine is all about. We'd like to solve these problems in such a simple way that everyone actually uses it.

How did Jobs know that people had shifted away from shoeboxes in the closet and began using their computer hard drives in their place? How did he know what would get people to actually use a backup solution? Total immersion within his audience.

Time Machine has been included in every single OS X release since 2008, and it's inspired products like iCloud backup and iCloud Photo Library.

iPhone

We all had cellphones. We just hated them, they were so awful to use. The software was terrible. The hardware wasn't very good. We talked to our friends, and they all hated their cellphones too. Everybody seemed to hate their phones.[†]

Call it talking to "friends" and family, but Apple didn't ask their customers to imagine OS X on a mobile phone. When you're Apple, you have access to people in the upper echelons of music, video, mobile, and computing. They're able to ask lots of "why" questions while immersing themselves in this environment, exploring their friends' problems, needs, and wants, and how they make decisions. But just because the people who work at Apple have different friends than the average person doesn't mean that they don't have to do the work to understand what people want.

Jobs revealed in an interview that the decision to create the iPhone could be broken down into this simple framework:[‡]

What do we hate? (Our cellphones.) What do we have the technology to make? (A cellphone with a Mac inside.) What would we like to own? (You guessed it, an iPhone.)

---

† *http://archive.fortune.com/galleries/2008/fortune/0803/gallery.jobsqna.fortune/index.html*

‡ *http://archive.fortune.com/2008/02/29/news/companies/amac_apple.fortune/index.htm*

iPhone 6 and 6 Plus

Fast forward to 2014. It was a different world from the one in 2007 when the original iPhone was released. Larger screen sizes had become a major form factor in mobile usage. And, much to the chagrin of iPhone customers, Apple had stuck stubbornly to the 4" form factor of the iPhone 5 released in 2012.

But Apple was listening. A leaked sales presentation revealed that Apple had been listening for at least a year. Growth rates were slowing. The strongest demand was coming from phones with larger screens that cost less. And competitors were spending "obscene" amounts of money to gain market share while simultaneously improving their hardware. "Consumers want what we don't have," a slide declared (Figures 1-9 and 1-10).

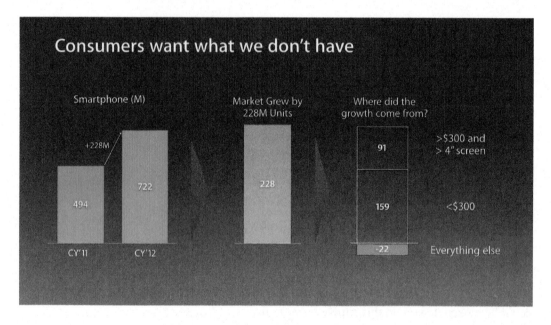

FIGURE 1-9

A leaked Apple presentation justifying phones with larger screens.

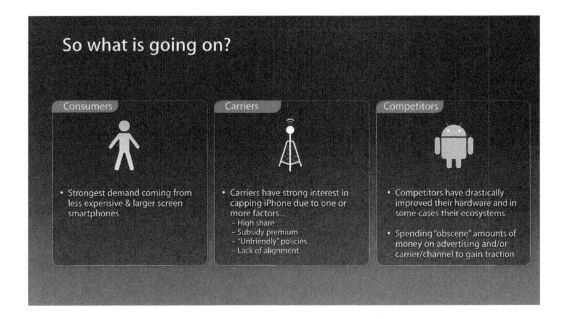

FIGURE 1-10

An Apple presentation outlining the landscape faced by the iPhone.

Just a year later Apple retooled its entire line of iPhones. The 6 and 6 Plus sported 4.7" and 5.5" displays, respectively—almost an inch larger than the iPhone 5.

The result? The biggest profit in corporate history after the iPhone 6's launch. A quarter-over-quarter growth of iPhone sales of 57 percent (74.5 million phones sold). And a drop for the first time ever in Android unit shipments (Figure 1-11).*

---

* *https://theoverspill.wordpress.com/2015/02/09/android-oem-profitability-and-the-most-surprising-number-from-q4s-smartphone-market/*

Smartphone Unit Shipments by OS World Market: 3Q 2014 to 4Q 2014				
Operating System	**Shipments**	**3Q 2014**	**4Q 2014**	**QoQ Growth %**
Android	(Millions)	217.49	205.56	-5%
Forked Android (AOSP)	(Millions)	85.47	85.00	-1%
iOS	(Millions)	39.27	74.50	90%
Windows Phone	(Millions)	9.02	10.70	19%
Others	(Millions)	3.18	2.34	-26%
Total	(Millions)	354.44	378.00	7%

Source: ABI Research

FIGURE 1-11

Apple sales figures after the release of the iPhone 6 and 6 Plus.

Devices, though, are only one side of Apple's products. The company has always prided itself on integration within both hardware and software. So it's important to make note of a perceived degradation within Apple's software efforts, as noted by user interaction expert Don Norman. He established the User Architect's Office at Apple, and rose to become vice president of Apple's Advanced Technology Group. He writes:

> I was once proud to be at Apple, proud of Apple's reputation of advancing ease of use and understanding. Alas, these attributes are fast disappearing from their products in favor of pretty looks, or as designers call it "styling."

> Apple has gotten carried away by the slick, minimalist appearance of their products at the expense of ease of use, understandability, and the ability to do complex operations without ever looking at the manual.

> Today, the products are beautiful, but for many of us, confusing. The fonts are pleasant to the eye, but difficult to read. The principle of "discoverability" has been lost. The only way to know what to do in many situations is to have memorized the action.*

---

* http://www.jnd.org/dn.mss/apples_products_are.html

PRODUCT HUNT

What started as an email list for friends and colleagues to share and keep track of new tech products is now one of the most fertile places for new products to launch, and for investors to seed new investments.

Ryan Hoover started Product Hunt after repeatedly being asked by people in forums and on social networks about what he thought of new products.[†] Hoover was spending so much time talking about these new releases, but the experience was fractured. He had to scan places like Reddit, Hacker News, TechCrunch, and Twitter to get the news and discussions he wanted.

He realized that others had the same problem.[‡] Product addicts like himself were also spending hours a day skimming these sites, including technology investors and founders eager to connect with willing audiences.

> *"What cool new products are you using?" We all ask this question. It's a common conversation starter, especially in the startup community. I'm particularly fond of this topic—I enjoy geeking out about products, writing design deconstructions, and swapping discoveries with smart folks. But these conversations provide more than just entertainment value: They are also a great learning opportunity. Understanding the subtleties of good and bad products is critical for product builders.*

Immersed within the audience, Hoover launched an early version of Product Hunt that was a simple email list. He reached out to people he knew would be receptive.

> *Years of blogging, relationship building, and projects like Startup Edition have given me an audience and network of supporters. The term "startup" is deceiving. Successful companies don't start up overnight; they are founded upon years of experience and help from others that must be earned.[§]*

A year later, Product Hunt announced a $6.1 million Series A investment from Andreessen Horowitz.[¶]

---

† *http://firstround.com/article/Product-Hunt-is-Everywhere-This-is-How-It-Got-There*
‡ *http://www.fastcolabs.com/3023152/open-company/the-wisdom-of-the-20-minute-startup*
§ Ibid.
¶ *http://techcrunch.com/2014/09/13/producthunt-raises-6-million-from-a16z/*

So What?

So how does all of this help you? How does reading a bunch of history enable you to end the cycle of throwing stuff against the wall and hoping that it works?

You don't have to be a statistic of failure. You don't have to be a part of the "fail fast" culture. You can change the trajectory of the technology industry by using the principles that worked for those who came before us—Dreyfuss, the Gilbreths, McElroy, and Cook.

Just because technology enables rapid adoption and instant access to audiences doesn't mean that humans have changed. People have problems. And people want other people to make those problems go away.

If this idea appeals to you, then you're going to love the next section. We're going to explore a modern version of ethnography invented by two entrepreneurs who were fed up by the culture of failure. Called Sales Safari, it's an entirely new brand of observation that takes place online.

Ready? Let's go.

Shareable Notes

- The idea of a product "failing fast" isn't the only way products get made. This technique, in fact, runs counter to the way products have been made for over a hundred years. It's a relatively new phenomenon brought about by technology's ability to distribute ideas around the world faster than any time in history.

- We can trace the origins of modern digital product design to our product forebears of the 20th century: Lillian Gilbreth, Henry Dreyfuss, Neil McElroy, and Scott Cook. Each conducted painstaking, extensive customer research in the field and used it to shape the products they made.

- Ethnography's central premise is that you can learn what people actually do when nobody's looking. You can tell how people live their lives by observing what they do and listening to what they say. By doing so, you'll understand how people behave on their terms and not on yours. It enlightens us about the contexts in which customers might use a product, and how that affects the relative value of your product in their daily lives.

- Dropbox, Apple, and Product Hunt are organizations that each demonstrate a deep understanding of their target audience and explicitly craft products to serve them.

Do This Now

- Spend some time researching Lillian Gilbreth, Henry Dreyfuss, Neil McElroy, and Scott Cook. Read their work. Research their methods. Look at the products they created as a result.

- The next time Apple has a keynote, listen to how they pitch their product. Where do they get their information? What data do they provide? Reading between the lines during these presentations can teach you a great deal about the value and practice of research.

- For the penultimate cautionary tale about the pitfalls of asking people what they think instead of observing what they do, research Margaret Mead and the controversy surrounding her study in the book *Coming of Age in Samoa*.

Interview: Keenan Cummings

Keenan Cummings is a product-minded design leader and strategist, writer, and occasional illustrator. He's currently at Airbnb, where he's a Product Growth Lead and Design Manager. He co-founded Wander, which was acquired by Yahoo! in 2014.

You wrote a timely and thoughtful exposition that sought to reach a "working definition" of product design. What compelled you to want to explore the meaning of this emerging field, and what did you learn along the way?

I've been exploring these ideas for the past year and a half. I spend about three years working in more traditional graphic design fields (marketing, branding, advertising, print, etc.) and was generally dissatisfied with the nature of the problems I was tasked to solve. When the core objective is always to move more product off of shelves (an unfair generalization of the industry, but I'm describing the feelings I had at the time), you're often left wanting something deeper. I saw admirable and interesting work being done in this field and people were calling it product design.

So I jumped into this pretty full force, taking on some serious risk at a very unstable time for myself and my family. It was a figure-it-out-as-you-go period (and still very much is), so product design became whatever I was doing. The more work we put in on our product, the more that definition grew. I knew product design was bigger than what I had been doing before, but now I was seeing what it takes to conceptualize and build a product from nothing.

The article was merely an ordering process. There was something that seemed a bit off in the way some fellow designers were thinking about product design. It seemed maybe too close to the kind of design I was doing before: narrow in scope and vision, and exclusive to the few that actually carried the title on the team.

Why is product design so hard to describe? What makes it "formless"? Is it because it's such an emerging field, or is it because it encompasses such a vast range of skills (or both)?

Product design feels like it has form. We make tools. But alone those tools are not products. Products shape, encourage, guide, and change behavior. A hammer is a formed, manufactured, aesthetic object. But the product of its creation is the extension of the arm, an empowered behavior. This is a very hard thing to define precisely because it is a hard thing to design. There are few rules, a million variables, and always unexpected outcomes.

Designers are always controlling the narrative, shaping audience perception, or walking viewers through an experience. But product designers have to give up that control and let the design process be about observation and response. You can see why an industry that has always defined itself by the associated hard skills (think of the traditional symbols of our discipline: letterpresses, Pica rulers, X-acto knives, Bezier curves) is at a loss when it is designing with behaviors and aspirations and impulses and motivations. The former process is so concrete that the latter can feel a bit like shaping a vase from smoke.

I also think designers want to own product design, but because it is so large it is open to many disciplines. We are used to being the tastemakers (the very idea of "taste" is a destructive idea to the product design process) and the visionaries. We don't have to give all of that up; we just have to be willing to share that responsibility with others. What seems to be the prime skill for a product designer is understanding people. And great typesetters or illustrators don't have a monopoly on that (although I do think designers can have a leg up here—more on that later).

How does one most effectively become a "cultural anthropologist" to 1) recognize behavioral patterns, and 2) understand the motivations behind them?

As I said before, product design is about understanding people. We have to get outside our own heads and that means tearing down a fortress of assumptions that keep us feeling comfortable in the world.

You have to constantly challenge how the world looks from your cozy spot in it. People will always surprise you. The only assumption I allow myself to entertain freely was something I read in *The Internet and Everyone* by John Chris Jones: "Design everything on the assumption that people are not heartless or stupid but marvelously capable, given the chance."

But that is merely the observation part. Discovering and understanding motivations is a process of empathy. This is what I was referring to when I said designers have a leg up in learning product design. Design really is just a practice of empathy. It is about synthesizing culture and movements of ideas and distilling that into something interesting. Designers do this without thinking. They work with the intent to spread ideas. And they are good at making things that are spreadable. That comes from empathy. They get outside their own frame of reference so they can make something that touches the masses.

And "taste" kills empathy. Taste is when you've amassed enough of those cultural influences that you start to believe the ideas and the cultural synthesis comes from within. The moment that happens, you stop observing. You stop absorbing the influences because you see yourself as the source. It's subtle, easy to miss. But slowly your source material narrows, your resources diminish, and you are left to repeat yourself. Culture goes on, dynamic and ever changing, and you are left with the same material to chew on. This is where "taste" leads you.

"Product design" is frequently equated with "entrepreneurship." How is product design different than entrepreneurship?

It's tough to draw the line between the two. Most entrepreneurs will need to practice some form of product design to be successful. But there is a distinction between starting and running a business and designing a product. I could go open up a furniture shop next week, following the well-worn path of smart business practices. My challenges might involve inventory, operations, and sales. For some entrepreneurs, these are solely business challenges that need to be managed rather than designed around.

But, instead of following that well-worn path, I could be IKEA. You could picture a corporate headquarters divided between the b-school grads on one side, running the operation, and the artists on the other side, dreaming up new product to fill their shelves. But what makes them who they are is that they are not, at the operations level, a bunch of businessmen. They are a company of product designers. They are always thinking about new ways of designing, shipping, building, and selling furniture.

Entrepreneurs that don't practice product design can build strong business, but they are usually not very interesting. It's the combination of business acumen and product design skill that yields companies that change things and endear us to them.

What steps have you taken to understand and build for your customers? How do you come to know their needs and expectations, and how do you build for those needs and expectations?

I have done some customer research in more formal settings. I've sat behind the two-way glass and watched dozens of users walk through the same set of questions. We had to reach benchmarks of comprehension to get approval by the FDA for a medication packaging project. This was rough work.

That kind of research has its place. But I think the more natural process most designers go through is ambient and semi-conscious. It's an attraction to what's cool, what's interesting. You might consider it an extroverted activity where art is introverted (although a lot of designers, myself included, might be socially introverted).

I am fascinated by what fascinates people. Early on, I wanted to find those interesting things and share them. I still do this, and can get embarrassingly passionate about a burger joint or a brand of shoes. But at some point, you realize you can make those things, and the easiest way to make them is by repurposing the stuff that you know is already working. Instead of making something entirely new, you mimic and mix until you get something that fits with everything else that was already interesting but has the integrity to stand on its own.

In concrete terms, I read and watch and collect all these cultural bits and try to dismiss nothing but experience as much as I can. That is hard to do—I am tempted to go deep on one thing—but getting a real range of influences starts to show up in your work.

[2]

How to Create Products
People Want

Avoiding "Ego-First Development"

"WHAT IF YOU LAUNCH your product...and nobody buys it?"

These were the words that compelled me, as a would-be graduate of the 30×500 bootcamp (a class that teaches people how to create and sell their first products), to become a student. It was a moment that would change my life.

Less than six months after graduating from the course, I created two products from scratch that made more money with fewer customers than the venture-backed startup I was a part of for almost five years.

This is a testament to the 30×500 approach: it forces product creators to cut directly to the heart of why a product should exist: *to find a customer.*

Again, these sentiments aren't new. I was paraphrasing Peter Drucker's words from almost 50 years ago: "the purpose of the enterprise is to create a customer."[*]

Talk about cutting directly to what's been causing technology's all-too-frequent product failures.

---

[*] Peter Drucker, *The Practice of Management* (New York: Harper Business, 1993), 317.

That's, in fact, one of the motivations Hoy and Hillman had for creating the 30×500 bootcamp: railing against the phenomenon they call "ego-first development": thinking that a product or idea is special just because it's yours.

It's a fallacy that sets you up for failure. It creates an endless cycle of throwing ideas against the wall with the hopes of finding something that works. Hoy puts it like this:

> *The core problem with so many businesses is that they're based on what the business owner wants. They're fantasizing about being the hero: "I'm going to ride in on my white 'software' horse, and save these poor people."*[*]

Their programs have produced some incredible statistics since starting in only 2011. Students who have never created a product in their lives have gone on to make tens of thousands of dollars for themselves in the first few months after following the 30×500 framework. Other product rookies were generating five figures in recurring revenue after only a few months. Their students have gone on to gross over $2 million in aggregate sales over the bootcamp's lifespan—despite the fact that the course is offered on an extremely limited basis.

One of their core teachings is this: creating a product based primarily on what *you* want focuses the product in exactly the wrong direction. When you do so, the primary benefit becomes the fact that *you've* created it, instead of what your product can do for others.

Ego-first development flies in the face of everything we've explored about how successful products are made. That's because, as we've seen, concocting a product idea is really an act of listening. And without knowing who you're serving and what they need, building product is simply another form of optimistic speculation.

But wouldn't the Build-Measure-Learn feedback loop that's been popularized by the *Lean Startup* model solve this problem? Isn't the right path to "validate" your ideas with a "minimum viable product" through customer interviews?

The methodology behind the 30×500 class openly challenges what's become common wisdom and all-too-frequent buzzwords in technologyland. Notions of "customer validation," "minimum viable product," and "pivoting" have successfully woven themselves deep

---

* *http://productpeople.tv/2014/02/07/amy-hoy/*

into startup culture. But startup deaths aren't letting up,[†] despite the influx of capital and talent into technology startups and the occasional high-profile successes like Facebook, LinkedIn, and Airbnb in recent years.[‡] Despite the flood of cheap and eager money, 70 percent of dead technology companies were in the Internet sector.

The core tenet of the ready-fire-aim approach found in the Lean Startup framework is believing that one can find customers—*and* the right product to build—by asking what they want.

But this is an inherently flawed notion, because doing so relies upon:

- Your ability to get your ego out of the way and to ask exactly the right questions at the right time from the right people.

- Your potential customers being rational or aware enough to identify their own habits, wax eloquently about what bothers them, and express what would make them happy.

- A freely accessible pool of people who aren't going to tell you just what you want to hear, and who don't change their habits after you interview them.

Hillman likens this belief to the dichotomy between observing lions in the zoo and how they behave in the wild:

> *Imagine going to see the lions on display in the zoo. Now imagine seeing the same species of lion in the wild on an African safari. Technically, you're looking at the same animal both times. But they behave differently in the wild than they do in captivity.*
>
> *You wouldn't make a judgment call about what MOST lions do based on a lion in a zoo, because MOST lions aren't in zoos.*[§]

So, what happens when you observe your customers like you'd observe lions on a safari? What happens when creating a new product *isn't* an exercise in the "extreme uncertainty" espoused by the Lean Startup model?

You'll know what your customers' problems are. You'll know what makes them happy and how they speak with each other. You'll know exactly what to say and how to say it to pique their interest. And, ultimately, you'll know how to make them want to use your product.

---

† *https://www.cbinsights.com/blog/startup-death-data/*
‡ *https://www.cbinsights.com/blog/billion-dollar-exit-venture-capital/*
§ *https://unicornfree.com/2014/validation-is-backwards*

This approach forms the basis of 30×500's modern ethnographic approach. Fittingly called "Sales Safari," it's a system that observes what your customers are already doing and turns those habits into the basis for product ideas.

Let's take a look at Sales Safari now.

Find Product Ideas with Sales Safari

Going on a Sales Safari is the process of uncovering product ideas hiding in plain sight. It places the work of coming up with these ideas on your potential customers, and lays a foundation for repeatable success. Based on the observation techniques used by Lillian Gilbreth and Henry Dreyfuss, Sales Safari is what Amy Hoy—the method's inventor—calls "net ethnography."

"Sales Safari is 'net ethnography,' combined with some close reading and empathy," she says. "[It's] step-by-step empathizing with your customer to understand them."

In case you've forgotten, ethnography's central premise is that you can learn what people *actually* do when they're not aware that you're looking. By observing what people do and say, you'll understand how they behave on their terms and not on yours.

Why's this important when creating products? Because this observation enlightens us about two really important things: the contexts in which customers might use a product, and how that affects the relative value of your product in their daily lives.

"The key is you start by observing what [your customers] actually already do," Hoy continues. "You don't try to persuade a vegetarian to buy Omaha Steaks. You look at what they actually do in real life on the Internet. What they read. What they share with each other. The problems they discuss. What things that they ask help for. How they help others."

What's particularly unique about Sales Safari is that it takes place entirely online, for a number of reasons:

Access

> You can reach almost any unique community that exists on Earth without leaving your chair.

Speed

Online research affords tons of conveniences like search engines, copy and paste, and more. Doing offline research is much harder to complete—and much harder to obtain without it being tainted by your presence.

A reliable record

When people are speaking in "meatspace," you either have to remember what they said, scribble notes, or awkwardly record your conversation. Online observation, though, is out there for you to read and parse at your leisure.

Time to analyze

Online observation provides "the ability to disassociate what someone is saying from what you interpret them saying," says 30×500 coteacher Alex Hillman.

Distance

You're not physically present to influence anybody's opinions, nor are you tempted to pull the *research pitch*—the act of pitching your product while asking people what they want. "People need to not know that you're there watching," Hillman continues. "That sounds really creepy to say it that way, but there's a reason for it. This is professional lurking if you want to look at it that way. You're there to watch what they do and say when they don't know that you're there."

Perspective

You literally have access to the entire Internet to find people in a particular audience. You're not limited to a local Meetup or user group; instead, you can get the full picture of an audience's pains from around the world.

Sales Safari's intentional distance is designed to avoid the pitfalls of asking questions and influencing your subjects. In ethnographic circles, this is known as avoiding the "Margaret Mead problem." Her story is a cautionary tale, and a predominant example of how being too close to the people you're studying can distort the truth.

It's 1928. Anthropologist Margaret Mead has finished writing her book, *Coming of Age in Samoa*, a study of the lives of teenage girls there: how they came of age, what their family structures were like, and so on.

The quick-and-dirty of the Mead story is that she lived with the villagers, asked about their lives, and listened to their stories—many of which were later revealed to have been made up by her teenage subjects. She took these stories at face value instead of observing their behavior.* Years later, anthropologist Derek Freeman returned to the village, where the now-elderly teenage girls from Mead's study admitted to making up stories just for fun.†

That's why *observing* people and not asking them is at the center of creating products that find a customer. And creating products that find customers depends on finding their *pain*.

Sales Safari's designed to root out people's pain. Because if you can discern what people's problems are, then chances are you're the one who'll be able to solve those problems.

"People walk around trying to tune out their problems, because they don't expect that they can solve them," says Hoy. "You have to reflect back to them. 'Hey, this is the problem that you're having. You know, it's a big deal, but also we can fix it together.'"

Pain and problems—revealed by observation and empathy. It's not a flashy notion, nor is it particularly groundbreaking. But it's been at the center of how successful products get made for over a century.

But by using modern online tools, Sales Safari can help you to start recognizing the patterns among your audience.

"In order for someone to go on the Internet and ask a question of a group of strangers about how to solve their problem, [it's] a very strong indicator of the level of pain they're in," Hillman says. "Even if it seems like very little pain to you. Like, 'Oh, that's so simple. Here's how to fix it.' It's awesome that you think that, but that's clearly not where they're coming from. Otherwise, they would have fixed it by now."

But how does Sales Safari help you uncover people's problems? How does it help you to create products that will be used by more than just a few people?

Sales Safari works by observing "at scale." That means spending not just a few hours, but dozens to *hundreds* of hours, analyzing your audience.

---

* *http://www.loc.gov/exhibits/mead/field-samoa.html*
† *https://en.wikipedia.org/wiki/Coming_of_Age_in_Samoa#Critique_of_Mead.27s_methodology_and_conclusions*

This, of course, implies that you've done the work beforehand to know where your audience or your customers hang out online. What forums, mailing lists, and link-sharing sites do they frequent? What are they writing in customer support emails or product reviews?

Then, it's on to what Hoy says requires "close reading," a study technique that's meant to uncover layers of meaning in text. When you close read, you're focusing on the way the person writes, how they see the world, or how they argue a particular point.[‡]

But we're not doing this for literary analysis. We're doing this to understand what people want.

And close reading, when used to understand an *audience*, uncovers a series of data points that will begin to form patterns.

"You start collecting jargon, some of their specific detailed language and words they use to describe the problem," Hillman says. "Elements and contributions to their worldview, their deep-seated beliefs that are unshakable. Then also the things that they talk about, they recommend. The things that they buy."

Doing this can be overwhelming at first. It certainly was for me when I started studying designers as an audience. But what I found through Sales Safari led me to create both this book and two successful products.

And, to be honest, this is hard work. Hours will tick by. Probably days, actually. Pages upon pages of the Internet will be scoured. But it's work that the average person doesn't do. Because it's so easy to base a product idea on a handful of data points—a few coffee shop interviews, or what your friends and family think.

But Sales Safari's power is that it's a system designed to do two things: gather tons of data and help you analyze that data.

"[People] get one data point or they get one potential client or customer, and they think, 'All right. This is it. I'm going to do [make this product].' That's really a recipe for failure," Hoy says. "You need to keep doing whatever research you're doing until it all comes together. It'll seem fruitless up until the point where it immediately, like the

---

‡ *http://writingcenter.fas.harvard.edu/pages/how-do-close-reading*

clouds will part and a ray of sunshine will burst through. People like to go on one data point, because it doesn't take any work and because it feels right. It's bad, though. Bad idea."

Gathering tons of data points means that you'll start to notice patterns trickling into your notes. Eventually, you'll be able to categorize them: How does your audience see the world? What do they dwell on? How do they speak? What products do they use?

And, eventually, you'll start noticing the most important element of all: what your audience's problems are, written in their own words.

So, what happens when you're able to empathize with a set of people, create something that they want, and pitch it to them in their own words? Sounds like you have an endless source of product ideas upon which to build.

As Hoy puts it, "The process is essentially, figure out what hurts them. Reflect that back to them in a very empathetic, understanding way. And then offer them assistance."

And, applied over time, Sales Safari will help you track how your audience gradually changes. Tastes evolve. Worries morph. New pains are uncovered.

It's really that simple, in theory—but only by actually putting it into practice will you and your product reap the benefits.

Plot the Pain

It can be difficult to sift through the heft of the raw data you gather during the course of Sales Safari research. Lots of your key insights will be tied up in text files or on sticky notes. There's a better way to visualize the data.

Enter the Pain Matrix (Figure 2-1). No, it's not a medieval torture device—it's a tool I invented to help me understand my own research data, and it can be a tool you use to help your team understand your customers better. This will help you zero in on your customers' pain, understand what makes them happy, and focus your product ideas.

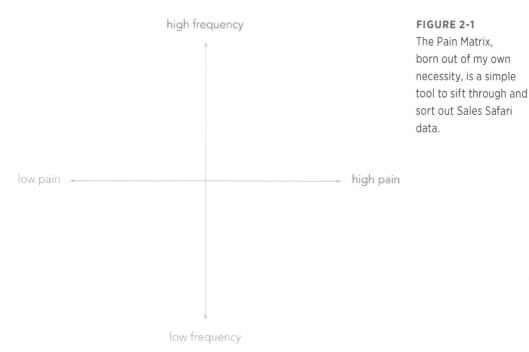

FIGURE 2-1
The Pain Matrix,
born out of my own
necessity, is a simple
tool to sift through and
sort out Sales Safari
data.

Note these characteristics of the Pain Matrix:

- The horizontal axis, from left to right, is where you'll track your audience's pain. What do they mention, and how intense is it?

- The vertical axis, from bottom to top, represents the frequency of pain. How often did you find this pain mentioned in your data?

When you plot out your research in this matrix, the four quadrants will emerge:

Upper right

Frequently occurring, intense pain. If a product can alleviate whatever is plaguing your audience in this quadrant, this is where you want to be to bring the most joy to your audience.

Lower right

Infrequent, yet intense pain. Products in this category might be nice-to-haves, surprising your audience if they were properly addressed.

Upper left

> Little pinpricks of pain that occur often. Products in this category might address smaller problems like administrative challenges or things that people label "it is what it is," and provide a customer "little wins."

Lower left

> Little pain happening infrequently. This is something that might appear like an opportunity while steeped in the details of your data, but reveals itself to be a low-opportunity product to build when you step back to look at the bigger picture.

What tends to emerge is that the four quadrants start to fill up with very specific kinds of pain:

Upper right

> Hate, fear, anxiety, feeling overwhelmed, feeling stupid, getting stuck, wasting precious time

Lower right

> Procrastination, self-doubt, guilt

Upper left

> Minor irritations, dislikes

Lower left

> Boredom

Doing all of this work takes time, yes, but the results you get are absolutely indispensable. You'll have confidence that you can build something that you know people will want. You'll discover the fastest route to building the right solution. And you'll be immune to the idea of "failing fast"—because failing is no longer part of the product creation process.

What Does a Product Designer Do?

[A designer] takes pride in a skill based on experience and an alertness sometimes interpreted as vision. He approaches every problem with a willingness to do painstaking study and research and to perform exhaustive experimentation. He is equipped to work intelligently with the engineer, the architect, the physicist, the interior decorator, the colorist, and the doctor. He must know how far to go and when to stop. He must be part engineer, part businessman, part

salesman, part public-relations man, artist, and almost, it seems at times, Indian chief. He operates on the theory that it is better to be right than to be original; therefore, he steers a course somewhere between daring and caution. If the merchandise doesn't sell, the designer has not accomplished his purpose.

—HENRY DREYFUSS, *DESIGNING FOR PEOPLE*

Barring any potentially politically incorrect characterizations in the preceding quotation, Dreyfuss might as well be talking about modern digital product design.

If we accept that a digital product's purpose is to serve a customer (and I hope that you can after all of the history we've explored together), then a product designer's primary job is to understand the audience they've chosen to serve.

Once that's in place, the product designer's job is crafting the product that will best serve that audience—and, in the process, taking on a slew of intersecting roles required to get the right product across the finish line.

But it's so easy to get caught up in the echo chamber of the self-congratulatory technology community. Product design has, in some circles, become synonymous with the glossy, the beautiful, and the stylish.

Sales Safari helps us understand that a product has to be built with a customer in mind, and it has to follow through on its promise.

In other words, product designers aren't artists, nor are they solely focused on the aesthetic.

"What am I helping them do? What am I helping them achieve or feel or whatever it is?," Kyle Bragger, cofounder of photography site Exposure, asks. "For me, those two things are way bigger than, 'How does it look? What are the features? What is the aesthetic? What does the stack look like?' Any of the other components of that don't really matter until you've figured out who you're building for and what it is that you're actually creating."

Everything else flows from the audience and what they want. Including the visual. It's *always* in service to the customer.

This isn't meant to discount the value of a so-called pretty experience. Aesthetics certainly have their place: they make a product appealing, more trustworthy, and more of a joy to use.

But we do a disservice to product design if we place too much emphasis on what's on the surface.

While it's constantly evolving, a product designer's role is an absorption of a number of disciplines into a single role that used to require separate positions.

Let's examine these merging roles now, and the characteristics they bring with them.

Entrepreneur

Identifies needs in the market and finds ways to satisfy those needs. It can be an opportunity great or small, external or internal, obvious or nuanced. This is the person who's willing to take a risk and back it up with hard work, determination, and team building. For a product designer, this typically means being able to identify opportunities to better serve one's customer and imagining tangible solutions to carry out this vision. It includes the ability to create and share this product vision with other teams.

Product manager

The product manager is, in the words of technology veteran Josh Elman,* helping "your team (and company) ship the right product to your users." While it's different in every company, a product manager builds a process to interpret ideas and feedback from all areas of the company—analytics, communications, trust and safety, support, operations, legal, international, and design (a technique at Twitter named "ACT SOLID"). This feedback also incorporates a deep understanding of the product's audience and the necessary research to achieve this understanding. The product manager then uses this feedback to decide the product priorities, driving the organization to build products in a timely manner that meet these goals.

Typically, the roles of a product manager and a designer have been separate. Designers have been responsible for the so-called *solution space*, inventing solutions to solve the problems found by

---

* *https://medium.com/@joshelman/a-product-managers-job-63c09a43d0ec*

product managers. Product managers, in turn, have traditionally been responsible solely for the *problem space*, uncovering customers' desires and problems and making market projections.

These roles, though, can be difficult to separate. Product designers are not only expected to possess the skills of problem-finding product managers, but they're also expected to be able to implement the solution. Combining these skills in one person can dramatically decrease time-to-market, increase a team's coordination, and improve quality.

A product designer should now be able to talk with customers, understand their needs and goals, and understand the market enough to design innovative solutions. Instead of creating product specifications with the designed solution to follow, they are able to work through the actual product designs themselves and create solutions with a firm foot in reality.

But in larger companies, a product manager might be required to manage the sheer volume of organizational coordination and team building. At Facebook, for example, product teams comprise both product managers *and* product designers. Both have overlapping skills, and if a product manager lacks a product designer on their team, they're expected to pick up the slack.[†]

Interaction designer

Envisions how people will experience a product and brings to life refined, inspired experiences with the goal of leaving a lasting impression. Thinks in terms of user flows and creates mockups of the user interface. This is an individual that can internalize what a user might need at any given stage and fight for their satisfaction. For product designers, this means having a strong ability to solve experience problems both within an existing visual system and with new, extensible patterns they create. Product designers should also be able to document these new patterns for the team.

Visual designer

Creates beautiful concoctions of color, space, typography, iconography, and illustration to help people navigate a product. Fluent in what constitutes so-called "good design" across all types of media,

---

† *http://www.quora.com/What-does-a-Product-Manager-at-Facebook-do*

including apps, websites, advertising, and more. For a product designer, this typically means having strong visual design skills that are both original and aesthetically intuitive.

Motion designer

Understands how motion influences interaction design and uses it to reduce confusion, lend a helping hand, and make the experience fun. Collaborates heavily with visual and interaction designers and uses motion to create a product personality instantly recognizable and wholly one's own. For a product designer, this typically means being able to identify well-constructed motion in other products or to invent original animations in prototyping tools or code.

Prototyper

Using whatever tools are best for the job, a prototyper brings to life interactions or user flows to determine what's the best experience. This person could create a prototype with a variety of tools with varying degrees of fidelity, including HTML and CSS, JavaScript, Adobe AfterEffects, Quartz Composer and Origami, Framer.js, InVision, or actual code. For a product designer, this means being able to implement one's own interaction and user flows. The benefit of this is being able to test ideas quickly, proliferate those ideas, and zero in on the best solution for the desired experience.

Data analyst

Understands the challenges a product intends to solve, and provides data on product usage for informed decision making. Able to create and interpret A/B tests, synthesize large volumes of data, and make sense of the trends. Knows how to set up tests and what user data to gather and when. For a product designer, this skill is typically demonstrated by a working knowledge of which data is significant to making a decision, an understanding of the impact of design decisions through data, and the ability to identify chokepoints where tests can be set up.

User researcher

A champion of customers and an expert at gathering both their insights and feedback. Designs, executes, and acts on ethnographic research and user experience evaluations to affect product strategy and product roadmaps. Helps the organization connect with the customer in a meaningful way. For a product designer, this skill is embodied by a deep understanding of the domain for which the product is being built. It's an individual who's able to translate what customers say into product vision, individual features, and marketing language.

Psychologist

Knowing that we're all human and each subject to various influences, base instincts, and emotional draws, a user psychologist brings a larger human perspective to the task of creating enjoyable, emotionally engaging experiences. Has a basic understanding of cognitive psychology, heuristics, empirical research, and empathy. For a product designer, this means being able to understand customer behaviors and the motivations behind them. It then provides the motivations to act on certain product features—creating habit-forming products by knowing what delights a human being in a particular context.

Copywriter

A person who's able to craft appealing, contextual, and easily understood copy to a specific audience. Has an excellent vocabulary and exercises proper grammar. For a product designer, this means balancing clarity with the personality of the product being built. It also means fighting for properly formed sentences.

Project manager

Has the responsibility of driving a project to meet its stated goals. This role requires balancing the four pillars of the project management superfecta: time, cost, quality, and scope. For a product designer, this is an essential part of the role and a constant dance between engineering and the needs of the business. What features are essential? What are nice-to-haves? What if *everything* seems essential—how do you choose what to trade to meet a deadline? Product designers must have the skills to navigate these muddy questions and deliver a satisfying product.

Product marketer

Is the link between the product and its intended audience. This can include internal groups like sales or public relations, as well as clients, customers, and partners. This person helps the product organization understand what should be built and keeps track of how customers and the market as a whole react to new product launches. Before the product is built, product marketers will perform market research to help determine where new product development should head. After the product is built, they take care of launch marketing and all relevant materials required to sell it. A product designer embodies this role when they work with marketing to make sure that the product's promise matches the public story. They'll determine what the release plan should be, and work with engineering through the launch process to fix problems and communicate what's happening with both the organization and the outside world.

Customer support representative and community manager

These are the people on the front lines, who regularly take the brunt of problems when things go wrong. And in the rare event of praise, they identify the parts of a product that are doing their job. They're advocates for customers having problems, and exude the product's and the brand's promise through their interactions. A product designer knows how to identify and categorize this messy feedback, from catastrophic to nice-to-haves. They'll be a bridge between Support and Engineering, and might even be a fixture in the community, serving as a nexus for their customers' candid feedback.

These have traditionally been separate roles in an organization. Many of them still are, and many will continue to be for some time. But they each have a role in the toolset of a product designer.

It's obviously impossible, though, for a product designer to be an expert in every one of these fields. The role lives at the nexus of all of them. Implementing a product requires knowledge and practice of each of these disciplines.

Typically, though, a person in this role tends to specialize in a set of these skills. It happens to product designers much like it happens to characters in role-playing games, or RPGs. RPGs typically start new games by requiring players to build custom characters. Players are asked from the start to choose characters specializing in a particular "class" of skills, such as a bounty hunter, a hacker, or a soldier. Over the course of the game's storyline, the player is given the opportunity to "level up" their skills, and can choose to either be a well-rounded character or one that has deep experience in a few particular skills.

Just because the words "product designer" may not be in your job title doesn't mean that it's not your role. Titles like "Product Manager & Lead Designer," "Product Owner," or even the classic "Product Manager" are going to require you to employ product design–like thinking and skills.

So how do you sift through the research you've gathered? How do you know where to point your product?

To answer that, let's take a closer look at the Pain Matrix, the tool I invented for analyzing my own research data, in the next chapter.

Shareable Notes

- Product design is a process that starts and ends with completely understanding your audience. This takes painstaking firsthand research *before* you even start building a product.

- Sales Safari is a modern approach to ethnography. It's the process of choosing an audience, seeing where they hang out online, and lurking in these communities to analyze their wants and needs.

- You can use the Pain Matrix to make sense of your original research by plotting your data.

- A product designer is a role that exists at the nexus of a slew of skills: anthropologist, product manager, copywriter, interaction designer, and more. It's a reflection of how important technology has become to our culture.

Do This Now

If you accept that product design starts and ends with an intimate understanding of how you can serve a customer, then identify the following:

- Who is the customer for which your product exists?

- Where do these people congregate online?

- What do you understand about them? What can you learn about them by reading their forum posts, App Store reviews, or support emails?

- Plot their pains on the Pain Matrix. Compare it to the problems your product is currently tackling. How do they match up? What has your product been missing?

Interview: Amy Hoy and Alex Hillman

Entrepreneur and teacher Amy Hoy invented Sales Safari, an online ethno-graphic technique she teaches in a course called 30×500. Sales Safari has transformed lives—30×500 students have grossed over $2 million in their individual product businesses within the past two years.* She teaches this technique, among many others, with her business partner Alex Hillman.

What is 30×500? And what is Sales Safari?

Amy: 30×500 is Alex's and my class for creative people. They can learn to create and sell their first products, because working and doing creative stuff for somebody else for hire, it's very different than selling directly. You're insulated from the market realities. You don't understand quite what people want, except your boss.

It's very difficult to go from school and job and then freelance to create a product. A lot of people fail, because they don't understand how different it is. So our class gives them those skills that they can go and launch something and make money.

Alex: And Sales Safari really started as just one of the components of that class. When we first set out to create it, the first version was actually called "the Year of Hustle."

What was interesting when we started teaching that version of the class, which is everything leading up to launch, a bunch of the components of that were...we didn't think they were all that high level, but we learned over time just through teaching that things like "take notes" and "go do research on your audience" aren't really specific enough.

So Sales Safari's really become the heart of the 30×500 class. Arguably, the majority of the lessons themselves, the exercises are tied directly to it, when originally, it was just one step of many.

Amy: I don't know if it was so much one step of many as that we would say things like "go study," "go read what your audience is writing, study it, and make notes. And use that." People don't understand how to go study, read, or make notes.

For a lot of college-educated people, none of that makes sense at all.

---

* *http://courses.30x500.com*

Alex: It's step-by-step. Every component is a "here's not just what to do," but specifically how to do it. Here's the results that you get. And here's to know whether or not you're doing it right, because you're going to use those results in the next component. Things like that.

Amy: What is really is, Sales Safari is "net ethnography," combined with some close reading and empathy. Like step-by-step empathizing with your customer to understand them.

Alex: Also sort of a built-in feedback loop. Once you start applying those Sales Safari data, you're collecting categories of notes, things like the pain that you notice in people. Not just the pains, like what the problem is, but also how they describe it.

You start collecting jargon, some of their specific detailed language and words they use to describe the problem. Elements and contributions to their worldview, their deep-seated beliefs that are unshakable. Then also the things that they talk about, they recommend. The things that they buy.

All these things where the individual data points can be valuable, but the goal of Sales Safari is to have a systematic and repeatable approach, so you can collect a ton of it. A ton of data, because without a ton of data, you can't find the patterns. Without patterns, you can't make smart decisions about the business.

Amy: Yeah, people who go and they, especially designers, developers, writers, they think, "I'm going to make a product." They get one data point or they get one potential client or customer, and they think, "All right. This is it. I'm going to do it." That's really a recipe for failure.

You need to keep doing whatever research you're doing until it all comes together. It'll seem fruitless up until the point where it immediately, like the clouds will part and a ray of sunshine will burst through.

People like to go on one data point, because it doesn't take any work and because it feels right. It's bad, though. Bad idea.

I cannot tell you how many friends, and early on students before we learned to discourage them, went and said, "All right. Well, my local bar, restaurant, salon has this stacked scheduling problem. I'm going to make software for it." They think they identified a problem that they were going to solve, but they didn't understand salons at all. They watch them misuse pieces of paper to do this rough scheduling, but they didn't understand that these people never buy software, ever. If they bought software, they wouldn't have this problem to start with.

We have seen staff scheduling issues for local businesses come up four or five times over the past few years. It's always a failure, because you can observe someone doing a task and not understand the bigger context. And the way that you understand a greater context is long-term observation, like many different intervals.

Alex: Then the other part to that is if you ask them to show how they use it, you're instantly at a disadvantage, because they know you're watching over their shoulder. That instantly creates changes, even if they're micro-changes, in how they use it, because they're trying to show you something, instead of doing what they normally do in order for you to observe.

There's an element to Sales Safari where there's a very intentional distance and a lack of participation. People need to not know that you're there watching. That sounds really creepy to say it that way, but there's a reason for it. This is professional lurking if you want to look at it that way. You're there to watch what they do and say when they don't know that you're there.

Amy: It's not that they're doing it in private. It's a public forum and mailing list and such, but they aren't *performing* for you.

Why is asking people what they want so unreliable?

Amy: People don't understand what they do all day. They don't pay attention to what they do all day. As a designer, I can tell you. It's just absolutely fact, because if I explain all these problems with enough software people, like, "Oh, but it's not so bad! Oh, that's just email or whatever."

I'm like, "Well, what about if it looked like this?" They're like, "Oh, I never thought of that. I never thought that maybe I should have a people view that will show the files Bob sent me, so I don't have to search for 'Bob.' And then click every email with that."

Alex: To Amy's point, there's a numbness to some pains. But the other side of it is, it's that people really ultimately train themselves to not think about it or to think about it in a certain and specific way. Or they've heard a certain thing that they think they're supposed to say.

Again, it's not an intentional act of deception. That's extremely rare. It's more that you're relying on them to be reliable. That's statistically—that's not going to be the case.

They're not aware. If they were so aware of their problem, there's a good chance the problem would be solved by now.

Amy: That's why every programmer makes their own tools, and they're all terrible. I'm a programmer. You all know what I'm talking about.

The other thing. If there's research that shows this, experts don't understand how they do what they do. They can't verbalize it.

When you start observing it, they start trying to explain it while they do it. Their performance worsens a lot.

I also remember the example you gave in a talk a while ago of the Walkman focus group.

Amy: Oh, yeah.

Where they said, "We want yellow." And then they all picked up black.

Amy: Yeah. All the kids were asked by Sony, "Which one is cooler? Which one would you want to buy? The cool, sporty, yellow Walkman—I think it was Discman—or the black one?" And then they were like, "Thanks for doing our focus group. Here's two tables' worth of Walkmen. Pick the one you want." And they almost all picked black.

People's vision of themselves is different than how they actually are. That's humanity for you.

It's this idea that people walk around looking for solutions to their problems. No. People walk around trying to tune out their problems, because they don't expect that they can solve them. You have to reflect back to them. "Hey, this is the problem that you're having. You know, it's a big deal, but also we can fix it together."

That's a good segue. What's the process that helps you understand what would make someone read that email, use this product, read that blog post?

Amy: The key is you start by observing what they actually already do. You don't try to persuade a vegetarian to buy Omaha Steaks. You look at what they actually do in real life on the Internet. What they read. What they share with each other. The problems they discuss. What things that they ask help for. How they help others.

And then you get in there with something that already fits their behavior and their worldview. If people don't watch videos or they exclusively watch videos or you find they pay more for videos, then you'll want to consider giving them videos.

The process is essentially, figure out what hurts them. Reflect that back to them in a very empathetic, understanding way. And then offer them assistance.

Alex: In order for someone to go on the Internet and ask a question of a group of strangers about how to solve their problem is a very strong indicator of the level of pain they're in. Even if it seems like very little pain to you. Like, "Oh, that's so simple. Here's how to fix it." It's awesome that you think that, but that's clearly not where they're coming from. Otherwise, they would have fixed it by now.

So keep that in mind, that in order for people to post a problem they're having for help to an Internet of strangers, that's a clue right there.

What made you build Sales Safari on the pains and not the joys that people mention?

Amy: Because joy is much more personal, and also a lot of cultural groups—and I don't mean like ethnic or country cultures, but industry cultures—don't talk about what's awesome. Or, if they do, it's sort of disingenuous, how everything's awesome.

30×500 focuses on providing business value. And business value always comes from something that is a waste to start with or a lack.

The thing is, if you just say, "I'm going to create joy," you'd be like, "Here's a cup of ice cream!" Doesn't actually tell you where to go. People like kitties. They like ice cream. They like jazz music, but those are harder things to sell unless they're in the need for them.

Whereas if you say, "You struggle with this problem every day. Imagine if it was actually a positive interaction instead?" Then you actually get people listening. If you can't stimulate demand for it easily, but if you work with something that they're suffering with, then you have a conversation opener.

Stimulating demand is difficult.

This interview has been edited for length. To read the interview in its entirety, go to http://scotthurff.com/dppl/interviews.

3

What Are We Building Here?

Defining What to Build

Design is a process of making dreams come true.
—THE UNIVERSAL TRAVELER

LET'S PLAY A GAME. (I'm imagining the computer voice from the movie *WarGames.* GREETINGS PROFESSOR FALKEN...SHALL WE PLAY A GAME? Alas, I digress.)[*]

How many people do you think are on the following product or feature teams?

- Apple's iMovie and iPhoto

- Twitter

- Instagram

- Spotify

Hint: the number is definitely smaller than you think.

- Apple's iMovie and iPhoto: 3 and 5, respectively[†]

- Twitter: 5–7[‡]

---

[*] *https://www.youtube.com/watch?v=ecPeSmF_ikc*

[†] *https://www.linkedin.com/in/glennreid*

[‡] *http://www.quora.com/How-are-product-teams-at-Twitter-structured*

- Instagram: 13 when acquired for $1 billion by Facebook[*]

- Spotify: 8[†]

We also know that the team that created the first iPhone prototypes was "shockingly small."[‡] Even Jony Ive's design studio at Apple—the group responsible for the industrial design of every product, as well as projects like iOS 7—is only 19 people.[§] And we can surmise that this group is broken up into smaller teams to work on their own individual projects.

Figuring out what product you're going to build is an exercise in working through the research you've gathered, empathizing with your audience, and deciding on what you can uniquely create that'll solve the problems you've found. But it's also an exercise in deciding how big the team is and who's on it.

Jeff Bezos of Amazon famously coined a term for teams of this size: the "two-pizza team."[¶] In other words, if the number of people on a team can't be fed by two pizzas, then it's too big. Initially conceived to create "a decentralized, even disorganized company where independent ideas would prevail over groupthink," there's some surprising science that explains why teams of this size are less prone to be overconfident, communicate poorly, and take longer to get stuff done. In actuality, that probably caps this team at or around six people.

Enter the work of the late Richard Hackman, a professor at Harvard University who studied organizational psychology. He discovered that "The larger a group, the more process problems members encounter in carrying out their collective work...worse, the vulnerability of a group to such difficulties increases sharply as size increases."[**]

Hackman defined "process problems" as the links—or, communication avenues—among the members in a team. As the number of members grows, the number of links grows exponentially. Using the formula $n*(n-1)/2$—where n is group size— Hackman found that the links among a group get hefty very quickly (Figure 3-1).

---

[*] http://www.dailymail.co.uk/news/article-2127343/Facebook-buys-Instagram-13-employees-share-100m-CEO-Kevin-Systrom-set-make-400m.html

[†] https://dl.dropboxusercontent.com/u/1018963/Articles/SpotifyScaling.pdf

[‡] http://on.wsj.com/1SJ4XqK

[§] http://www.newyorker.com/magazine/2015/02/23/shape-things-come

[¶] http://www.wsj.com/news/articles/SB10001424052970203914304576627102996831200

[**] David M. Messick and Roderick M. Kramer, eds., *The Psychology of Leadership: New Perspectives and Research* (New York: Psychology Press, 2004), 131.

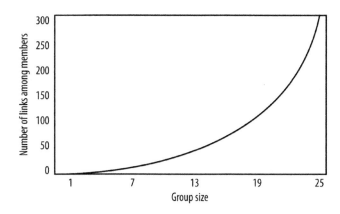

FIGURE 3-1
The larger a group gets, the more "process problems" a group faces. This requires increased communication and can slow down decision making. (Source: Messick and Kramer, *The Psychology of Leadership*.)

Even though math wasn't my favorite subject in school, let's go through a few team size scenarios. Let's start with Bezos's recommended team size of six—assuming that two pizzas are appropriate for six people (although, I've been known to put away a whole pizza on my own from time to time):

- Bezos's preferred team size of 6 people has only 15 links to manage.

- Increase that number to 10, and you already have 45 links to manage.

- If you expand to the size of where I work every day, Tinder—70 people—the number of links grows to 2,415.

But managing more communication links isn't the only problem groups face when they increase in size.

Larger teams get overconfident. They believe they can get things done quicker, and have a tendency "to increasingly underestimate task completion time as team size grows." In 2010, organizational behavior researchers from the University of Pennsylvania, the University of North Carolina at Chapel Hill, and UCLA conducted a number of field studies confirming these findings.[††] In one of their experiments, they observed teams tasked with building LEGO kits. Teams with two people took 36 minutes to complete the kit, while four-person teams took over 44 percent longer.

But the four-person teams believed that they could complete the LEGO set faster than the two-person team.

[††] *http://www.opim.wharton.upenn.edu/~kmilkman/2012_OBHDPb.pdf*

That's why the notion of the two-pizza team is so powerful. It's a simple concept that's easily understood by anybody within your organization, and can be used to combat the "let's throw more bodies at the problem" mentality that some organizations might be used to using.

OK, so we've figured out how big your team should be. But who should be invited to the party?

Everybody loves to be in product meetings. Especially when you're in the *deciding* phase of deciding what to build.

Even Steve Jobs loved being in the room during this phase. "He told me once," said Glenn Reid, former director of engineering for consumer applications at Apple, "that part of the reason he wanted to be CEO was so that nobody could tell him that he wasn't allowed to participate in the nitty-gritty of product design."[*]

Treat this process like you're the bouncer at Berghain nightclub in Berlin.[†] (Hint: it's practically impossible to get in if you don't speak German. And even then, Sven the bouncer, "a post-apocalyptic bearded version of Wagner," enforces an obscure dress code that nobody can seem to crack.)

So, who's in the room together? How much do they know about the pains you've found? And how do you frame the discussion?

At this point, you should have everyone who's going to be involved in the creation of the product on the team. An example of this could include:

- The product designer or product manager (depending on how your organization is set up, and if you'll be working with someone else who will be designing the product).

- The engineer(s) with whom you'll be working to build the product—typically frontend and backend.

- A representative from the team that will be launching and promoting the product; this could be someone from marketing or public relations to create a feedback loop between what will be promised to your customers and what your product is actually capable of doing.

---

[*] *http://inventor-labs.com/blog/2011/10/12/what-its-really-like-working-with-steve-jobs.html*

[†] *www.telegraph.co.uk/travel/destinations/europe/germany/berlin/10601482/Berghain-how-to-get-into-Berlins-most-exclusive-nightclub.html*

While at KISSMetrics, Hiten Shah structured these teams with

> ...a product manager, a designer, and an engineer. Sometimes
> it's multiple designers, multiple engineers, and sometimes it's an
> engineering manager.
>
> At times it can even be, sometimes, someone from marketing, if
> that makes sense, or even someone from sales. I mean, we have
> tried different methods. I'd say for different things, small things,
> big product releases, a whole product, it's going to be different and
> for the stage of the company it's going to be different.

Party Like It's 1991

Regis McKenna had something to say about this process. When he saw
how fast technology was changing society in 1991, he realized—like
our friend Neil McElroy at Proctor & Gamble—that a new role would
need to be formalized. This person would be "an integrator, both internally—synthesizing technological capability with market needs—and
externally—bringing the customer into the company as a participant
in the development and adaptation of goods and services."[‡]

If your eyes glazed over reading that, well, you should read it again.
Because McKenna was responsible for launching some of the hall-
marks of the computer age: the first microprocessor at Intel, Apple's
first PC, and The Byte Shop, the world's first retail computer store. Oh,
and one more thing: he was the guy behind the "startup in a garage"
legend first made famous with Apple's early days.

So, did you read it again? Did anything seem familiar?

Hey, he's describing you!

You're the product designer. The integrator. You're the customer's
champion, their expert, their advocate.

This process requires you to lead your team through the research; to
propose product ideas to eliminate your customer's pain or find their
joy effectively.

That, of course, means that everybody involved in building the product
must be intimately familiar with the research that's been conducted
on your audience.

[‡] *http://onproductmanagement.net/2010/03/14/the-origins-of-product-management-
part-3/*

Take the opportunity as an "integrator" to build on your strengths as a team: what innovative technologies and design can you apply to the problem at hand? Even better, what can you and your team uniquely build for this audience?

I thought Josh Elman (Greylock Partners, Zazzle, LinkedIn, Facebook, Twitter) had a great insight on this part of the product creation process:

> *The first thing is you have to trust your team. I think that sounds obvious, but it's much harder in practice. I think a lot of structures and processes are built on the fact that there isn't innate trust... next, get your team's help in how to solve the problem. The team knows what they can build. The team knows how it can be developed. The designers know what kinds of things are designable and natural in the product and what kinds of things are not. All of this matters.*

Don't forget the Pain Matrix (Figure 3-2). What are the observations you made that fit into the upper-right quadrant where there is the most acute, frequent pain? How can you build your customers' dream product? What are the pains that you're uniquely capable of solving?

FIGURE 3-2
The Pain Matrix, a simple tool I created for myself. It's intended to make sifting through and making sense of the research you've gathered much simpler.

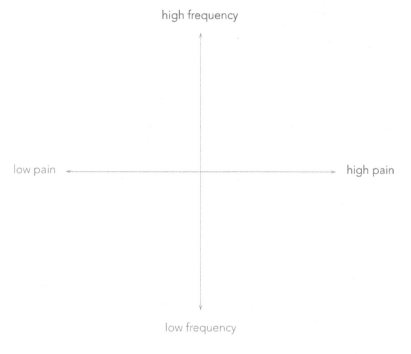

The Pain Matrix is the perfect piece of collateral for when you're hashing out what to build. This document becomes a communication device, an advocate for your customers. Everybody can see it and you can back it up with your data. Bonus points for direct quotes from your research.

"The thing to focus on is that yes, 100 percent of your users are humans," Diogenes Brito, a product designer most recently at startup Slack, reminds us. "While technology is changing really, really rapidly, human motivations basically haven't at all. Like Maslow's hierarchy of needs, that's still the same. Designing around that, the closer you are to the base level of what humans desire, the more timeless it'll be."

To reiterate: don't lose sight of the actual, observed, tangible pains and joys that you've researched. Resist the temptation to delve into hopes and dreams. Just throwing an "MVP" out into the wild to "validate" something you spend time building is a waste of time, money, and talent.

You're better than that.

Now, all you have to do is keep everybody focused.

Keeping Everybody Focused

There's always a big problem when the club-like euphoria from a product meeting starts to turn focus into chaos. How do you keep everybody on task and debating healthily?

I highly recommend a whiteboard for idea collection and harvesting. This serves three practical purposes:

- It's difficult to remember what was said. You don't want good ideas getting lost simply because there were too many thrown around the room.

- It allows you to be visual. Not all ideas can be verbally explained; a low-fidelity medium allows anybody to sketch the central core of the idea without unnecessary detail. This allows your team to get ideas out of their head on an equal playing field.

- It lets you take advantage of the natural tendency for the group to forget which idea was contributed by whom. This naturally allows the best ideas to float to the top and the worst ones to sink to the bottom. It's hugely beneficial, especially if the group has a lot of ideas. The key here is to avoid attaching names to ideas, so you can avoid hurt egos and the so-called *not invented here* syndrome. Called the Cauldron, this was a technique used by Apple—sometimes even with Steve Jobs in the room. According to Glenn Reid, the former director of engineering at Apple, the Cauldron "let us make a great soup, a great potion, without worrying about who had what idea. This was critically important, in retrospect, to decouple the CEO from the ideas. If an idea was good, we'd all eventually agree on it, and if it was bad, it just kind of sank to the bottom of the pot. We didn't really remember whose ideas were which—it just didn't matter."[*]

There's also the benefit of timed techniques, like one used at online publishing startup Medium. With the right group of people in the room, the problem that needs to be solved is defined and "you have two minutes to write down as many ideas as possible [to solve it]," director of product design and operations Jason Stirman told me. "Then you have five minutes to put the ideas on a whiteboard and explain them. Then you have another two minutes to add to ideas...the end result is you just get as many ideas as possible. So we do that a lot here. We brainstorm a lot."

The "Working Backwards" Approach

There's another technique used by Amazon that's particularly powerful. Known as the "Working Backwards" approach, this technique calls upon the product owner to literally write a future press release for the product—as well as fake customer quotes, frequently asked questions, and a story that describes the customer's experience using the product.

In your case, this could be a future blog post that you'd put out about your product or feature instead of a press release.

What's particularly unique about this technique is that this document involves every part of your organization that's required to make the product successful—not just product and engineering, but marketing, sales, support, and every other part of your company. In other words, it forces you to think about all of the aspects that can inform your product.

---

* *http://inventor-labs.com/blog/2011/10/12/what-its-really-like-working-with-steve-jobs.html*

Werner Vogels, Amazon's CTO, describes the rationale behind the process:

> *The product definition process works backwards in the following way: we start by writing the documents we'll need at launch (the press release and the FAQ) and then work towards documents that are closer to the implementation.*
>
> *The Working Backwards product definition process is all about fleshing out the concept and achieving clarity of thought about what we will ultimately go off and build.[†]*

According to Vogels, there are four documents included in Working Backwards:

The press release
What the product does, and why it exists

The "frequently asked questions" document
Questions someone might have after reading the press release

A definition of the customer experience
A story of what the customer sees and feels when they use the product, as well as relevant mockups to aid the narrative

The user manual
What the customer would reference if they needed to learn how to use the product

This all might seem like a lot of frivolous upfront work, but the method's been used at Amazon for over a decade. And if you use it in conjunction with the Sales Safari method outlined in Chapter 2, you'd be hard-pressed to find a more customer-centric approach to building products. That way, you'll be working on ideas that have their foundation in what real people need, as opposed to coming up with ideas that you try to plug into an amorphous audience.

At the center of Working Backwards lies the press release. A document that should be no longer than a page and a half, it's the guiding light and the touchstone of the product and something that can be referred to over the course of development.

---

† *http://www.allthingsdistributed.com/2006/11/working_backwards.html*

"My rule of thumb is that if the press release is hard to write, then the product is probably going to suck," writes Ian McAllister, a director at Amazon. "Keep working at it until the outline for each paragraph flows."*

Amazon's view is that a press release can be iterated upon at a much lower cost than the actual product. That's because the document shines a harsh light on your answer to your customer's pain. Solutions that aren't compelling or are too lukewarm are easily identified. Nuke them and start over. All you're working with at the moment is words.

"If the benefits listed don't sound very interesting or exciting to customers, then perhaps they're not (and shouldn't be built)," McAllister writes. "Instead, the product manager should keep iterating on the press release until they've come up with benefits that actually sound like benefits."

So what does this press release look like? Thanks to McAllister, we have a very specific outline of the documents Amazon uses in their product meetings:

1. Heading: this is where you announce the name of the product. Will your target audience understand its meaning? Will they be compelled to learn more?

2. Subheading: declare in one sentence who your product's target market is, and how they'll benefit from it.

3. Summary: summarize the product and and its benefits. McAllister cautions that there's a large chance that your reader will only make it this far, so "make this paragraph good."

4. Problem: this should be easy since it's been the focus of your customer research. What's the problem your product solves? What are the pains your customers are experiencing that justify this product's existence?

5. Solution: how does your product annihilate your customer's pain in the most frictionless way possible?

6. Quote from a Spokesperson in the Company

---

* *http://www.quora.com/What-is-Amazons-approach-to-product-development-and-product-management*

7. How to Get Started: how does a customer take their first step into the larger world that's your product? Describe your ideal first step that provides an immediate benefit.

8. Customer Quote: what would your ideal customer say after they'd had their pains destroyed by your product?

9. Closing, with a Call to Action

I think that this process—however laborious—endures at Amazon because it provides such clarity about what the product is going to be, and how it's going to help your customers.

"Once we have gone through the process of creating the press release, FAQ, mockups, and user manuals, it is amazing how much clearer it is what you are planning to build," writes Vogels. "We'll have a suite of documents that we can use to explain the new product to other teams within Amazon. We know at that point that the whole team has a shared vision on what product we are going to build."

Create a Product Guide

Before you finish defining what product it is you'll be building, you're going to want to leave with some paper in hand.

I love Cap Watkins's approach. The vice president of design at Buzzfeed and former Etsy senior design manager keeps his team on task after the meeting by creating a key internal document. We'll call this a *product guide* for the sake of discussion:[†]

> At the end [of the product definition meeting], leave with:
>
> What you're doing.
>
> Why you're doing it (problems you're trying to solve).
>
> What success looks like (quantitatively and qualitatively).

The product guide helps you "keep yourself and your team focused and prevent design creep: if it doesn't solve the problem or meet the goals, it doesn't go into this version."

The only two elements missing from this approach are who's responsible for what pieces of the product, and when they'll be done.

---

† *http://blog.capwatkins.com/my-design-process-part-1*

Pre-dating Steve Jobs, Apple created a rule for every project they undertake: the "Directly Responsible Individual," or *DRI*. It's a simple yet effective rule. By placing one's name next to a task-to-be-completed in front of the entire company, you can be sure that individual feels more responsibility to perform.[*]

In your own internal product guide, use this rule and make sure that every line item has a DRI. Assign someone (or recruit volunteers) to complete each task. Make sure this is in place before you break up the meeting. Include it in your guide's circulation.

It's not enough to put people's names next to line items. You and your team need dates, too. Do you need to do research for technological or data considerations? Do you need to build a prototype to see if a particular interface component is possible? Did you misinterpret something in your audience analysis? What can be executed upon immediately to challenge any outlying assumptions? Who needs to see what and when (other product teams, clients, bosses)? At what fidelity?

By giving every task a deadline, you'll maintain momentum even when the initial enthusiasm of creating something new dies down.

But how should you build in accountability? How do you race against the clock to get something valuable out to your customers?

Customer retention company Intercom—whose clients include Shopify, InVision, and Rackspace—gives their product teams weekly goals to hit. "We believe you can achieve greatness in 1,000 small steps. Therefore we always optimise for shipping the fastest, smallest, simplest thing that will get us closer to our objective and help us learn what works. All our projects are scoped into small independent releases that add value to customers."[†]

At AngelList, Graham Jenkin places a similar pressure on himself and his team to execute on a new product as quickly as possible—with a bias toward small chunks. "We're always thinking about how are we going to execute this by the end of the day, or 'how are we going to get this done this week? Can we get it done this week?' If we can't, maybe it's the wrong problem to try to solve." His approach is more of a rolling set of needs, rather than standing, arbitrary deadlines.

---

[*] *http://allvirtual.me/2012/09/04/what-inside-apple-teaches-you-about-product-marketing-and-product-management/*

[†] *https://blog.intercom.io/how-we-build-software/*

And my current employer, Tinder, holds product update meetings every Monday, Wednesday, and Friday—but only if there's something to discuss. These meetings typically consist of the product team gathering feedback from each other on their own projects and asking for critiques or help solving any design challenges. Every Monday is a roadmap meeting where engineering, product, customer support, and marketing leads get into a room and update each other on the progress of their projects, while alerting the group if something new needs to be addressed.

Whatever the setup is at your company, remember that you're the integrator. So be the leader. Be the customer's advocate. Don't settle for hand-waving and bravado.

You're better than that. More talented. And probably better looking.

Shareable Notes

- Defining what to build starts first with who's in the room.

- When choosing who's in the room, follow Jeff Bezos's "two-pizza team" rule: your team should be small enough that two pizzas could feed them. Typically, this comes out to about six people.

- Only allow team members through the door if they're educated on the research you've conducted on your audience. Use the Pain Matrix liberally.

- Whiteboards are your friend. They help you remember what was said, allow you to be visual (sketching together brings teams together), and disassociate ideas from their inventors. This allows the best ideas to win without any regard for who invented them.

- Amazon's "Working Backwards" approach can help you pinpoint the product ideas that'll solve your customer's pains, versus creating something that's too flashy or uninspired.

- Leave this meeting with a key document: the product guide, which outlines what you're building and who's responsible for doing it.

Do This Now

- Re-examine the knowledge your team has of your audience. Encourage them to study up on the research you've done so they can make more informed product decisions.

- Think about how your product can really make your customers happy. Are you really bringing them joy? Are you truly able to alleviate their pains and satiate their needs?

- Take stock of how your team conducts meetings and makes decisions. See if any of the techniques mentioned in this chapter can help you make more realistic decisions in a smaller time period.

Interview: Sahil Lavingia

Sahil Lavingia was on the original Pinterest team, where he helped invent the famous pinboard design, as well as the Pin It button and the Pinmarklet—before even finishing college at the University of Southern California. He then left Pinterest to design Turntable.fm's first iOS app, and started Gumroad shortly thereafter. At Gumroad, as founder and CEO, he's making it easy for artists to sell any good—digital or physical —to customers around the world.

So I noticed this distinct thread that runs through your thinking of everything you work on. You want to create something that solves a problem simply that gets in the hands of other people. What kind of philosophical steps along the road did you take to have this epiphany?

Yeah, I think the first thing that I figured out pretty quickly was that it's really hard to predict what people want, like it's hard to sort of guess in a year how your product is going to look.

And two, it's just you're forced to make simple stuff because you're not going to work on it for more than a weekend, right? And like now I think it's sort of obvious like, yeah, release something MVP, iterate, etc. But I think I was just like, "I want to build 50 things over the next year," and the only way to do that was to release MVPs. So that sort of built itself into the cycle.

How did you get started on this journey?

I was at [the University of Southern California] in the fall of 2010 with the intention of getting a degree; I was not really even considering leaving. But I started publishing a lot of my work online and I was like, "Wait, I'm finally in the U.S., I'm finally in California, I should start trying to get in touch with a lot of these people that I had followed for a long time." And that got me into doing contract work with these startups, that got me full-time job offers, and I sort of realized I could do this full-time; I didn't need a degree to do what I wanted to do. That led to me leaving USC after a semester, four months.

So I joined Pinterest, I was 18 at the time. I started contracting while I was doing school so I wanted to at least finish up the semester and end it cleanly.

Then I was there for a year, working on all sorts of stuff—design, frontend, backend. The mobile app was sort of my primary baby, but I worked on sort of everything. I joined the same day as another guy so I was number two and a half, three, or whatever, or we were both two.

And I was the most design-y frontend person at the time, so it was like, "You have to do that." So I learned a lot through that, then I left; I did some contract work for this startup called Turntable.fm based out in New York. I built their mobile app, designed it, and then I started to go on my own and that was already two years of stuff that happened really quickly. But [during the course of those two years] I think the things that got me excited—there are two big things—one was this constant emphasis on value creation.

I think Ben [Silbermann, cofounder and CEO of Pinterest] is really good about talking about it, especially now. But we were never really a super well-known Valley-like startup; no one really knew what we were. TechCrunch didn't really give a shit what Pinterest was for a long time. But we had these really core engaged users, even though we didn't have a lot of them—the people that used us were really psyched about us.

And so there was always this focus on building stuff that will make these people's lives better, which I think is the ultimate goal anyways—but you forget when there's all these other things that are going on, like raising money and trying to recruit people and pitching a different story there and press and things like that.

The other thing that I think really helped was just the volume of sort of feedback that I got. Like I had built these [different products] and sure, I had maybe a few hundred thousand users, maybe 1,000,000 combined over all the things I had built myself.

But with Pinterest I could launch something, I could try out a new thing, I would be able to get this massive amount of feedback. And we never ran A/B tests or anything at Pinterest, at least not when I was there. But with most of the things we worked on, it was very easy to figure out very quickly what was working, what wasn't working—and typically they're the same things. Simpler is better. Making things intuitive rather than complicated. Things like that. They're obvious to say out loud, but they definitely influenced a lot of the design that we did at Pinterest and a lot of the interactions that we built that really I don't think were very common before them and now are a lot more common. So I do think there was some amount of nonobvious stuff that we built to solve the needs of our users and that expanded from there.

Tell me about how you used the invitation-only system in the early days to spur growth.

Typically if you talk to someone in tech [about this technique], they're like, "this is stupid." First of all, no one actually thinks that this is a secret and closed beta. You get 1,000,000 emails a day, right? So another one just actually hurts you—but if you look at the normal person, even today, at least the normal people, the first people that used Pinterest and probably still sign up today, they didn't get a lot of email. Now, if you look at their inboxes, it's typically Facebook and Pinterest.

So, in that case, it's actually great that we said they loved the emails. They love getting invites to secret stuff, they're like, "Holy shit, I have this amazing secret new service and I can only tell five friends about it. So I'm going to take the time to really invite the best people I can invite because I only have five of them." They don't know that they don't expire, that there's actually an infinite amount of them or whatever. Yeah, those things still work.

That seems to have been one of the strengths of Pinterest's early growth— that Silicon Valley discounted you.

Yeah, it's pretty funny. I remember this one specific moment where I think Ben [Silbermann] said, "I was just in the meeting with somebody and they're like, 'You guys are building a site for women, right? Are you guys scared that your site is only going to be used by women?,'" or whatever. And, he jokingly replied, "Yeah, I'm really scared that we're only building a thing for 50 percent of the world's population."

And it's true. More women use Facebook than men I think by far—I think the engagement on females is typically a lot higher. And Instagram I'm sure is majority women, I think; Snapchat is probably the same. But yeah, things like that were unsexy in the Valley and I think a lot of people probably didn't focus on problems like the ones we were focused on. Because it was unsexy or uncool or not the hot hip thing to do.

But that's kind of a common thread between what you get at Pinterest and what you're doing now: you're going after people that are hard to get to, they're under-served, and if you give them some tools they'll run with it.

Yeah, and I like how you said "tools." [At Pinterest] we always thought about that piece of it too—we were always like, "How do we build tools to help our users solve their problems?" I think a lot of people focus on the network. They focus on the big picture—but you only get to the big picture if individually everyone is gaining value out of your service.

Most of the people—our competitors, you could argue—like for me at least, that's how I always considered it, is we stole users away from the Internet Explorer bookmarks folder. That was our competitor—we stopped more people from using that than any other service ever. And when you think of it like that you're like, "We need to build a better feature set that lets people bookmark stuff, scrapbook stuff, collect things, the sharing and other things like that.

They just want to find a better way to organize the 5,000 different things they might want to buy for their new house. And it doesn't matter how many recommendations or how many freaking gamification badges, leader boards, whatever you work on to provide, it's really just like, "I just need a better way to bookmark stuff."

This interview has been edited for length, and you're missing out on thousands of words of insights. To read the interview in its entirety, go to http:// scotthurff.com/dppl/interviews.

4

User Interfaces Begin with Words

Really? Start with Words?

As far as the customer is concerned, the interface is the product.

**—JEF RASKIN, HUMAN-COMPUTER INTERACTION EXPERT
AND THE CREATOR OF THE MACINTOSH PROJECT AT
APPLE**[*]

IMAGINE IF YOU'D WITNESSED the birth of the Macintosh project in 1979.

Disco. Bell bottoms. Anticipation for *The Empire Strikes Back*. The Iran hostage crisis.

But in a dingy office in Cupertino, you'd have seen the implementation of the first commercial graphical user interface. The invention of the one-button mouse. The creation of some of the most essential, foundational apps in computing.

But, even more powerfully, you'd have been exposed to the idea that the computer could be something used by regular people—not just scientists, businesspeople, or engineers. The dream was that the computer could be like any other household appliance, winning space in the living room next to the television or the solar-powered calculator.

This was a huge step in thinking at the time. *Computers are business machines*, went the conventional thinking.

---

[*] Jef Raskin, *The Humane Interface* (Boston: Addison-Wesley Professional, 2000), 5.

Not only was a man named Jef Raskin there to witness this spectacle, but he helped to make this dream into a tangible reality. Raskin was the one who started the Macintosh project at Apple. Seeing that the Apple II was still too complex for everyday use, he believed that the computer could be as easy to use as a regular home appliance.

So Raskin decided to define the guiding principles of what a so-called "easy-to-use" computer should be. And in his book *The Humane Interface*, published about two decades after he left the Mac project, he revisited and refined his ideas about human-computer interfaces.

Raskin believed that the success of a product's interface was dependent upon how well the designer understood two parties: the human using it, and the capabilities of the machine on which the software ran.

One of his core beliefs was that a designer should start designing the UI with...*copy.*

> *The place to start the implementation is to list exactly what the user will do to achieve his or her goals and how the system will respond to each user action.**

This is where the foundation of your product's user interface is laid. And you've earned the right to be here because you've already defined the tasks that the product needs to accomplish—because you know your audience, you've done the research (you *did* use the Pain Matrix, right? :)), and you know what your team is capable of delivering.

So go into this stage with the confidence that what you're creating has a soul and a direction. Will the product change as you're developing it? Perhaps, as you learn more about your customer and determine what you're capable of building. But that's part of the process of being flexible.

The foundation you lay here will help you understand *exactly* how your product can annihilate your customers' pain. You'll understand *exactly* the steps required to make your product tangible.

And don't forget—doing this will save you time. How long does it take you to type words into a text editor? How long does it take you to draw squares and arrows with words in it?

---

* Ibid.

Not long. So it's easy to shuffle the cards, so to speak, if what you came up with feels wrong, or bloated, or impossible to pull off.

The other added benefit of writing your interface first is that you're not worried about which font you should use, the border radius on your dialogs, or the interaction convention of the week. You're focused on your customers' productivity.

But a lot of us get this backward. We get sucked into the dopamine rush of inventing novel interactions and layouts, worried too much about impressing our peers in the product design community.

Words are the building blocks of practically all user interfaces. That's because interfaces are really just a set of tasks driven by words and symbols—and by focusing on good copywriting, you'll vastly improve your product and its design. Words are the nucleus of the interface, the design built out of them.

I love how Jason Zimdars, a designer at project management company Basecamp, puts this (Figure 4-1):[†]

> *My favorite sketching tool: iA Writer [a minimalist text editor].*
> *I'm not joking. UI design starts with words. Writing first makes*
> *me treat UI as a conversation. How would I tell a friend what*
> *they can do here and now?*

FIGURE 4-1

Jason Zimdars of Basecamp describing how he starts his UI design process.

Words get you, in old-school engineering parlance, "close to the metal"—closer to the *who* and *why* of your product, versus jumping into the *how* and *what*. It's beginning your user interface as a dialogue

---

† *https://twitter.com/jasonzimdars/status/365111733410463745*

with your future customers, versus trying to invent UI components right out of the gate. Because, as Raskin writes, "Users do not care what is inside the box, as long as the box does what they need done."

So how does one go about writing out a user interface? There are three key steps:

1. Map out the sequences of interactions—otherwise known as *flows*—that your audience will use to complete every task in your product.

2. For each screen in these flows, list out the components that are required to make each step in the flow do what it's supposed to do. Forms? Buttons? Pieces of data? List everything out.

3. Write the actual copy. What's the headline going to say? What's the context? In what tone should you write it, and should you reflect a certain personality? Don't settle for *Lorem Ipsum* here.

In the end, there's no one perfect way to do this. The goal is, as a famous stormtrooper once said, to "move along now," and get something working as quickly as possible without having to juggle all of the product's variables in your head. Clarity around what you're building and opening a line of communication with the people who are building it is the primary goal of the copywriting process. Systemic design problems can be thought out and designed on paper or in text first— before even a single pixel is created, or a line of code typed.

With that in mind, let's talk about mapping your product's user flows.

Creating User Flows

Science fiction, fantasy, and thriller writers who have to handle a bunch of plot lines need a way to keep track of what's going on. Writing a book—especially a *series* of books—with separate and intertwining plot lines demands an overarching method of organization. Can you imagine what George R.R. Martin, J.R.R. Tolkien, or J.K. Rowling had to do to keep track of all their characters and subplots?

Well, you're in luck, because you can jump inside the head of Rowling while she wrote *The Order of the Phoenix*. A sample page of her handwritten plot spreadsheet surfaced online in 2010. The columns dividing the spreadsheet consist of chapter numbers, story timeline, main plot points, subplots, and chapter titles (Figure 4-2).*

---

* *http://mentalfloss.com/article/26346/jk-rowlings-plot-spreadsheet*

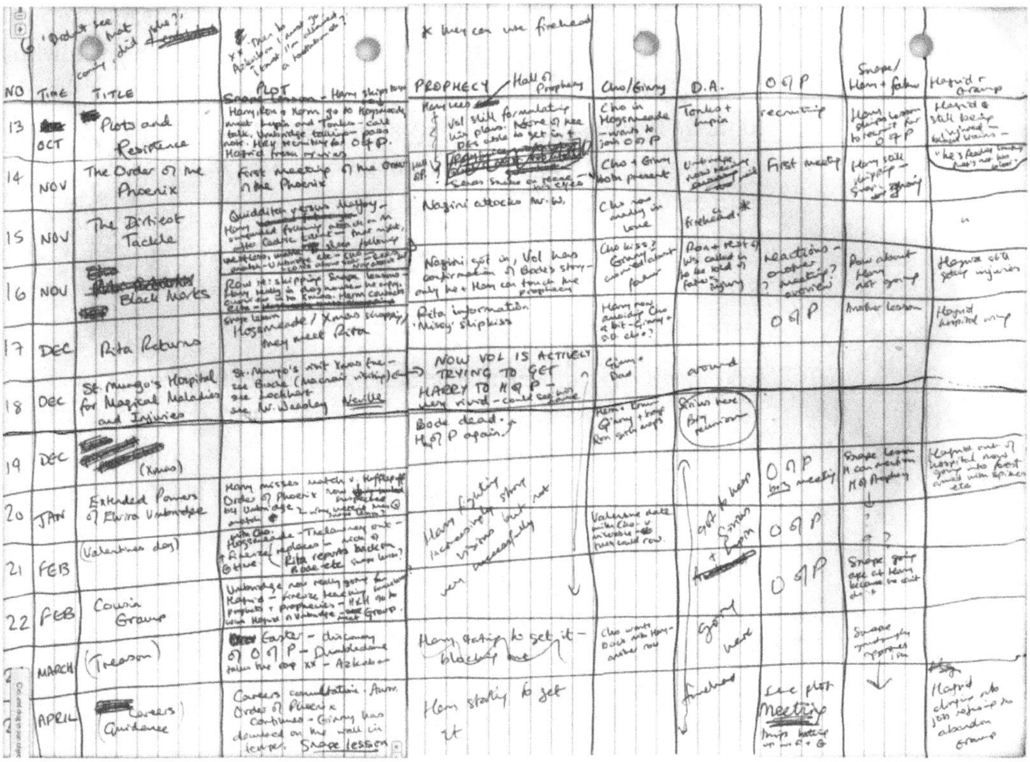

FIGURE 4-2

Harry Potter author J.K. Rowling used handwritten matrixes to map out the plots of her novels, like this one for *Harry Potter and the Order of the Phoenix*.

If you're familiar with the Potterverse and have read the books, you'll notice some events that took place that were never explicitly mentioned in the novel—namely, the subplots near the right of the page. Rowling made sure to note that these events were happening in the context of the universe she created so she could keep track of what was going on, even if she never explicitly exposed them.

There are also many elements present here that were changed in the final novel. Note, for example, that "Elvira Umbridge" is mentioned instead of Dolores, and that Dumbledore's Army and the Order of the Phoenix swap names later.

Even if you haven't read the Harry Potter series (hold on—you haven't read *that* and you're reading *this*? I recommend fixing this problem as soon as possible), the lesson here is clear: Rowling didn't just dive into writing her book. She didn't create a successful story without forethought. She meticulously planned it in a way that forgave mistakes and bad ideas, and without much overhead. At worst, Rowling would have to crumple up a piece of paper and throw it away if the plot didn't make sense. You can even see how she crossed out mistakes and bad ideas in the spreadsheet—imagine the cost of having written an entire scene instead?

Creating a user interface for your product really isn't much different. By mapping out the flows of your interface first, you're outlining the story, your characters, and your subplots.

And flows are important, because your customers aren't going to accomplish the task you've laid out before them in just one screen. From signing up, to taking a photo, to even confirming something with a simple "OK," everything in your product is going to be judged by how well the *flow* of screens...well, flows.

Creating user flows that are both smooth and logical is an essential hallmark of a great product. It is rare that a feature exists within a single screen. In many cases, mapping out your product's flows will help you determine the type of interaction best for each step. For example:

- Does this step need to be a single screen, or could it just be a pop-up window?

- Do you need another form on this step, or could you just reuse existing data from a previous screen?

- Will you need a double confirmation because you're dealing with a potentially destructive action?

More generally, flows are so essential at this stage of product design because all of the following details are getting out in the open:

- Where are people starting in your design: from within your product? Or are they coming to a page from outside of it?

- What are the assumptions your customers have at this point: are the customers new? Exploratory? Cautious? Or are they experienced and trying to get a task done as quickly possible?

- What are the possible decisions your customers can make on each screen—and where does each decision take them?

- What pieces of data do you need to have available?

- On the flip side, what pieces of data do you need your customers to input?

- What happens if something goes wrong—or right? What do you display? Where do you direct customers?

Doing this early legwork relieves you of the burden of keeping these details in your head. It's also an iterative process with your team: by keeping them aware of what you're thinking, they know how their pieces each fit into the overall product and can adjust them as the flows change.

That's why it's fine to be as verbose as possible. There's nothing to lose at this stage, and it's best to put all of the variables that you're dealing with out in the open. Furthermore, there's a high probability that these flows will change as you turn them into interactive prototypes, and, eventually, a fully refined experience.

But where to begin? Start by focusing on what makes up the essence of the product—the centerpoint of your product's use case—and then work out from there. By mapping out the most essential flows first, you can then orient every other flow around them. In other words, the secondary functionality of your product should be in service to the primary flows. This approach has the effect of leading customers back to what makes your product unique and the most useful.

As an example, Snapchat famously made the camera the first screen a customer sees. So whenever someone opens up Snapchat, the app opens the camera first. This places every other action—viewing other people's Snaps, playing with settings, adding friends— as secondary. It makes content creation the most encouraged flow. It also had the side effect of creating new customer expectations within the photo sharing space (Figure 4-3).

FIGURE 4-3

Snapchat for Business presentation deck.

PRODUCT OVERVIEW

Snapchat is one app with several functions. People use it to communicate one-to-one, one-to-few, and one-to-all. They share moments, not just pretty pictures, through stills and videos with added with captions, doodles, or filters to make them even more fun and personal.

APP OPENS HERE

One-to-one messaging and live video — Feed of directly sent Snaps and messages — Photo and video capture with optional filter, doodles and captions — Story feed — Mix of your own, your friends, brands, celebs and events — Friend and follower management

SWIPE BETWEEN SCREENS

So how do you write out these flows? What's the most efficient, flexible way to get this stuff out of your head and into a format that can be consumed by your team?

One of the most unique methods for mapping I've ever heard of—and one that I've actually adopted myself—was created by Jon Troutman, cofounder and chief creative officer for home security startup Canary. Based in New York City, Canary sells a security device and suite of software services that makes it easy to not just see, but understand, what's happening in your home from anywhere. Troutman's responsible for the company's hardware and software design, which includes a suite of mobile and web applications.

Troutman eschews anything visual in this phase and instead maps all of the flows in the text editor TextEdit. His philosophy is that by preventing any ability to focus on visual or layout details, he's better able to focus on the content and purpose of each screen. And since copywriting is a major part of interface design, he's simultaneously crafting large swaths of the interface.

> I like to start in TextEdit as a content inventory canvas where I start to type out things that I know are going to be on the page or on the app. I like to organize things in TextEdit just because—it's comfortable now, because I've been doing it for a while—but at least starting out there were uncomfortable constraints that forced me not to get visual, but instead think in terms of content.

It's also a convenient way to collaborate with the team, and creates a quick way to start experiencing the flows you've built.

> We used [the raw HTML flows] as a way to collaborate with other members of the team to make sure, "hey, is this the content that we're going to want on this page?" By getting the right content in there, it was then super easy to turn the text into an HTML prototype with no styling. Then we all tested it by clicking through, making sure it felt like the right flows and things fit together right and the information architecture was right, then increasing fidelity from there.

Troutman found that this was a way to quickly determine if a page or section of the user flow was overloaded:

> TextEdit forces you to be linear. Then you start to think about importance. What's going to be further down within the content, or what's going to be higher within the content—whether or not you break them into separate pages or different flows, you start to prioritize and give the content a hierarchy just based on the amount of things before it. Doing this forces you to whittle down your content and make things shorter and smaller and more succinct and you start to rearrange stuff around. It's actually pretty key to my process and I use it all the time.

The goal of mapping your flows is to answer the following questions: How does the customer get into a position to complete a task? How do they complete these tasks? Where do they go afterward? What are the potential hangups?

And how are these communicated? Sketches? Diagrams? Mind maps?

Troutman's method may not be for you. Maybe it's not visual enough, or maybe it's too minimalist.

Katelyn Friedson, when she was mobile product manager at publicly traded Care.com, used flowcharts to communicate the general flows of a new product with her designers and engineering counterparts (Figure 4-4). "While it's important to get something in the hands of a developer quickly," Friedson said, "I think it's also important to put as much thought into the flow or feature or product as possible before handing off something that's half-baked. This is done to avoid waste."

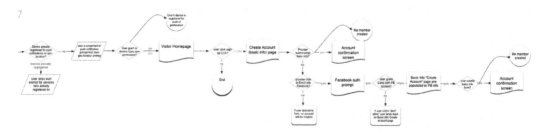

FIGURE 4-4

Katelyn Friedson worked with designers at Care.com to develop a product with this map of flows.

But she doesn't let the fear of handing off something that may be ill-conceived at the moment prevent developers from thinking about what's going to be required for a new feature:

> *That said, developers are looped into what we'll be working on building for a specific iteration cycle. For example, at Care, we were building a peer-to-peer payments flow. We knew which payment vendor we'd be integrating with, and we knew of 4–6 use cases that we were sure we would need to build out. This gave our developers time to begin researching, even coding, these flows— integrating with APIs, testing, etc. It also allows them to prepare questions they have in the event they aren't covered in the product specifications.*

In other words, Friedson uses her user flow maps to enable developers to get more specific in their thinking:

> Forget about design and flow, and focus on areas and use cases that developers can start tackling right away from a backend perspective. These use cases can be easily and very quickly communicated through user flows, which are essentially made up of boxes and arrows, showing the various use cases a user would take. For example, if a user's credit card were to fail, what would we present to the user?

Just because a designer hasn't worked through every loading state or error screen doesn't mean that you should keep your cards close to your vest. Friedson's thought-through-but-evolving user flows let the organization start moving forward even when everything isn't finalized.

Diogenes Brito, product designer at LinkedIn, uses this flow-mapping phase more as a personal step to organize all of the variables in his head:

> What ends up mostly in my notebook, which I always have and I think is an important part of any designer's toolset, is more mindmap kind of stuff. Listing all the requirements, the kind of problems you should think about and related problems, and things we might want to keep in the back of our heads as we're designing a certain thing.

> I'm going through all the options and arrangements, and what really [ends up] I think in my logbook specifically are questions about information architecture. It's complex categorization. What if we think about it this way in these other categories? What if we think about it this other way in these other categories?

For my own projects, I personally like to invoke J.K. Rowling's technique—by first scrawling text and arrows on a piece of paper. And, like Brito, this is an exercise first for myself. It's a way to organize my thoughts and account for all of the variables flying around. Here's an example from a signup flow I had to create for a mobile product on which I worked as product designer (Figure 4-5).

FIGURE 4-5

I mapped these user
flows when working on
mobile products.

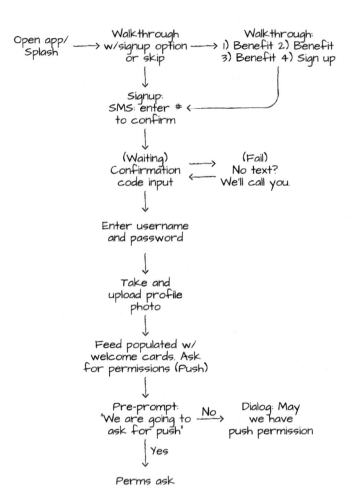

With these broad user flows, I'm seeking to communicate only the broadest strokes of the essential functionality of each screen. Once I have the broad flow down, only then will I go and sketch out the specifics of each screen. You can see this sentiment in the "Walkthrough" section of the signup flow—I know that I want to highlight three benefits, but I don't know what those are yet. There's no need to represent those here in specificity yet.

Here's a more complicated flow that includes a series of forks—importing photos into one's profile from two possible sources. What happens if you choose Instagram? Or Facebook? What happens if you're not authorized with Instagram yet, and what happens if authorization fails (Figure 4-6)?

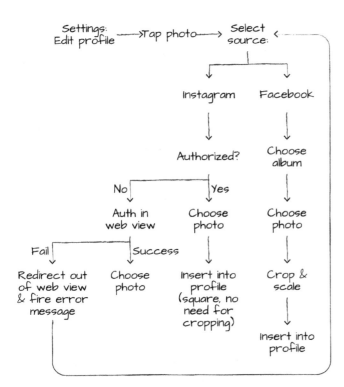

FIGURE 4-6

A more complicated flow on the surface can make it obvious where you can reuse certain segments. This can simplify development.

What I like about this technique is that it easily highlights where and when to reuse flows. For example, if I attempt to authorize Instagram and my login fails, we'll just pop you back to the "Select source" step and throw an error message.

From here, I like to sit down with the lead engineer on the project and work through each step together. We'll literally scratch out, flip, and invent new steps in the flow during these sessions based upon what's right for the customer and what's technically feasible.

Sometimes, if it's necessary, we'll turn these into a higher-fidelity flow-chart like the one created by Friedson in Figure 4-4. This is usually in response to a need to "socialize" the user flows more widely within the company.

So, these are the broad strokes, but what about each screen?

Let's look at those next.

Writing Your Screens

Writing out flows is one thing. But writing out the specifics of what's on each screen is where some of the most meaningful user interface work happens—because, as Raskin wrote in *The Humane Interface*, "as far as the customer is concerned, the interface is the product."[*]

The reason why it's so useful to map out the key product flows ahead of time is because every screen lives in context. Successful screens are aware of the screens that came before them and appear after them.

So how do you make sure that you've accounted for all of the elements required to make a screen successful?

Well, the first step is to relinquish all fear. Ernest Hemingway—whether he actually said these words or not—is now universally credited with saying, "the first draft of anything is shit."[†]

Ryan Scherf, a product designer at Quirky, gets this. "I think sketching is super important. There's no such thing as a bad idea. So as we're thinking through these things and throwing ideas out, it's really important to me to have a team that understands that there's no such thing as a bad idea, and someone has to have the first idea, and usually the first idea is the worst idea."

Think of your screen sketch as a canvas where nothing's impossible. Just as J.K. Rowling used a blank piece of paper to spreadsheet out her plot lines (if *spreadsheet* is even a verb), take this chance to get every crazy, dumb, implausible, or ridiculous idea out of your system.

So list everything that you think needs to be on this specific screen of your product. This could possibly include:

- User information like name, age, biography, job title, etc.

- Common connections like friends, interests, or visited locations to which two or more people could share

- Photos, videos, and any kind of rich media

- Core and secondary actions the user could take

---

[*] Raskin, *The Humane Interface*, 5.

[†] *http://www.writersdigest.com/writing-articles/by-writing-goal/write-first-chapter-get-started/get-messy-with-your-first-draft*

Really, this list includes anything that your product requires to successfully fulfill its promise to your audience—namely, a prompt to the user about what they should do, the primary action you'd like them to take, and any bits of information that you can supply to them that makes their decision easier.

I recommend making this list next to a rough sketch of what you've envisioned the interface to be in your mind's eye. For example, in Figure 4-7, I created a list of potential elements for a hypothetical profile. I listed out all of the possible pieces I could include—with a rough sketch of where they might go, so I could visualize these elements as I listed them.

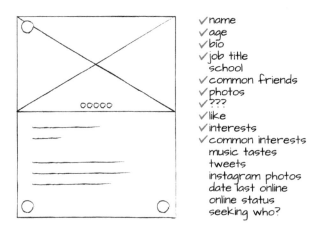

✓name
✓age
✓bio
✓job title
 school
✓common friends
✓photos
✓???
✓like
✓interests
✓common interests
 music tastes
 tweets
 instagram photos
 date last online
 online status
 seeking who?

FIGURE 4-7

List out the requirements for each screen alongside a rough sketch.

Note that I didn't list these interface items with any priority in mind—it was a stream-of-consciousness exercise in what could possibly make sense on the screen.

What's great about doing this is that you get all the insane, crazy ideas out of your system. Once you write it all down, you can take a step back and really look at what you've written down on paper.

That's because you're dealing with reality. You've got a dataset from which to load data. You've got constraints on the client for which you're designing—desktop, iPhone, Android, Windows Phone—you get the gist. What are the essential interface elements that you need to convey the purpose of this screen? What's everything you need for the ideal state of this screen?

We'll explore the ideal state in Chapter 6, but for the sake of this step, you're creating the ideal version of this screen by hand. And the ideal version of the screen starts at its center—what's its primary purpose? What functionality can you exclude that doesn't fit within the purview of the screen's function?

A great example from Internet history lies in Jack Dorsey's initial conception of Twitter (Figure 4-8).* In 2006, Dorsey drew the components of an interface that you'll recognize even today. That's because he was able to identify the core components (however straightforward they might have been) of an interface that aligned with the product's use case.

FIGURE 4-8
One of Jack Dorsey's original sketches of what would become Twitter.

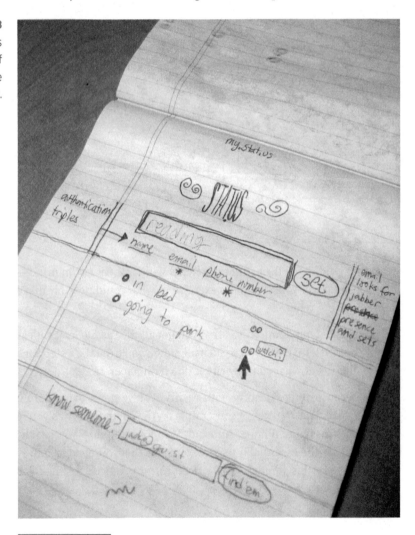

* *https://www.flickr.com/photos/jackdorsey/182613360/in/photostream/*

Also, notice how Dorsey's notes about potential avenues to pursue on this screen never endured in the Twitter interface. While we might have the benefit of hindsight here, Twitter has maintained the core tenets of Dorsey's original interface sketches even 9+ years later (Figure 4-9).

FIGURE 4-9

Twitter has maintained the core tenets of Jack Dorsey's original interface sketches even 9+ years later.

In the end, writing and drawing out your product's interface before you even put pixel to canvas has immense benefits—because you're weeding out the bad ideas before you make big investments. But even in these early stages you can flesh out another massively important interface element—an interface's actual copy.

Traits of Good Interface Copy

Here's the beauty of starting your design with words: it can help you set the tone of your product, especially if you've researched your audience as we discussed in the previous chapters.

These early words are the foundation on which the walls of your interface will be built. So they'd better be good.

Jon Troutman of Canary eschews any efforts at this phase to insert fake text like *Lorem Ipsum* (or, even my favorite, Riker Ipsum, as tempting as it may be):*

> *I write out what it would actually say. I think it forces you to not let yourself put in* Lorem Ipsum *and just* headline goes here *and things like that. You put all the content in and when you first start, you're not playing with font sizes or anything. It's all inline.*

Here are four broad principles that you can use to make sure your copywriting starts off on the right foot.

Who's the Audience?

Who's using your product? How comfortable are they with your product on any given screen? Are they just now being introduced to your product's capabilities, or are they veteran customers? Have they paid for anything yet, or are they on a free plan?

Use the jargon you found while researching your customers to ingratiate yourself with them. What words and terminology will be most recognizable?

But don't mistake your customers' jargon for your own. Internal terms—like project nicknames, error codes, acronyms, inside jokes, or placeholder copy—have no place in your product's interface. Your job is to make it make sense for your audience, not for you.

In What Tone Is It Written?

Good interface copywriting isn't overly technical, vague, or laden with branded or internal buzzwords. It's helpful and forgiving, and it's aware of when it's delivering good or bad news.

---

* *http://rikeripsum.com*

Is your product for stockbrokers? Teenage girls? Book authors? Eco-conscious mothers? The tone of your product's copywriting should be conscious of this. Humor, seriousness, dryness, and other tones each have their place.

The ultimate tone to strike, though, communicates your product's capability of fulfilling its promise—that it can be relied upon to do the job it said it can do.

What's the Context?

Is it a landing page? A signup form? Settings? The first time a customer sees a screen? Your shipping policy? In response to something on which they explicitly took action?

Good interface copywriting takes into account where a customer is reading. And it helps them to decide which action they should take next, if any. Most of the time an interface is presenting information to a person so they can make a decision. Be as clear as possible about which decision might be best for your customer in this moment.

Effective interface copywriting also takes into account the limitations of the context. For example, if you're sending information via text message, you should be courteous and write your message in less than or equal to 160 characters.

The best way I've heard the copywriting process described is to act like a newspaper editor. You're trying to create short, direct, easily absorbed copy that succinctly describes every decision in which a customer might find themselves. The goal is to make those situations effortlessly understandable—so your customer knows what to do next without question.

Are You Being Consistent?

Humans are creatures of habit and your customers will quickly adapt to the patterns and cadence of your product. That's why being consistent within your product with labels and commands is essential.

Can you "Log In," then "Sign Out"? Do you advance by tapping "Continue" or "Next"? Do confirmations come with "OK," "Okay," "Submit," or "Confirm"? Universal commands should be consistent across your product.

And, when possible, buttons should reflect the action they're performing. The best button titles are written with one or two words that describe the result of using the button. "Send Message," "Take Photo," "Leave Comment," and "Not Now" are all much more descriptive than a generic "Submit."

Be aware of common industry terms and the geographical region in which your product is being used. If people know a camera as a "camera," then call it that.

Considering regional differences is also an exercise in consistency. "Zip code" versus "postal code" is a real thing—so is "state" versus "province." And be aware of how you're representing dates. Most countries present the day before the month.

And different cultures have different norms. The United Kingdom, for example, might take offense to an excessive use of exclamation points. Who knew? *It's your job to know.*

In the end, this is the canvas that you can go crazy on at little cost. Writing actual, tangible copy turns it back into reality, because the next phase increases the fidelity of your product—by turning these screens into interactive prototypes that you can socialize among your team.

Shareable Notes

- Interface design begins with words. Before you invest inordinate amounts of time creating the next great user interface, spend your time mapping out each user flow in your product. Then, dial down into each screen.

- But with each screen, keep it low fidelity. Write out all of your hopes and dreams for each screen, even with a rough sketch of what you envisioned the interface to be in your mind's eye. List every element that could possibly be on the screen.

- Assess what it'd take to load all of the data for what you listed on the screen. Then, eliminate what you don't need. Remember the centerpoint and purpose of each screen—what does your audience need to understand what's going on? What elements do they need to make the right decision along each step?

- Ultimately, you're creating flows and screens to create the product that'll annihilate your customer's pain. So start crazy, then reel it back in—because, in the next phase, we'll turn these screens into prototypes.

Do This Now

- On your next project, challenge yourself to start with the most intimidating blank slate of all: the blinking cursor on a white background.

- Think about the tone your product should strike. Playful? Witty? Comforting? How can you use this tone to make your product more useful for your customers?

- Just say no to Lorem Ipsum (or, even my personal favorite, Riker Ipsum)!

Interview: Jon Troutman

Jon Troutman is the cofounder and chief creative officer at Canary, a hardware and software home security monitoring startup. It launched as a crowdfunding campaign on Indiegogo, becoming the most successfully funded project in Indiegogo history and raising almost $2 million. Jon is also the cofounder of Designer's Debate Club and a former product designer at coworking company General Assembly.

I like trying to drill down in the tactics you use when you start building something. Do you start with sketches? What's your personal workflow? What are the tools you use?

One of my most important tools in my process, I would say, is my collaborators—who I'm working with. I think earlier on in my career was a lot more me wanting to be able to solve everything on my own, and even though I still have a little bit of that in me, I feel super empowered by the team that I'm working with. I think having discussions and making plans and learning from each other early in the process, being collaborative as opposed to a designer just going off into a corner and a developer being in a different corner—actually being collaborative early on in the process—I would even consider that a tool just because it's so key to the process.

Then, maybe more physical tools. This is kind of funny. I start a lot of design work in TextEdit.

Really?

Yeah, it's funny, but because it's not design software it's impossible to even focus on any visual or layout details. I like to start in TextEdit as a content inventory canvas where I start to type out things that I know are going to be on the page or on the app. I like to organize things in TextEdit just because— it's comfortable now, because I've been doing it for a while—but at least starting out there were uncomfortable constraints that forced me not to get visual, but instead think in terms of content. Then, if what I'm working on is a website or web app, then it's really easy to take stuff from TextEdit, then just throw it into HTML and just start wrapping tags around it.

That's a great point.

I redesigned the General Assembly website maybe six months into working there. Completely from scratch. We started with the content.

This is how we did the process: it started in TextEdit.

We used it as a way to collaborate with other members of the team to make sure, "hey, is this the content that we're going to want on this page?" By getting the right content in there, it was then super easy to turn the text into an HTML prototype with no styling. Then we all tested it by clicking through, making sure it felt like the right flows and things fit together right and the information architecture was right, then increasing fidelity from there.

If you're designing with code, you can then start to add in some basic CSS around things to make it look a little bit nicer and get a sense of hierarchy.

That's sort of my sketchpad, because, like I was saying earlier, I'm quickest in design. It works really well to just do sketches and start to hone out some of the more visual details there—but then just going back into the CSS and start adding in rule sets that match up with that design. That's how it works when I do work on websites. Right now I'm working on this process of doing a native iOS app, and I think maybe at a high level, the tools and the process will be similar. But it's kind of been a fun challenge so far since it's the first native app I've worked on. It's a little bit different.

There's something about text. I know text seems not very designer-ish, but the Internet is text. It's really all about the content and it forces me to think that way when I do that.

I write out what it would actually say. I think it forces you to not let yourself put in *Lorem Ipsum* and just *headline goes here* and things like that. You put all the content in and when you first start, you're not playing with font sizes or anything. It's all inline and it also goes along with this mobile-first line of thinking, which, regardless of whether or not you're building a mobile responsive site—which, maybe you are, but even if you're not, sort of this line of thinking of, hey, if the user can only see one thing at a time or see things in a linear format, as opposed to columns and a lot of stuff on the screen—TextEdit forces you to be linear. Then you start to think about importance.

What's going to be further down within the content or what's going to be higher within the content, whether or not you break them into separate pages or different flows, you start to prioritize and give the content a hierarchy just based on the amount of things before it. Doing this forces you to whittle down your content and make things shorter and smaller and more succinct and you start to rearrange stuff around. It's actually pretty key to my process and I use it all the time.

Do you find that it makes your copywriting tighter because that's all you're focusing on at first?

Yeah, totally. I think copy is part of design, also like how voice is a part of design. When you're doing it this way, it forces you to not write copy to fit the design. It's just the wrong way to do it.

That's super cool. So, just to recap, how do you make these HTML prototypes more high fidelity? What's the process?

With the GA website as sort of a case study, I would be working on the information architecture and getting stuff structured right, and then I would actually just share the files. I would actually zip up a bunch of the HTML files and share that folder around to some team members and let them play with it. They unzip it on their computer. They just drag one of the HTML files into their browser and they can just kind of click through the either unstyled or roughly styled site. And while they're doing that, I'd let them sit on that for an afternoon while I'm just playing with it and with the design, starting to move stuff around—questioning stuff that I had and then changing it in HTML. I just jump back and forth a lot between those two, working up to designing in higher fidelity.

At what point do you make the final push and get everything locked down? How does your team agree on how it looks and feels, and at what point do you firm that up?

It's always changing. If you're not delivering something to a client, if you are married to the product and you're working on it all the time, you firm it up. It firms up naturally as you increase the fidelity as you're working on it.

You have to be decisive. I like doing stuff that's iterative because you're always thinking of everything as iteration. You're always improving and willing to throw stuff out and try new things—but at the same time, I'm very decisive about the work that I'm involved in.

So you're making decisions all along the way and when something is working you're like, OK, that's probably not going to change. You kind of just lock that in. I don't know if there's a moment where you firm it up and you say, "now we're moving out of this format and into this format" because you've made a decision. It just kind of happens and that process to me just happens naturally.

I think product design includes everything and so does user experience. It's definitely not about an app. User experience design and product design, it's not about an app, it's not about a screen, it's not about a user flow. It's about a person.

It's about the experience of a real human being, and that includes both what they're looking at and whatever screen they're using. It includes how they're feeling in the chair that they're sitting in or the streets that they're walking down while they're doing it—these products that we're developing, they include the feeling that a user has while they're interacting with it.

This includes marketing and the voice and the copy and the feeling is that this is going to stay with that person after they stop interacting with the screen.

I'm working on this product right now called Canary and we built what we call "the world's first smart home security device for everyone"—because it's this simple device that you literally just plug in, and it has all these sensors and an HD camera and it monitors your home and allows you to keep an eye on your home from your smartphone.

The reason I bring it up is because the product that we're designing is definitely not the app, and it's not even the device. Both of these things are included—that's the physical thing that you use, the device that you set on your bookshelf or whatever and there's a smartphone app that you're going to be interacting with every day—but the product is that experience. The technology that's in the device and the streaming and the flow and the interactions and the app are important, but only because they allow the user to be more connected to their homes, to be more connected to their family, and to have this experience that they couldn't have before this product existed.

Product design is all-inclusive and almost impossible to define, because the list would be so long of what's included in product design. But it's everything that touches the experience you're creating.

I think part of product design, and being a designer in general, is caring about people, and thinking about people, and trying to put yourself in other people's shoes. When you do things like that—the more experiences you have that are unique and different—the more you are able to have empathy for people that are different than yourself and people that do other things on a regular basis. You've got to try to have experiences that allow you to move past your own closed-mindedness, which we all have even though we like to think we don't.

You've got to do things that help you have empathy for others, and think about how others experience the world. It makes you a better designer, I think.

This interview has been edited for length, and you're missing out on thousands of words of insights. To read the interview in its entirety, go to http:// scotthurff.com/dppl/interviews.

5

Tangible Trumps Theoretical

Prototypes: Worth 1,000 Mockups

To design is to communicate clearly by whatever means you can control or master.

—MILTON GLASER

FOR TWO SIGNIFICANT SEQUENCES in 1977's *Star Wars*, George Lucas wanted to do the unthinkable: create dogfights in space.

"I had no idea at that point how I was going to accomplish it," Lucas said of the sequences. "[So I] got together with some of the people who I brought in to start ILM. We had to create different technology to accomplish [those shots]."*

At the time, film sequences were commonly represented by static, drawn storyboards. But for these particular sequences, Lucas knew that he'd have to put together something more robust to get the scenes he envisioned out of his head.

> *We had to do it by sleight of hand…[we cut together] videomatics, crude animation, footage from actual dogfights and various documentaries to create a sequence of visual motion.*

With the help of his then-wife and legendary film editor Marcia, Lucas cut together an eight-minute long 16mm film that represented every cut of the battle sequences.

---

* *http://www.starwars.com/video/george-lucas-interview-aerial-dogfights-in-star-wars*

Before the storyboards were done, we recorded on videotape any war movie including aircraft that came up on television, so we had this massive library of parts of old war movies—The Dam Busters, Tora! Tora! Tora!, The Battle of Britain, Jet Pilot, The Bridges of Toko-Ri, 633 Squadron *and about forty-five other movies. We went through them all and picked out scenes to transfer to film to use as guidelines in the battle.*[*]

Shot-for-shot, the spliced footage would match the film's final sequences almost verbatim. In the documentary *Empire of Dreams*, for example, there's a sequence that shows the *Millennium Falcon*'s escape from the Death Star playing next to black-and-white clips Lucas spliced from the 1943 war film *Air Force*.[†] The cuts, the on-screen movement of the models, and the reactions of the actors are almost verbatim.

Lucas would continue to use whatever tools he had at his disposal to get the ideas out of his head and onscreen.

We have always had to use some kind of device to give you a sense of motion. For the end battle of A New Hope, *I used bits and pieces from documentary films about World War II and war footage of airplanes flying, that sort of thing.*

On The Empire Strikes Back, *we had to do little cartoons of the walkers walking and explosions and stuff. For* Return of the Jedi, *we built little models [of speeders on Endor] and took a video camera and we shot little videos of these little models on sticks going through the frame.*[‡]

Lucas's desire to have more control over his shots *before* shooting had, unknowingly, stumbled upon a technique he'd use to pioneer digital filmmaking techniques. In essence, Lucas devised a way to *prototype* scenes before getting cast, crew, or locations involved.

And prototyping, in turn, is changing the way products are made—by improving their quality *before* you go through the costly and time-consuming process of fully creating a product that isn't quite right.

---

[*] Sally Kline, *George Lucas: Interviews* (Jackson: University Press of Mississippi, 1999).

[†] *http://kitbashed.com/blog/war*

[‡] *State of the Art: The Pre-Visualization of Episode II* (*http://www.imdb.com/title/tt0425481/*).

"When we finally got to *The Phantom Menace,* we were actually able to use digital animation to do our videomatics in a more sophisticated way," Lucas described. "Eventually, we came to rely on that department to define how the movie would go together. We'd create the semblance of the film as if you went out and shot with thousands of people. You can't do that with storyboards, but you can do that with pre-visualizing sequences within a computer" (Figure 5-1§).

JARVIS- Yes sir.

FIGURE 5-1
Examples of a computer pre-visualization for scenes in the film *Iron Man 3* by Westlawn Productions. These are the techniques that Lucas helped to pioneer with his digital filmmaking techniques in the *Star Wars* prequels. This "pre-viz" included no dialogue, temporary music, and repurposed sound effects that matched the intended tone of the scene. In the film, the final sequence closely matched the pre-viz—but with the inclusion of the real actors, new sound, and finished effects.

The documentary *The Pre-Visualization of Episode II* describes how Lucas would define a particular sequence with a one-page summary. From there, storyboards would be drawn that defined the broad swaths of the motion that'd be taking place onscreen, along with a rough definition of the scene's visual style.

---

§ *https://www.youtube.com/watch?v=GiZRuOxiCGw*

Using these static storyboards as a template, an editor would literally go "into a barn" with a handheld digital camera and film stand-in actors reading the script's lines. Stand-in props like Lucas's Ferrari or Luke's old landspeeder prop from *A New Hope* would be used.

"You need to develop videomatics to tell you editorially where you're going, how long the shots are going to be, and whether it's working because it's a purely kinetic thing...it all has to do with movement," Lucas said.

Lucas would then use the rough cuts to mold the sequence into what he'd envisioned first in his one-page text treatment. Over time, they'd reshoot the sequence, filming new shots and adjusting the timing until it was just right—then, a digital reconstruction would be built and played in front of the real actors (such as Ewan McGregor) while they filmed their actual sequences. The digital reconstruction would then be used as a basis for the final effects shots.

Getting usable shots as quickly as possible—shots that could be critiqued, modified, and improved—was key to the entire process.

"I couldn't [make these films] without some kind of pre-visualization process," Lucas said.

As I watched this documentary, a wave of déjà-vu washed over me. The process sounded eerily familiar. And I realized how much we, as product designers, could learn from it.

The parallels to creating products are incredible. Lucas's one-page sequence script? Sounds similar to the flows and screens we wrote out in the previous chapter. Rough storyboards and video sequences filmed in a barn?

That's Lucas's version of prototyping.

Product design thrives when exposed to the power of prototyping. It's the embodiment of externalization—getting out the ideas in your head for your team, clients, and potential customers to see and experience for themselves.

Once the copywriting has been roughed out and the user flows mapped, the goal in this phase should be to get something working as quickly as possible—*working* being the operative word. What's defined as working for your product will differ wildly, intersecting at the center of these four constraints (Figure 5-2):

Fidelity

Does the format communicate your design ideas with the appropriate level of precision?

Timeframe

How much time can you spend communicating your design ideas?

Audience

Who's going to be vetting your design ideas? What do they need to see to understand them?

Comfort

How comfortable are you with the tools you're using?

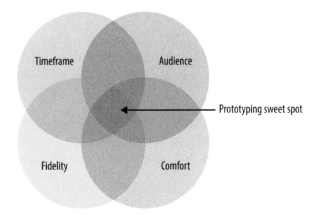

FIGURE 5-2

A prototype is at its most powerful when you're aware of who's seeing it, when you need it done, how polished it needs to be, and how familliar you are with the tool.

Working doesn't mean pixel perfection, fully fleshed-out color schemes, or, in some cases, even any code.

Kyle Bragger, cocreator at Exposure*—a tool for photographers launched within software studio Elepath†—sees prototyping as "more about just getting something running...something that feels polished enough to trick your brain into thinking, 'Oh, this is a product, I can use it.' I can play with it and I can see how it feels to use."

Bragger uses these early prototypes to challenge his assumptions. "Why does it have to be this way? Why are we doing it this way? This is what's most important—it's not the aesthetic, and it's not the latest bells and whistles, [or] the latest design fads. It's 'Why am I designing this? Who am I designing this for?' What problem am I solving?

---

* *http://exposure.co*

† *http://elepath.com*

And really just being thoughtful about it, being able to articulate those things and understand every aspect of it and not just, 'Well, we did it this way, because it was popular.'"

There's an old writing adage that advises writers, whenever possible, to "show, don't tell" when bringing characters to life. The goal is to reveal the story through the character's own experiences instead of the author's.

When designing a product, we have a similar burden. Dammed up inside our heads are creative waterfalls of fresh interactions, transitions, and animations. But how are we supposed to communicate them? How do we get them out of our heads?

Through a game of charades? I'm sure some of us have resorted to these antics. Confession: I have as well.

Not being able to "show" the interactions and animations for our designs is one of the core, common struggles plaguing how we design products.

The static mockups that we used to look favorably upon in the past are no longer good enough. They simply don't do the job. Static screens, manually strung together, don't communicate the motion or velocity of moving through an experience.

Staticness, in other words, prevents us from telling our product's story.

And exacerbating this situation is the fact that we now design for screens that can be tapped, pinched, swiped, zoomed, and more. There's no way around the fact that our interfaces must become transitional, alive, and reactive to fingers.

So as the mouse becomes a relic of the past, let's embrace movement and flows—let's experience the product as early on as possible so we can avoid polishing the wrong gemstone—or, in our case, mockups.

Bigger Than a Buzzword

There's a saying at famous design firm IDEO that if a picture is worth a thousand words, then a prototype is worth a thousand meetings.[*]

That's because prototyping is a form of communication. It's transmuting ideas into the physical realm where they can be experienced by yourself, your team, and your customers.

It's been surprising to me how bigger companies have been leading the way here. Organizations like Airbnb, Evernote, Facebook, and Google have been surprisingly benevolent by publicly showing us how they integrate prototyping into their product workflows. Even better, they're showing us the practical and positive results of doing so.

Efforts to bring prototyping tools down from the mountain and into designers' hands are happening all around us.

Let's start with the obvious: InVision.[†] I haven't seen a simpler, more democratic tool for helping designers and nondesigners alike to externalize the flows they have in mind. Hand-drawn sketches, wireframes, or even mockups of any fidelity can be strung together with convincing transitions that feel native. Then they can be distributed to the team member—who can leave feedback directly inline.

"InVision is my first go-to prototyping tool, largely because it's so fast and simple to set up with the added benefit of being able to share it seamlessly," said Pauly Ting in our interview. Ting is a product designer who's worked with *Fortune* 500 clients, major retailers, and some of the largest automotive manufacturers in the world. "It requires no technical knowledge, which means when working with nontechnical stakeholders, it's easy/low barrier for them to collaborate, participate, and more constructively contribute to the design process. It's easily the fastest tool to use to create a polished-feeling experience."

Apple Keynote and Microsoft Powerpoint are also enjoying a growing role in the realm of prototyping.

"Especially with app design, animations are key—I've done a number of quick, low-fidelity animations to explain what happens after a user taps or swipes," said Timoni West, a product design veteran from Flickr, Foursquare, and Alphaworks who currently runs her own design studio, Department of Design. "Often they'll be presented

[*] *http://www.ideo.com/images/uploads/news/pdfs/hemispheres_1.pdf*

[†] *http://invisionapp.com*

alongside static wireframes. Sadly, Keynote is still best for this. I don't know of another simple product that allows you to cut-and-paste in vectors and perform core animations on them with an immediate preview."

But if there's any organization that's opened the floodgates to building wholly original interactions within prototypes that feel native, it's Facebook. They've been driving the state of prototyping forward ever since the release of Origami—a comprehensive set of tools and extensions built on top of Apple's Quartz Composer.* Originally created in-house by the Facebook Creative Labs team to invent new interactions for iOS app Paper (Figure 5-3),† it paved the way for competing tools like Pixate,‡ Google Form,§ and Framer.js.¶ Even design firm IDEO jumped into the pond when they released their own suite of prototyping tools called Avocado.**

It's also been a poorly kept secret for some time now that Apple has a set of their own advanced prototyping tools. Rumored to be called "Mica," it's the tool that Apple created so that their UI designers could create interactive interfaces more easily.†† This has been rumored to replace Quartz Composer inside 1 Infinite Loop's walls, and is used to create everything from interfaces to Final Cut Pro plugins.

---

*   *https://facebook.github.io/origami/*

†   *http://www.wired.com/2015/02/facebook-shares-smartphone-design-tool-apple-app-store*

‡   *http://pixate.com*

§   *http://www.relativewave.com/form/*

¶   *http://framerjs.com*

** *https://github.com/ideo/avocado*

†† *https://www.designernews.co/stories/23355-is-facebooks-origami-the-savior-of-quartz-composer*

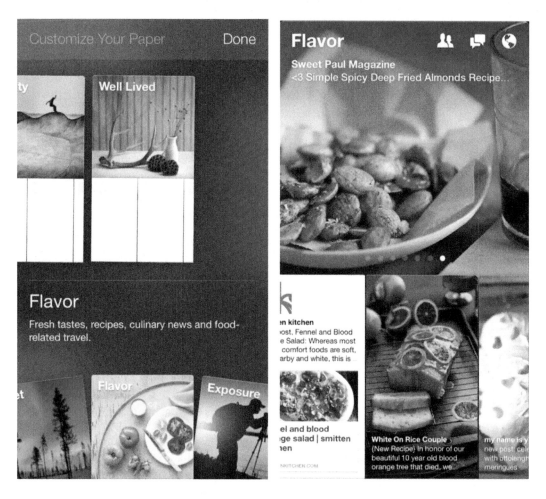

FIGURE 5-3

Facebook Paper's interactions took the design community by storm. WIRED later revealed that they were developed with help from Origami.

This isn't to say that prototyping is just a corporate fad—something akin to transparent glass whiteboards or Six Sigma. Or something that only elitist organizations with lots of time and money can afford to do.

Prototyping can help all of us who build products create better products. And if that weren't enough, when prototyping has a presence in your design process, it has immense practical benefits. It has the power to bring your team closer together, help you make decisions faster, and, overall, make your end users happier.

It just might be the Holy Grail.

[cue John Williams's Indiana Jones theme]

I was, in fact, previously a prototyping skeptic. I thought it was something that I didn't have time to do and that my business partners would balk at introducing something new into our process.

While I set out both to learn how to prototype and to incorporate it into my workflow, I also went into the field to learn from designers who are prototyping veterans: Steve Meszaros, product designer at Wildcard, and Pauly Ting, a product designer who's worked with huge companies like Macy's, SiriusXM, and Jaguar.

Meszaros is building Wildcard's nascent product with Khoi Vinh, former design director at the *New York Times* and named by *Fast Company* as one of the 50 Most Influential Designers in America. With Vinh, Meszaros is responsible for Wildcard's interface design and interactivity, which aims to combine the performance and experience of native apps with the breadth of the entire Internet.

Ting was head of user experience at Tigerspike, a design firm that builds apps and mobile sites for *Fortune* 500 clients, from big-box retailers to Internet giants. His work had to operate at a massive scale from day one to satisfy not only his clients, but his client's bosses and his client's customers as well.

From our combined experiences, I distilled down what we learned about prototyping, how you can incorporate it into your workflow, and how you can avoid the early mistakes we made.

Goals of Prototyping

The first goal of a prototype is to test, prove, or conceptualize an idea that's in your head within a limited timeframe or budget. You're using this to focus your already-limited time. Prototyping cuts out fluff, tangents, and feature-creep to help you focus on demonstrating a very specific use case or workflow.

"It's much like a hackathon," says Ting.

The entire purpose here is to get your ideas out of your head as quickly as possible, at a fidelity that presents the concepts in your head clearly enough.

"Prototyping interactions and animations has been pivotal to the development cycle here at Wildcard and allows us to articulate complex ideas more clearly," says Meszaros.

Many designers who are just starting out with prototyping begin by trying to do too much. But the entire purpose of prototyping isn't to design the interactions of your entire product at once, or to just make *pretty* things. It's to demonstrate bite-sized pieces of interaction or specific workflows.

The second goal of a prototype is to reflect who's going to see it. That'll help you understand how far it must go—does it have to include an entire flow or user track? Or just a simple interaction? How low or high fidelity does it have to be? A successful prototype speaks directly to its audience.

But that's not all. What are your time constraints? This can help you choose the right tools for the job.

Depending on how these factors are configured, a prototype can take on different forms. These are questions you need to answer before you start each prototype.

I love how Paul Stamatiou, product designer at Twitter, describes the give-and-take of these factors he experienced while designing Twitter Video:

> While I love preaching about prototyping, I also clearly recognize when it's useful and when it's a waste of time. Prototyping takes a nontrivial amount of time and can very often be an unrelated technical challenge when you start needing to think about storing state and array manipulation. So I only went to prototyping if I needed to answer some big questions about how it might feel; things I couldn't figure out in "my mind's eye" as one of our designers says. I would get the prototypes functional enough to get the point across but wouldn't spend an extra day or two trying to get every bit of functionality coded.*

"Rapid prototyping is about focusing an intentionally limited block of time in order to cut out fluff, tangents, and feature creep," Ting adds to this line of thought. "Naturally, the more 'polished' the experience, the more impressive it feels and thus a higher chance of stakeholder buy-in. That said, we must prove every decision we make. If an

---

* *http://paulstamatiou.com/twitter-video/*

interaction is critical to demonstrating a new/better/easier way to navigate or work through an experience, then yes, we would build it. But if it's simply chrome, then no."

Remember, as a product designer, your job is to determine the product and features your team needs to build. You need to understand, define, and communicate this as quickly and as thoroughly as you can. The product you define and design must solve the right problem and be something your team is capable of building within a reasonable timeframe.

"A prototype can serve many purposes. It can be just for demonstrating an idea, it can be for exploring and testing an idea, it can be for selling an idea, or it can be to build an MVP," says Ting.

But prototypes are ultimately storytelling tools. If you can tell a better story because of the prototype, then you've already come a long way toward building a product that solves your customer's pain.

That's because a prototype that tells a story helps to sell one user flow's improvements over another, while emotionally connecting a user to the experience—however "faked" it might be. It enables users to get lost in the experience, while effectively illustrating key differences or improvements to pre-existing product flows with which they're familiar.

This can be more powerful than simply prototyping a single interaction, since single interactions are best understood by dedicated product teams. Decision makers or test users will better understand where in the flow the interaction sits, how it's different from any existing interactions, and how it will make an improvement over any previous iterations or their current product.

Once the prototype is ready for consumption, it should immediately be used to drive discussion and an eventual decision about how to proceed.

Here's a great example of this in action—Twitter (again), but in a form you probably have never seen it. In mid-2006, Twitter could've been mistaken for a Craigslist clone. No CSS. Two, simple images (a yellow star and an outline of a start). Just a text box, a submit button, and an unstyled `<ul>` that listed in reverse chronological order the status updates of the people you followed (Figure 5-4).*

---

*   *https://www.flickr.com/photos/jackdorsey/182614595/in/photostream/*

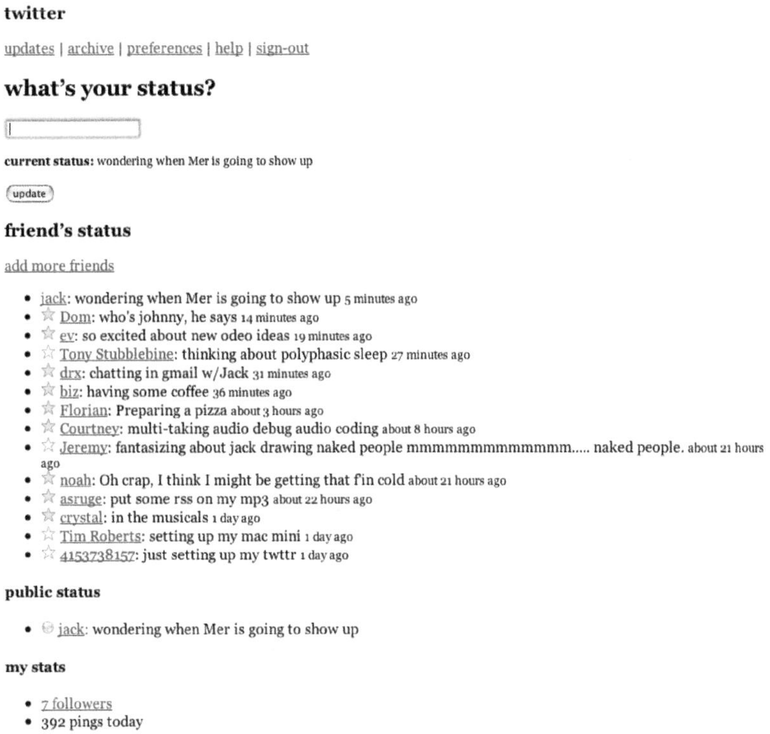

twitter

updates | archive | preferences | help | sign-out

what's your status?

[|]

current status: wondering when Mer is going to show up

(update)

friend's status

add more friends

- jack: wondering when Mer is going to show up 5 minutes ago
- ☆ Dom: who's johnny, he says 14 minutes ago
- ☆ ev: so excited about new odeo ideas 19 minutes ago
- ☆ Tony Stubblebine: thinking about polyphasic sleep 27 minutes ago
- ☆ drx: chatting in gmail w/Jack 31 minutes ago
- ☆ biz: having some coffee 36 minutes ago
- ☆ Florian: Preparing a pizza about 3 hours ago
- ☆ Courtney: multi-taking audio debug audio coding about 8 hours ago
- ☆ Jeremy: fantasizing about jack drawing naked people mmmmmmmmmmmmm..... naked people. about 21 hours ago
- ☆ noah: Oh crap, I think I might be getting that fin cold about 21 hours ago
- ☆ asruge: put some rss on my mp3 about 22 hours ago
- ☆ crystal: in the musicals 1 day ago
- ☆ Tim Roberts: setting up my mac mini 1 day ago
- ☆ 4153738157: just setting up my twttr 1 day ago

public status

- ☺ jack: wondering when Mer is going to show up

my stats

- 7 followers
- 392 pings today

It required no fluff, no fancy UI, and no pixel-perfect mockups. Once the flows and copy were mapped out, the product was easily constructed with the most basic elements. Then, the entire team was able to play with a rough-and-tumble version to test how it worked and to see if it satisfied the stated goals of the product.

Beyond speed, this is another huge benefit of prototyping. It allows for greater buy-in across your organization and even among your clients. The prototype becomes a common language that can be experienced and understood by everyone.

Your goal with a prototype is to understand where your interaction or flow falls short. What parts are implausible to build or too over-the-top? Where do people get confused? What parts could use more personality or ingenuity? How could these changes inform other parts of your product? Get it in front of your developers, decision makers, customers, and clients, and you'll have quick answers to these questions.

FIGURE 5-4
One of the earliest Twitter prototypes.

TANGIBLE TRUMPS THEORETICAL | 111

"Visualizing [and experiencing] interactions allows us to have more constructive conversations with the larger team," says Meszaros. "Prototypes have been instrumental in bringing together and facilitating feedback across all areas of the team, from strategy to engineering and design. By developing prototypes, we have greater control of our consequences. At Wildcard, discovering whether or not a build may be expensive is critical to staying on target," he continues. "That's why I strongly advocate designing and prototyping in context whenever possible. I find it best to build with all attributes of the UI in place as it would be in the final product."

So, how long should the typical prototyping process take? After comparing notes, we found that the entire loop usually took about a week—and, at most, two weeks for each prototype to be created, tested, iterated upon, and readied for implementation.

"[One to two weeks] is a good blend between being able to come up with some quality ideas and delivery without all the fluff, tangents, and politics. It's long enough to stop, breathe, and make smart decisions, but not long enough to waste time," he said. "The biggest thing I've learned about rapid prototyping is that it's a great equalizer," adds Ting. "Using tools like InVision or Quartz Composer really puts the onus on UI, UX, PMs, and engineers to understand each other's disciplines and thus work together. We've had little conflict; everyone feels informed and it's very organic in feeling. Rapid prototyping allows that. It's not just a tool or even a methodology, it's a culture."

This timeframe will obviously vary with the type of project you're working on and the people involved. For many small teams, though, the typical turnaround of this process can be as fast as a typical business day.

"We can refine and tweak very quickly, at times, in a matter of minutes or seconds," Meszaros said. "This level of control is really quite amazing. There is an art to interactive design, and prototyping gives us an edge."

Readying for Consumption

Once the prototype has been vetted by your team and, ideally, your customers or clients, it's your job to make it easy for your counterparts in engineering to implement.

Making it easy for your engineering counterparts to piece apart the experience you're trying to achieve, the logic required to get there, and specific values for timing, speed, bounciness, and other particulars means you're providing the connective tissue between each phase of the product creation process (Figure 5-5).

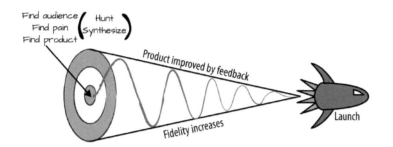

FIGURE 5-5

The product creation model thrives through the power of prototyping.

Remember, with each iteration, your product increases in fidelity. So it doesn't matter if your prototype is made up of a series of screens with simple transitions, or if you're using a high-powered prototyping tool that exports code written like a robot. And it doesn't even matter if you write sloppy code. By taking these steps, you've contributed to an increase in your fledgling product's fidelity and gotten it closer to being realized.

Depending on your tools of choice, getting messy code into the hands of your engineers can take many forms. For some, it might be just handing off code you wrote in Framer.js, or sharing your Xcode storyboards. If you used Quartz Composer/Origami, share your composition files and extract key values, such as transition and animation timing. Include the type of easing curve, such as "quadratic in-out," if applicable. Providing as much information up front about how to implement your ideas will increase the speed at which you can ship your product.

Bleed as much into the development process as you can, and hone this skill over time.

The payoff is that you can start getting micro-builds of features onto people's phones, tablets, or desktops. They'll test your assumptions. And through the process, your engineering counterparts will start to grasp fully just how much effort it'll take to build your product with these features and designs.

Ultimately, you'll be amazed at what you can accomplish through prototyping. Not only is it a great unifier for your team and your customers, but it also builds excitement for what you're building and makes everyone feel like they're a part of the design process. It brings joy and momentum to design reviews. And it helps your team make better decisions.

"Prototyping helps us to make more deliberate and calculated decisions as a group, and that is what may be the most important aspect of prototyping," says Meszaros. "It's an engaging way to review new features or updates and brings a bit of joy to our design reviews. Don't be intimidated to prototype; you'll be amazed by what you can accomplish."

But perhaps the most powerful side effect is that it can make you a better designer. You'll become both more productive and more creative. When you're building rapid prototypes, you begin to create feedback loops that improve your designs. You'll stumble upon ideas as you work through the core problem you're trying to solve.

"There are regular situations where I would literally change a design in front of everyone mid-discussion and ask, 'is that what you mean?'" recalls Ting. "And then we'd test and discuss that. It saved hours and days of emails, meetings, side conversations, politics, and debate."

Shareable Notes

- Depending on who you talk to, a prototype can be worth 1,000 meetings, mockups, or specs. The truth? I don't care. Even if just one of these suppositions were true, I'd say that the value of prototyping your product—and increasing its fidelity over time—more than pays off.

- The intersection of timeframe, intended audience, required fidelity, and the comfort you have with your tools should help you choose the right prototyping method.

- Prototyping will help you gain a new respect for the engineering process. It'll help you understand the cost of building the features that you dream up and the logic required to create seemingly simple interaction ideas.

- Use prototypes to break down the *great product spec wall* between you and engineering and to gain feedback from internal testers and your potential customers. They help you trick people's brains into thinking that they're using a real product, and, as a result, get you feedback you wouldn't have otherwise gotten.

Do This Now

- Prototypes don't have to be made with some fancy tool. String together unstyled HTML pages with links that you open on your phone. Take photos of sketches you drew and make them linkable. Do whatever it takes to trick your brain into thinking that this is a product you can use. Then you'll be able to test your assumptions and start gathering feedback.

- If you want to go to the next level, though, teach yourself a prototyping tool. Play to your strengths. Don't know code? Try InVision. Know JS? Go for Framer. Feeling experimental? Go Origami.

- Use prototypes to smash bad ideas, wasted time, and misunderstandings before they start. Get something in the hands of your teammates and people in your target audience. See how they react without "leading the witness."

Interview: Pauly Ting

Pauly Ting is a product designer who's worked with Fortune 500 clients, major retailers, and some of the largest automotive manufacturers in the world to create mobile apps, ecommerce experiences, and more. He's brought huge teams together by using prototyping as a leveler and a massive collaboration tool. He can be found at http://paulyting.com.

What's the biggest thing you learned after making prototyping part of your design process?

The biggest thing I've learned is it's a great equalizer. It's the first time I've really found teams understand what agile really is.

Using tools like InVision or Quartz Composer, etc., really puts the onus on UI, UX, PMs, and engineers to understand each other's disciplines and thus work together.

For example, when I was working with Macy's, their PM told me: "in all my years here, this is the first time everyone's engaged and excited about working together, and the UX, UI, and devs all want to work together."

So we've had little conflict, everyone feels informed, and it's very organic in feeling.

That's because rapid prototyping allows inclusion. It's not just a tool or even a methodology, it's a culture.

It's about including people. About giving people the soapbox at the same time and not in a linear fashion. It's about giving people the opportunity to be involved and to empower them—but also then to draw lines in the sand that everyone is aware of.

I'd say it's giving up some power [as a designer] and sharing the work around. But, honestly, it's really a much faster way of working. It's the whole issue of when you're trying to make a decision with someone who isn't there with you—like, "what color pants should I buy?" I can send you photos, I can describe it, I can email you the link, etc.—it's just nowhere near as efficient, simple, or even accurate as you standing there in the store.

Because when you're in the store, you are part of the entire context in which the decisions are being made. And that's critical to project delivery and team engagement.

But why? It's the revisiting of old questions, re-explaining things (which mind you, people are *not* good at).

Prototyping breaks down the silos and attempts to stop "offline" conversations where decisions are made outside of scope.

Do you think that prototyping gives designers more respect for the engineering process? That it helps them temper some of those "crazy ideas" that creep into user interfaces?

Sadly, too many UX designers have no dev background. So they see something "cool" in an app like an interaction. Path's "+" symbol menu is a great example. And they "want that," despite an ignorance of what it takes to make, and, particularly in my situation, [it's a minefield with] legacy systems, branding guides, marketing/legal teams, etc.

So, being a UX with a semi-tech background means that I annotate in real-time with them to understand where and how information will be pulled, parsed, and handled. And that's important because it means engineers *are* involved at the product design stage and not at the "we designed this so now you have to make it" stage.

One of my biggest pieces of feedback for Macy's and clients alike was needing to have multidisciplined teams. Sure, have specialists, but UX needs to have some UI and dev skills, UI needs to have UX and dev skills, and devs needs to have UI and UX skills.

And most importantly, PMs, the lynchpins and leads, need to have all three skills. They don't need to be necessarily experts (although I believe it makes for significantly better product), but they can't be ignorant.

Help me understand the specific journey of a prototype. What information do you need to start building one? The workflow of your target user?

I like to know what the intent is. Usually a rapid prototype is to test/prove/conceptualize an idea in a limited timeframe and budget—much like a hackathon. What usually prevents these from being successful is when people approach this like a long-winded, heavily funded project with a million years up their sleeve, or don't have a purpose or objective in mind other than "make stuff."

Second, I would work out if we're trying to create something focused on one particular user to track, or all. Sometimes we are focused on just one user in a specific context; others we need to consider everyone involved and show gains/benefits for all. I always want to design for and consider all people involved, but in a system that might have a consumer-facing side and an admin-facing side, knowing you're designing for the consumer helps to keep focus, and where necessary, allude to an expanded admin area without having to design it for the sprint.

I like to take the time to identify what success looks like for both the business and the user, so that we can set a standard in whatever we create.

Third, I would interview the end users we're designing for, looking particularly at their workflows and keeping questions without bias. A way that helps me really focus their feedback to inform our work is to create a User Sentiment Journey, which is a detailed workflow of the *entire* experience, not just the digital one.

Lastly, I'd create a new workflow over the old one (to show gains, e.g., less steps or less variables, etc.). This includes the entire experience and I would color-code what "screens/views" need to be created, but also so the team understands the context of where a digital experience would sit within the greater experience.

I do all this before I sit in front of a computer and start drawing stuff.

How much functionality do you typically include in a prototype? A whole flow? A specific animation?

It depends. I like to create a whole flow so that I have a story to tell. Telling a story helps to sell gains, emotionally connect the users/stakeholders, and to show a comparison. A single function is fine if all involved have a deep understanding already (like a dedicated product team) of how that function will improve the product, but it will feel out of context/undervalued by a team peering in. Kind of like me trying to show you the value of cedar-wood windows for a house you haven't been part of designing versus one that you have been.

When does a developer get involved? How does that feedback loop look?

I like a multifaceted engineer to be a resident on my prototyping team. My ideal team is a PM, UI, UX, multidisciplined tech lead/engineer—but they all must have the ability to understand each others' role (i.e., a PM must understand at least some code, a designer must have a design/UX eye, all must communicate well and demonstrate a strong blend between commercial pragmatism and the technical work).

More often than not, engineers have been my biggest and best source of better design suggestions simply because they can provide "what if we could?" and "why does it need to be designed this way?" type questions. This is invaluable for real-time feedback about how a function might work. I would regularly design something and run it immediately past the engineer to say, "what if we did it this way?" This really helps them understand my thinking—what I'm trying to achieve—and offer suggestions, alternatives, and support.

When do you show it off internally or to a client? How does that feedback loop work?

It depends on the client relationship. My favorite is when I augment their team and we work together, side-by-side, as opposed to a client/agency model which is going away, doing something, and coming back for approval. I've had a lot of success working with clients using tools like InVision, particularly when there's a lot of work and they want to feel included, kept in the loop, and want to see progress. Most clients are very excited by the tools and become quite engrossed in the design process, which always leads to better product, more ownership, easier buy-in, and a better relationship.

As a result, everyone's excited, everyone's motivated, and people feel professional, part of the team, and ownership over their contribution.

What's the typical turnaround of this process?

I've done a rapid prototype in 24 hours all the way to three months. Ideally, the longer the sprint, the harder it is to maintain momentum—it's called a sprint, after all! Naturally, though, the bigger the project profile, the more detail we want/need about users and their experiences, and the scope will warrant more work, meaning more time.

My favorite timeframe is 1–2 weeks. It's a good blend between being able to come up with some quality ideas and delivery without all the fluff, tangents, and politics. It's long enough to stop, breathe, and make smart decisions, but not long enough to waste time.

One key tidbit—it's important for the entire team to stick together. One big problem is teams who are resourced across multiple projects/teams and contribute an hour here and there to a sprint. You're either on the bus, or you aren't.

Do you find prototyping helps you come up with better ideas?

Of course. Anything that forces you to articulate and arrange your thinking will help you identify strengths, weaknesses, opportunities, and threats. The great thing about rapid prototyping is that you learn to let go of ego in your work, largely because the time invested per iteration is a lot less.

Rapid prototyping helps teams come up with better ideas because it's an inclusive process. Everyone involved in the project can now contribute their expertise along the way, as the work takes shape. It does require a multidisciplined and pragmatic team, though, as it can still fall victim to design-by-committee, but generally, I've worked in a team with me and one other, all the way to me and 40 others—with great success.

Sure, the bigger group was slower, but surprisingly the mood/attitude was much more receptive, positive, and people felt a sense of ownership and inclusion, which led to less conflict.

There are regular situations where I would literally change a design in front of everyone mid-discussion and ask, "is that what you mean?" And then we'd test and discuss that. It saved hours and days of emails, meetings, side conversations, politics, and debate.

And regularly, we'd find awesome and better ways of doing things from suggestions from customers, designers, developers, product managers, marketers, and business teams. My role of UX shifted from being the designer "presenting to the room" to facilitating and leading the user experience design, injecting my expertise and professional opinion at times when there needed to be a decision, and to constantly cross-check the team's feedback and thoughts with the goal at hand, and the users we were designing for.

It also helped nondesigners to make better sense of why some decisions are made that could impact the product, and equally to designers why some business/engineering decisions are made that affect the product.

This interview has been edited for length, and you're missing out on thousands of words of insights. To read the interview in its entirety, go to http:// scotthurff.com/dppl/interviews.

[6]

The Mechanics of Interface Design

The Push and Pull of Prototypes Versus Pixel Perfection

I keep a large number of details that will later go. I first do the animal with almost all its trappings. Then I gradually eliminate them...

—FRANÇOIS POMPON, FRENCH SCULPTOR AND ANIMALIER

BORN IN 1855, ONE of my favorite new artists, François Pompon, applied his coveted talents as a sculpting assistant for legendary artists Auguste Rodin and Camille Claudel in Paris. It wasn't until 1922 at the age of 67, however, that Pompon became famous for his own work.

Called *L'ours Blanc*, or *The White Bear*, Pompon's huge sculpture of a polar bear is something truly unique (Figure 6-1). It lacks any ornamentation or flourish. It eliminates every unnecessary detail. And it makes no attempt to be realistic. Without these elements, the viewer is struck by the raw presence and personality of the bear. Pompon eliminated the unnecessary details to help us focus on what makes the bear, well, a bear.

In this case, both the product *and* the process fascinate me. Pompon would actually sculpt his subjects (at this point in his life, they were mostly animals) with most of the details intact. Then, over time, he'd eliminate these details—the waviness of the fur, the texture of the feathers, the sharpness of the claw—to focus on only the necessary aspects of the subject's form. Without these details, he let the viewer focus on the purest elements of the animal's character.

FIGURE 6-1
Pompon's L'ours Blanc.
Photo by Rodney
(*https://flic.kr/p/4jq2HD*).

As product designers, our job in this phase is similar, albeit less physical. We're gathering all of the information we can, completely immersing ourselves in the problems faced by our potential customers. We're binging on current alternatives in the marketplace, sampling heavily to get inspiration for our own yet-to-be-invented solutions. Then, we're iterating rapidly through the most plausible solutions to see what works best.

At this stage, we're already moving along the process of stripping away the unnecessary. Increasing fidelity. Moving toward something we can *ship* (Figure 6-2). In Chapter 4, we created the copy for our product's interface and began turning that copy into user flows and screens. In Chapter 5, we began morphing those flows into something tangible, something we could use to test ideas and start *feeling* how the product might behave.

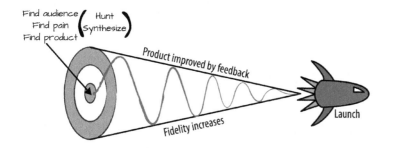

FIGURE 6-2
Remember the product creation model? We're moving toward launch, but we're still not quite there yet.

Now, we're finally going to refine these elements into the ingredients necessary for a badass user interface.

I think a lot of product designers make the mistake of jumping *directly* into Photoshop or Sketch or Illustrator. They misinterpret what it means to be *interface first*, and get caught in a loop of trying to achieve pixel perfection before really knowing which direction they're going.

Look, there's a push and a pull between all these axes. If interface copywriting, pixel-perfect mocks, and functioning prototypes were on a spaceship together, they'd be the directional thrusters responsible for lining up the ship for a clean seal on the airlock.

Like I said in Chapter 5, this push-and-pull depends on your time-frame, your internal audience, the required fidelity at any given stage, and your comfort with the tools you're using.

But at some point after you've written out your interface and its flows, you're going to have to deliver pixel-perfect mocks.

Here's why. See, regardless of the internal living document that is your product plan and milestones—call it a spec, call it a user story, call it whatever buzzword your people use—combined with the prototypes you create, you're still going to need the "hero" version of your product's interface.

Apple, unsurprisingly, takes this approach to the extreme. Called *10 to 3 to 1*, Apple product designers are expected to design 10 wholly different, high-fidelity mocks for each feature to be built. The 10 ideas are narrowed down to the best three, and then the team combines the best ideas of the best three into the final product.*

---

* *http://pragmaticmarketing.com/resources/you-cant-innovate-like-apple?p=0#sthash. JmgfLmPI.dpuf*

While this approach might seem too systematic or wasteful to some, it balances the pressures of creativity with a production mentality. It codifies the fact that most ideas will be left on the cutting room floor, but also sets limits on creative exploration. The goal is to drive a designer's imagination in the right direction.

Why? Because pixel-perfect mockups are the ultimate communicator, because they can be integrated into your prototypes and filled out with the real copy you've already created. Then, *boom*. Suddenly, you're fooling everybody that this is a real product. Disbelief is suspended, and true opinions flow out. On top of that, pixel perfection, combined with prototypes, are the ultimate guidebook for engineers.

So when the final product launches, nobody's going to be taken by surprise.

I'll take those benefits over a so-called *functional spec* any day.

But while pixel perfection is critical, it sure ain't easy. It takes a crazy amount of time. There are multiple screen sizes. Different platforms. Landscape mode. Portrait mode. Ergonomics to keep in mind. And five states for every interface.

But if you plan for these contingencies, the process becomes less overwhelming.

Let's start with the *UI stack*. In the next section, you'll learn how to avoid the pitfalls of what I call "awkward UI" by always remembering how the five states of an interface work together.

The UI Stack: Five States of Interface Design

Have you ever experienced a user interface that feels lifeless? Have you created a UI that just seems to be missing...*something*?

If that's the case, you've probably experienced a case of awkward UI.

Awkward UI is a missing loading indicator. It's forgetting to tell your customer where something went wrong (bonus points for doing so with a scary error message). It's a graph that looks weird with only a few data points. It's a linear *snap* into place when a new piece of data is introduced.

Still not clear about what awkward UI is? Here's a simple real-world example: I use Apple TV. A lot. (In fact, I have the latest episode of *Star Wars: Rebels* playing in the background as I write this.) Whenever I pull up my Purchased movies, I see the screen shown in Figure 6-3.

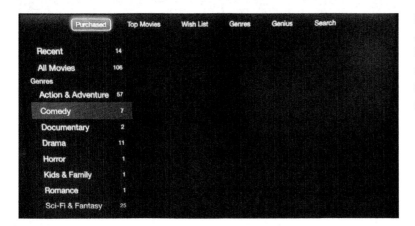

For a second, I get scared. Every time. And I use this screen often. I know what to expect.

But why am I scared? What are the mechanics that cause my brain to think I'm seeing what the Apple TV intends for me to see?

There's no loading indicator. No sign of activity. So in the span of seconds, scary questions race through my head. Where are my movies? Are they lost? Deleted? Hijacked?

Then, after my heart stops racing, the movies I own suddenly and unceremoniously pop into place.

Man, that's jarring.

Contrast this with playing a movie. After clicking "play" on the Apple remote, I see a nice indicator that *Back to the Future* is getting ready to play (Figure 6-4).

FIGURE 6-4
The comforting signs of
progress.

Notice the experiential difference?

Creating interfaces that are easily understood by humans puts us product designers right up against the sad fact that computers are lazy. They don't care about helping people understand what's new, what to do next, or how to react when something goes wrong.

In a computer's ideal world, all it would have to do is throw obscure error codes and scary-sounding alerts when something unexpected happens. Or, better yet, it would just talk with you in binary.

But we don't speak binary. We think in flows, and we're used to the physical world. When a door opens, it swings on an arc. When something travels, you can see it move. When something falls, you can see it bounce.

Awkward UI is when a product designer doesn't take these things into account. That means that somewhere along the line, some rules have been broken.

But which rules?

The rules of the *UI stack*. Let's talk about that now.

What's the UI Stack?

Every screen you interact with in a digital product has multiple personalities. Five, to be exact (Figure 6-5).

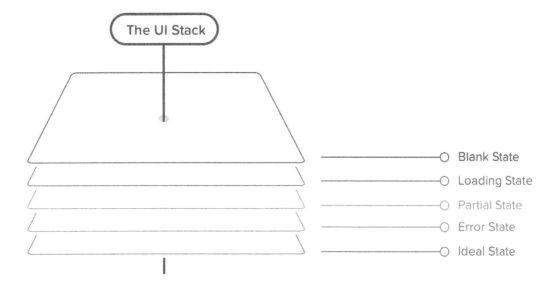

FIGURE 6-5

The UI Stack consists of the five states of a single screen's user interface, as well as how the user moves through those states.

Depending on the context, these personalities are revealed to your customer. In designer-speak, we call these *states*. And you should consider these states for every screen you make.

That's because following the rules of the UI stack and the five states helps you create a cohesive interface that's forgiving, helpful, and human.

Be honest with yourself. When's the last time you created a screen that had only one state? Even if you're creating weather apps (cue Dribbble joke), one state won't cut it.

The reality is that the world in which we live isn't perfect, and things go wrong. Servers take time to respond. And your customers won't always use your product the way in which you intended.

So, as a product designer, you've got to take these realities into account.

That's why every screen you'll design for your product can have up to five states:

- Ideal state
- Empty state, including first-time use

- Error state

- Partial state

- Loading state

As your customer moves through your product's flows, they're also going to move seamlessly between between each state within those flows. In other words, each state in the UI stack is built with the notion that *UI states smoothly transition from one to another*, and as many times as necessary. We'll explore this notion together in the section "A Hypothetical Example" of this chapter on page 152.

But first, a brief interlude into Internet history. Back in 2004, Basecamp, the company formerly known as 37signals, wrote, in my humble opinion, a groundbreaking piece entitled *The Three State Solution*.* (And no, this isn't a plan to end the Israeli-Palestinian conflict.) They outlined that every screen should consider three possible states: "regular, blank, and error." This blew my mind. And changed how I thought about design for the Web forever.

But things change on the Internet. First, there was the AJAX revolution (coinciding with the rise of *Web 2.0*, as it was then known). Then came mobile apps. Next came the mass consumerization of mobile and tablets and the Web in general.

Demands and expectations for UIs changed. And so the UI stack is my adaptation of the decade-plus idea from Basecamp.

With that noted, let's talk about the ideal state.

IDEAL STATE

This is the first state to create, since it's what you want people to see most often. Aptly named, it embodies the zenith of your product's potential—when your product is providing maximum value and is full of useful, actionable content. It'll serve as the foundation for every other state you'll create for this screen. Think of this as the quintessential marketing page or mobile app store screenshot.

Let this state set the tone of each of the other states. Because as you iterate on your core interface, this UI could change completely over time. That's both the beauty and the risk of iteration.

And this has vast consequences for all of the other states.

---

* *https://gettingreal.37signals.com/ch09_Three_State_Solution.php*

All UI states lead to the ideal state. So start with this first, and let all of the other states fall into place as your designs get closer to solving your customer's problem.

Still not sure what I mean by the ideal state? Let's take a look at some examples to clarify (see Figures 6-6 through 6-8).

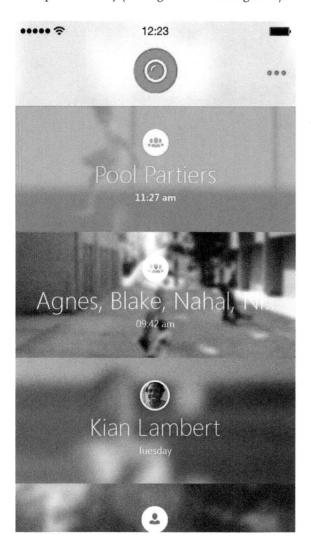

FIGURE 6-6

A picturesque view of the ideal state for Qik, Skype's standalone video app. Here, we have many groups from which to choose, with active users presumably at the ready to receive your compelling video messages.

FIGURE 6-7

Tinder works best
when there are new
people to meet. Here,
we see the dating app's
ideal state—a customer
you haven't seen
before, with many more
options only a swipe
away.

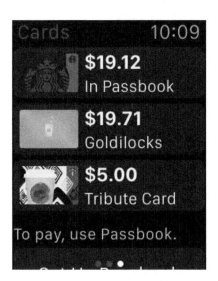

FIGURE 6-8
The ideal state of Starbucks's app, which shows one's various cards and their relative balances. The only sad part is that keeping my balances this high on a weekly basis requires a significant investment. At least it's a relatively cheap addiction.

EMPTY STATE

An empty state really is bigger than just one screen. It's about providing your customer an incredible first impression as you introduce them to your product—to spur them to action, keep them interested, and remind them of the value your product's going to provide.

There are three broad versions of the empty state. The first is what's seen by your customer the first time they use your product. The second is what's seen when your customer voluntarily clears existing data from the screen, like when you attain the exalted "Inbox Zero," for example. And the third is what happens when there isn't anything to show, say, for a search result.

Broadly speaking, the risk with empty states is that it's easy to tack them on as an afterthought. Most of the time, doing this either creates an overwhelming experience (see Figure 6-9) or a cold, impersonal one.

FIGURE 6-9

As George Takei would
say: "Oh, my..." While
I love Propellerhead's
beat-making app
Figure, the coach
marks are oppressive
and overwhelming.
Where does one even
start? How am I going
to remember all of this?

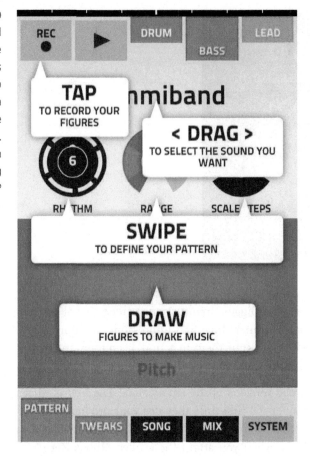

Coach marks—or instructional overlays—are, in my opinion, the
best examples of an underthought first-time experience. They place a
burden of learning on the customer that includes more interface and
more memorization, all done with a pretty big mental interruption.
What a buzzkill.

Let's explore the first-time use state more in depth.

First-time use/onboarding

If a customer is using your product for the first time, this state is your
one shot to describe what your customer will see when data exists. It's
your opportunity to encourage action, to help them understand the
value they're going to get out of this screen. First impressions happen
only once, and this is your chance to make a great one.

I liken this state partially to what's known in the literary and screen-writing world as the "hero's journey" (Figure 6-10). Introduced by Joseph Campbell in his amazing work *The Hero with a Thousand Faces*,* it's the foundation of mythological stories found throughout the world, from *The Odyssey* to *Star Wars*. Here's the basic premise:

> *A hero ventures forth from the world of common day into a region of supernatural wonder: fabulous forces are there encountered and a decisive victory is won: the hero comes back from this mysterious adventure with the power to bestow boons on his fellow man.*

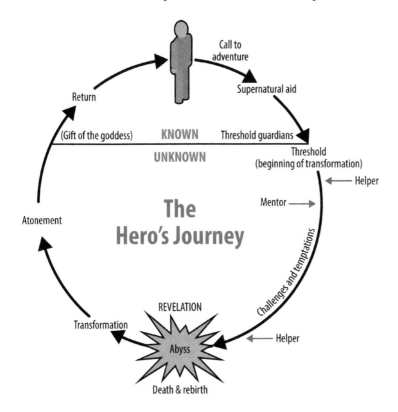

FIGURE 6-10
The hero's journey.

Propel your customers down the hero's journey with the empty state. Call them to adventure, take them through known challenges and the temptations of the abyss, and transform them into more powerful individuals.

---

* *http://amzn.to/1C6SgTo*

But how? Some ideas:

- Lead a horse to water. Be encouraging and uplifting in your copywriting, and speak plainly about what to do. For example, saying things like "Nothing to see here" really says nothing about what your customer should expect, and it's a bit depressing that this would be the first thing they'd see. Instead, telling your customer the exact button to press and why they should press it is a much more helpful prospect.

- Use your product's content to instruct your customer about what to do. For example, if you're building a messaging product, your first-time experience might automatically include a message in the customer's inbox. The subject line could say "tap to open me," while the text within the message discusses more about how to manipulate and reply to a message.

- Offer an example screenshot of what the screen will look like in the ideal state. It brings a bit of hope to your customer that they'll achieve something similar while showing off how potentially useful your product can be.

- Monitor your customer's progress and respond accordingly. If they pause too long on a certain screen, for example, you could message them with a live chat asking if they need help.

FIGURE 6-11

Hipchat comes right out and tells you what to do while hinting at some fun, extra functionality that's hidden beneath the surface. This state reminds you of the product's purpose and, hopefully, demonstrates its value by getting you a response back in real time. One critique is that the copy isn't aware of the fact that Kyle is currently idle, what this means, and that he may not respond immediately.

Figures 6-11 through 6-14 show a few first-time-use empty states that I love.

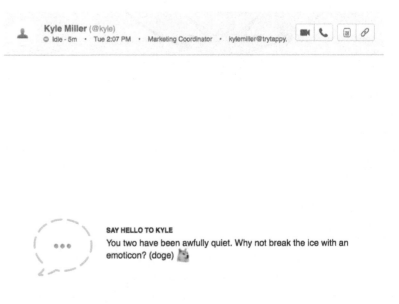

Kyle Miller (@kyle)
Idle - 5m · Tue 2:07 PM · Marketing Coordinator · kylemiller@trytappy.

SAY HELLO TO KYLE
You two have been awfully quiet. Why not break the ice with an emoticon? (doge)

FIGURE 6-12
Facebook Paper
gradually introduces
you to its functionality
while teaching you key
gestures. My critique of
this flow is that, while
beautiful, it's triggered
almost immediately
after I sign up, giving
me little time to grasp
the product. And
having to tap the X to
exit the "tutorial" can
be annoying for some.

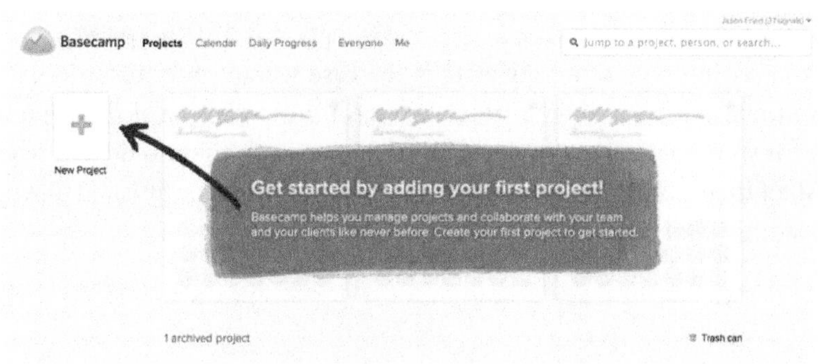

FIGURE 6-13
Basecamp has no
content to show you—
but instead of filling the
screen with nothing, it
places stand-in content
for you to visualize the
product's potential.
The completionist in
me wants to create
projects so I can see
this screen full of
utopian productivity.

FIGURE 6-14
Tapping into Airbnb's
Wish List for the first
time gives you this
stylishly simple empty
state. What I love about
this design is that it
doesn't try too hard
(fitting with Airbnb's
design language), but
it also has a very clear
call to action to get you
to start gathering data.

Your Wish Lists will live here

Explore thousands of fairytale
destinations and add your favorite
spaces from around the world.

Start Exploring

The subject of onboarding and first-time states is a topic big enough for another book. And it just so happens that one exists. If you want to jump into the user onboarding pool, I highly recommend Samuel Hulick's excellent *The Elements of User Onboarding*.*

User-cleared data

The second type of empty state is the case where your customer has voluntarily removed data from the screen. An example of this would be if your customer completed all of the items on their to-do list, read all of their notifications, archived all of their emails, or finished downloading all of their music.

---

* *https://www.useronboard.com/training/*

These types of empty states are great opportunities to reward your customers or to spur further action (Figure 6-15). Achieved "Inbox Zero"? Great! View this amazing photo. Downloaded all of your music? Good—now go listen to it. Sifted through all of your notifications? Here's something else you might want to read.

A customer clearing data is a customer who's engaged with your product. Keep them in the flows your product has in place by doing the work for them. Don't put the onus on your customer to make the next leap.

FIGURE 6-15
A vintage screenshot from iOS 6, yes, but one that still illustrates the slight dopamine drip that comes with achieving Inbox Zero. Your reward is a hand-selected Instagram scene from somebody's coffee shop or sunset—and you can share it out, where you'll celebrate your Inbox Zero and also advertise for Mailbox. Triple win!

No results

In cases where your customers are browsing or searching for a piece of data in your product, there's a chance that they won't find what they're looking for. These scenarios are amazing opportunities to infer what your customer intended to find and to make intelligent suggestions.

Amazon employs one of the best examples I've seen of this technique. Accounting for misspellings and similar searches, Amazon's search rarely gives you an empty result (Figure 6-16). Instead, it'll give you the closest matching result while showing which terms it didn't match.

FIGURE 6-16

The example where I finally reveal my love for metal, and for Metallica. Oh, well, it had to come out sometime.

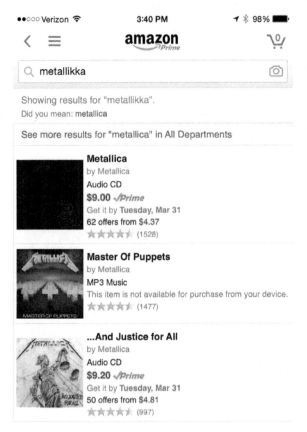

As for Pinterest (Figure 6-17), well, not quite the same results as Amazon, but this is Pinterest, after all. Based upon how their search parsed my query, it should be relatively easy for a customer to adjust their search terms to get what they want.

FIGURE 6-17
Notice the search
results are categorized
("Handmade"), and the
search term is turned
into a pillbox for easy
deletion.

The lesson: don't just drive your customer off a wall in this state. Give them something they might be able to work with, or suggest an alternate path.

ERROR STATE

This is the screen when things go wrong. Typically, this is more complex than just one screen, since errors can occur in surprising combinations. Error states can include anything from missing or invalid form data; an inability for your app to connect to the server; the app trying to move forward to the next step without finishing an upload, leaving a page without text submitted; and more.

Error states should also be comforting in the sense that your product keeps all user input safe. Your product shouldn't undo, destroy, or delete anything entered or uploaded by your customer in the event of an error.

It's apt to paraphrase Jef Raskin, creator of the original Macintosh and author of *The Humane Interface*. He writes:

> The system should treat all user input as sacred and—to paraphrase Asimov's first law of robotics, 'A robot shall not harm a human, or, through inaction, allow a human to come to harm.' The first law of interface design should be: A computer shall not harm your work or, through inaction, allow your work to come to harm.*

This advice could be well heeded by some particularly vile offenders of this rule: airline websites. Missing a tiny form field for a credit card security code, for example, frequently results in a page reload that blows away all of your meticulously entered details while highlighting the missed field with an offensive red hue (Figure 6-18).

---

* Jef Raskin, *The Humane Interface* (Boston: Addison-Wesley Professional, 2000), 5.

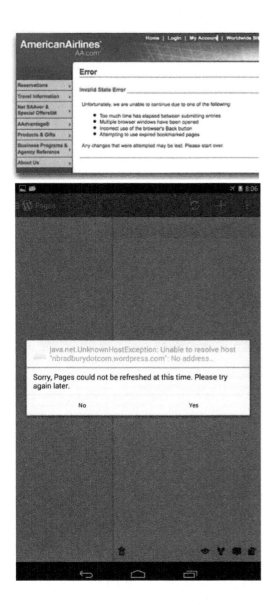

FIGURE 6-18

American Airlines has learned better by now—and I'm sure WordPress has, too. But freaking people out with gibberish-laced error messages or apocalyptic-like reasoning for blowing up one's work is simply unacceptable.

No! Yes! Maybe?

Ah, finally, a contextual error message we can follow. Bonus: we get a little sense of humor to humanize it (Figure 6-19).

Just last week, 5,535 companies signed up for Basecamp.

- Prices start at just $20/month. Jump to the full price list.
- Every customer gets a **no-obligation, 60-day unlimited-use free trial.**
- No credit card required. Just fill out the form below and you're in!

Your full name

Jack

Company or organization

Company

Email

asd.com

Enter a valid email

Password

Easy to remember, hard to guess

Start my two month free trial

Already use Basecamp? Start a new Basecamp trial with the username you already have.

FIGURE 6-19
Basecamp's delightful, human, and highly specific error message upon signup for a new account.

Ideal error states, like Basecamp's, occur dynamically without destroying any data input by the user. If a page or screen reload must occur to detect an error, please do everyone a favor and save whatever data—however flawed—was input into your product. Typically, though, reloading a page to detect an error is a sign of laziness. For the sake of your customers, ensure you and your developers go the extra mile to handle errors in graceful and accommodating ways.

Additionally, error states shouldn't be dramatic, nor should they be vague. Remember the "Blue Screen of Death"? The Mac's "Kernel Panic"? Or—for those computing veterans—"Abort, Retry, Fail"? Each of these error states, by necessity, marked a significant system error requiring a computer reboot or retry. But to this day, each is well remembered because of the shock, fear, and confusion it conveyed to the end user.

Microsoft's Blue Screen of Death (Figure 6-20) became so infamous because it simply freaked people out. The blue screen—while better than a red one—was out of context, abrupt, and filled with scary-sounding jargon, even if it was useful in debugging the problem.

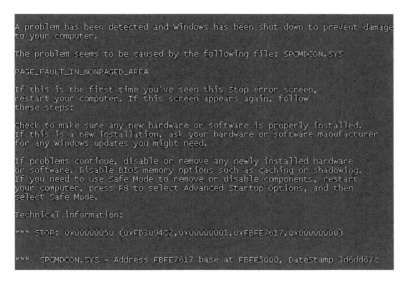

FIGURE 6-20
The legendary
Microsoft Windows
"Blue Screen of Death."

That's because error states must incorporate concise, friendly, and instructive copy as to what to do next. Vague error codes, hexadecimal numbers, and confusing advancement options are only going to scare and frustrate the people who experience these errors.

Of course, your product's audience might consist of rocket scientists or computer engineers. That's a case when these highly technical error messages may be well suited to your customer. But as most of the world adopts software in their everyday lives, these types of error messages become less and less appropriate.

Generally speaking, great error messages are:

- Written with your specific customer in mind.

- Constructive, clear, and helpfully specific.

- Positive—not intimidating or overly dramatic.

- Presented with the core of the error first, and, if possible, an inferred solution.

- Specific about exactly what is in error.

- As timely as possible.

- Written in grammatically and thematically correct language, without jargon and excessive abbreviation.

- Offered with clear paths or options to resolution, and without excessive requirements (especially in the event of password security).

The error state is such a widespread occurrence, and one of the least desirable states for which to design. But I promise that if you put as much care into this state as you do into the previous two states, your product will be infinitely more joyful to use—and, more helpful, as you'll have thought through common customer pitfalls and solved them in advance.

PARTIAL STATE

The difference between an error state and an ideal state is like night and day. But how does the screen look when there's only one row of data? A few photos? A half-completed profile?

The partial state is the screen someone will see when the page is no longer empty and sparsely populated. Your job here is to prevent people from getting discouraged and giving up on your product.

This is a great opportunity to design micro-interactions to guide people toward the full glory of the ideal state. It's a journey on which you take your customers to help them realize the true value of your product. This implies an accomplishment—that your customer has spent some time in your product to see a glimpse of its potential. Keep them hooked.

Some game design principles can be useful here. I'm not referring to the scourge-like yet addictive practice of making your customers gather crystals to advance à la *Clash of Clans* (Figure 6-21), but instead building what is called *acceleration* into this state of your product.

FIGURE 6-21

Big, huge arrows in Clash of Clans lead me to build a cannon so I can expend
more crystals so I have to buy more crystals. Yep!*

Acceleration helps a player visualize how they'll be more powerful in
the future, guiding them along a predefined series of tasks to complete
to achieve this vision. The trick is to make the player not realize they're
performing what could be perceived as tedium in order to extract the
maximum value from your product.

> *Players entering [an acceleration phase] aren't thinking about the
> tedious repetitions they have to perform in order to level up, they're
> just doing them, and enjoying the accelerating rate of the results...
> Rather, those players are caught up in a future in which their
> character(s) will be powerful in a way they can't even understand
> yet. To put it more technically, they're inferring an exponentially
> increasing power structure that vanishes beyond their player pre-
> diction horizon. It's not exactly the same as traditional flow, but
> the exhilaration of the players is subjectively very similar.†*

---

*   *hhttp://clashofclans.wikia.com/wiki/Flammy's_Strategy_Guides/Total_Newbie_Guide*

†   *http://thegamedesignforum.com/features/acceleration_flow_1.html*

Figures 6-22 through 6-24 are some great examples of the partial state in the wild...

FIGURE 6-22

LinkedIn's famous "Profile Completeness" bar, encouraging you to perform exact tasks to achieve 100 percent. Completionists cheer. Flow achieved.

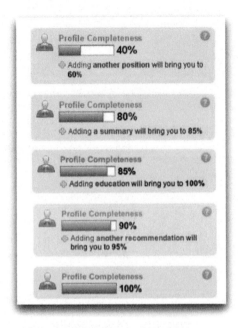

FIGURE 6-23

Dropbox shows you how close you are to achieving some extra storage space, which is a major attractor for most Dropbox customers, I'm sure. Not only does Dropbox show you how many steps you have left to complete, but these steps also have the side effect of making customers more valuable through education and activation.

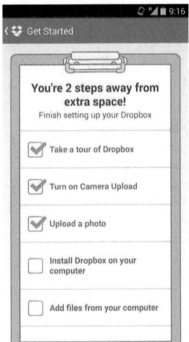

FIGURE 6-24
Apple Watch and its fitness app. Its entire goal is to get you to "fill up" the activity circles.

LOADING STATE

It's easy to overlook this state, and many product designers insert it as an afterthought. But there's a very real burden that comes with setting expectations. When your app is loading data, waiting for an Internet connection, or transitioning to another screen, you must take great care to be mindful of how you represent situations where you're fetching data. This can consist of an entire page takeover, lazy loading of content panes, or inline loading, potentially used when one might look up username availability from a form field.

And the perception of loading is equally important. Too often designers simply fill their screens with whitespace and spinners, placing a massive burden of responsibility on the content that isn't there. This, in turn, encourages your customers to figuratively watch the clock—putting the focus on the indication of progress versus actual loading progress being made.

Such is the belief of Luke Wroblewski, a product design expert that's led design teams from eBay to Yahoo! to Google, where he now resides after selling his mobile polling startup Polar.

Wroblewski and his team discovered that after they implemented a series of loading spinners for each poll, Polar customers began complaining that the app seemed slower, saying things like "There seems to be an excessive amount of waiting around for pages to refresh and load—it doesn't seem as quick as the previous version."

Wroblewski realized that:

> With the introduction of these progress indicators, we had made people watch the clock. As a result, time went slower and so did our app. We focused on the indicator and not the progress, that is making it clear you are advancing toward your goal not just waiting around.*

Skeleton screens

This realization directly resulted in the creation of what Wroblewski calls "skeleton screens" (Figure 6-25). They're a technique that's been co-opted by at least Pinterest and Facebook in both their web and mobile versions.

Skeleton screens are an innovative take on the loading state—they place the focus on the content as it loads versus the fact that the content is loading. They accomplish this by displaying the basic structure of the page and gradually filling in the missing pieces as they download. The beautiful thing about this technique is that it can eliminate spinners completely. And it can increase the perceived performance of your product.

---

* *http://www.lukew.com/ff/entry.asp?1797*

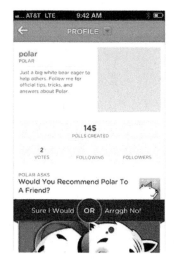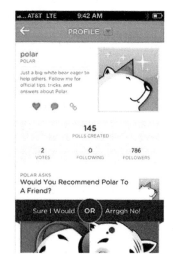

FIGURE 6-25

Luke Wroblewski's app, Polar, and its pioneering skeleton loading screens in action.[†]

Pinterest, while employing the use of the skeleton screen loading state concept, put a unique twist on its implementation: deriving the "average color" of the pin's image and using that color to fill in the pin's background. So before the pin's image loads, you feel like you get a preview of what the pin will be. This technique is now used in Google Image search results, too.

Facebook invented a similar technique, used in their mobile app Paper and later implemented in their web version (Figure 6-26). The Facebook experience displays a stylized skeleton screen with shapes resembling content. And to communicate that the content is loading, the shapes will pulse with what Facebook calls a "shimmer effect."

---

† Ibid.

FIGURE 6-26

Facebook invented a loading screen technique similar to Wroblewski's "skeleton screen" concept. They combined this technique with the "shimmer effect," which pulse the shapes to indicate loading activity.

Assuming success with optimistic actions

"Nobody wants to wait while they wait," said Instagram cofounder Mike Krieger in 2011 as he described how his engineering efforts achieved the app's perceived speed (Figure 6-27).*

Krieger, in fact, pioneered the notion that actions should be performed "optimistically" by a product. When an action's success is assumed, actions appear to take place much faster.

---

* *https://speakerdeck.com/mikeyk/secrets-to-lightning-fast-mobile-design*

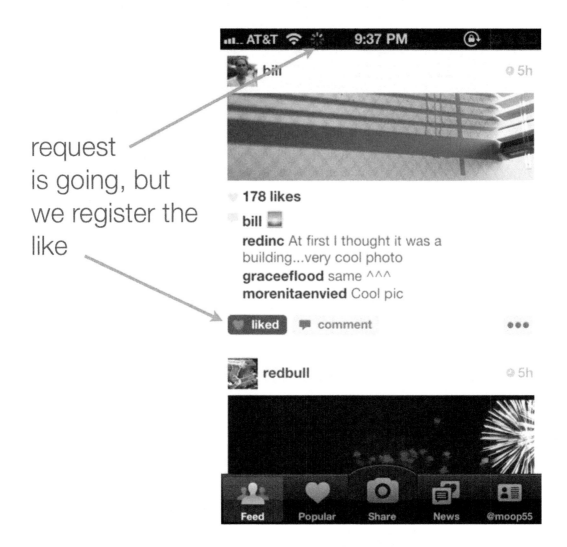

request is going, but we register the like

FIGURE 6-27
Optimistic success in action in an early version of Instagram.

Take the case of "liking" a photo or leaving a comment. In both cases, the action is registered as completed instantly from the perspective of the customer. And in the background, the product is making server requests to actually complete the action.

Optimistic actions can also greatly help to reduce the perceived speed of uploading media. Instead of uploading when a user taps "Done" at the end of the photo upload flow, Instagram starts uploading the photo immediately after a filter is selected. While it's not an optimal engineering solution—and data might get thrown out if your customer backtracks—it makes uploads appear to happen very quickly. Following the "move bits when no one's watching" mantra can help make your product's speed one of your assets.

A HYPOTHETICAL EXAMPLE

You've seen a number of examples of the UI stack and its five states in isolation (Figure 6-28). But how would they work together? How does the UI account for the transitions between each state?

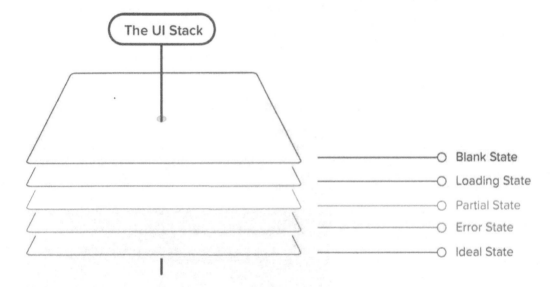

FIGURE 6-28
A reminder of the UI stack and its elements.

That's the power of the UI stack. These states don't exist in vacuums. They exist on a vertical axis that can be called at any time by the product. It's your job not only to account for each of these states, but to dictate how the screen *moves* between each state.

I've created a hypothetical messaging app to illustrate these ideas.

Why a messaging app? Because it's not an immediately obvious example of these states at play. But I think it's a great example of how even temporal UIs like messaging interfaces follow the rules of the UI stack. And, even further, it's an illustration of how immense our responsibility is to ensure that each screen's states flow smoothly from one to another.

So what do we have to deal with in a messaging app?

We have to account for when there's no messages. This is our blank state.

Our partial state is when only one party has sent a message.

Then, there's receiving a message—the typing indicator. This, in other words, is our loading state.

But wait. There's another series of loading states—when *we* send a message out. And then there's the delivery confirmation.

An error can happen along the line, too. That's when our message fails to send.

And you can't forget the mechanism by which we recover from an error, and attempt to send again. There's *another* version of the loading state.

Finally, we reach our ideal state: when messages turn into a conversation.

Our hypothetical messaging app

Let's say Marty and Doc just exchange numbers and Marty wants to message Doc about what he's just seen at Twin Pines Mall.

Since there are no messages, we have an opportunity to exploit the empty state and encourage the customer into acting how we want them to act—in this case, that's sending a message (Figure 6-29).

FIGURE 6-29
The blank state transitions into the partial state.

But what happens to this state when a message is sent? We need to gracefully wash away the empty state and shift it into a partial state: in this case, that's when Marty sends only one message.

Let's fast forward to when Doc has responded (Figure 6-30). He's sent one message—but he's not done yet! Hence the typing indicator, another form of a loading state.

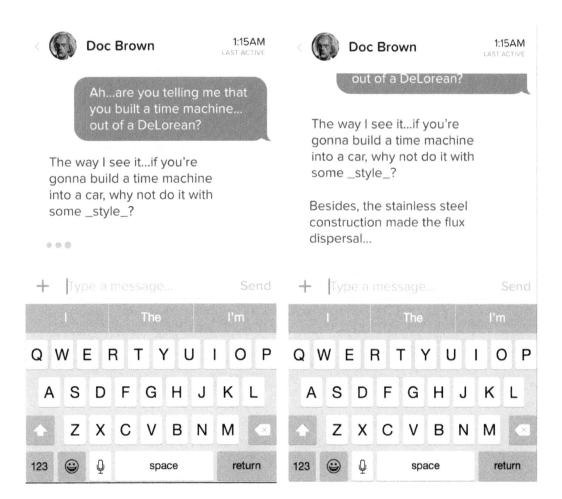

FIGURE 6-30

The loading state—in this case, the typing indicator—transitions into a new incoming message.

Once the typing is done and the message is sent, we transition out of the typing indicator and bring in the new message, pushing the others out of the way.

But what about when Marty wants to reply back (Figure 6-31)? First, we have to show some state awareness when there is text in the field— notice how the "Send" button turns from grey (a disabled state) to blue (an enabled state). Then, once we send the message, *another* loading state occurs for our send process. We keep the message dimmed during this time because there's not a successful delivery yet—until the "delivered" stamp tells the customer that all is well.

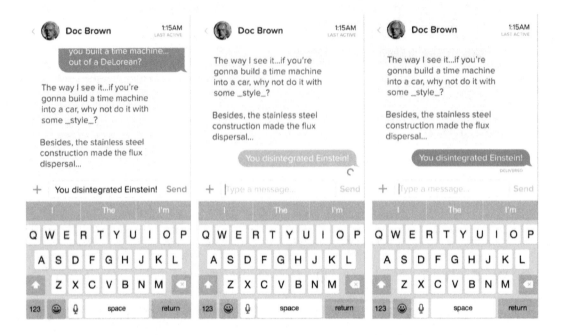

FIGURE 6-31

Sending a message requires state awareness changes on the "Send" button, as well as a series of loading states and a delivery confirmation.

But what happens if the message isn't successfully delivered (Figure 6-32)? Here comes our error state. The red marker replaces the loading spinner, and we're left with a message in the "undelivered" dimmed state. Tapping (or, in this case, clicking into the Quartz Composer prototype) on the undelivered message retries the send. We're in luck this time, and the message fills in after the angry red "!" disappears and we can register a delivered indicator.

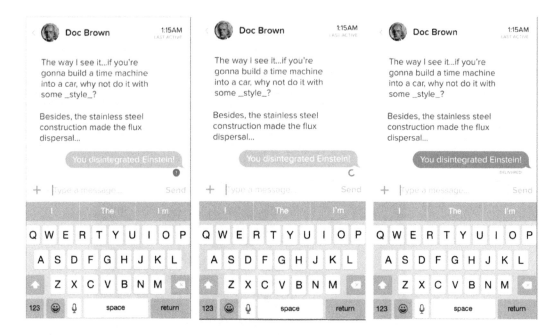

FIGURE 6-32
Retrying a message delivery after a failed attempt. Getting out of the error state requires some careful considerations.

And that, my friends, is the UI stack in action.

It's the five screen states and the seamless transitions between them. Without these transitional elements, we risk confusing or surprising our customers as new states appear and disappear. Making people uncomfortable and confused isn't exactly in our job description, now, is it?

Speaking of comfort, let's shift over to the ergonomic considerations UIs need to consider in this world of touch screens and wearables.

Ergonomics: Thumb Zones and Tap Targets

In the last section, we dove into the five states of a user interface: ideal, partial, empty, error, and loading. These constitute the UI stack. And they exist on every screen you design—these user interface states are universal, no matter the context. Desktop. Mobile. Tablet. Wearables. TVs. Cars.

Now, we're going to talk about how your interface should take into account the physical world.

No, we haven't suddenly jumped into the world of *Minority Report,* *Back to the Future* 2015 style, or gotten to play with those awesome holograms Tony Stark made with his friend JARVIS (or *is* he his friend? Hmmm...)

We're actually going to be talking about natural thumb arcs and why they're important for touch screen design.

See, if you aren't designing yet for touch screens, you soon will be.

Don't believe me? Look at Figure 6-33. IT'S A BABY USING AN iPAD.

FIGURE 6-33
Babies using iPads.
Soon, dogs and cats
will be living together.
Mass hysteria ensues.

For the first time ever, a generation is growing up touch-screen-first. Let's just say touch-based interactions aren't going anywhere anytime soon. The mouse is becoming a relic of the past. We now must design for screens that can be tapped, pinched, swiped, zoomed, and more.

So how do we handle this?

Well, remember when we explored the history of product design in Chapter 1 together? We looked at the work of Lillian Gilbreth, Henry Dreyfuss, and Scott Cook. What was the big theme?

Research. Namely, we need to understand how people hold their phones, tablets, and wearables, and how they use touch-enabled desktops.

And we're in luck.

Mobile expert Steve Hoober conducted a study with 1,333 people in early 2013.* He discovered that people held their phones in the following ways (Figure 6-34):

---

* *http://www.uxmatters.com/mt/archives/2013/02/how-do-users-really-hold-mobile-devices.php*

- One-handed: 49%

- Cradled: 36%

- Two-handed: 15%

Handedness figures were also instructive:

- Right thumb on the screen: 67%

- Left thumb on the screen: 33%

Hoober notes that left-handedness figures in the population are around 10 percent. So the observed higher rate of left-handed use could be correlated with people doing other things at the same time—smoking, riding a bike, drinking coffee, eating currywurst, and so on.

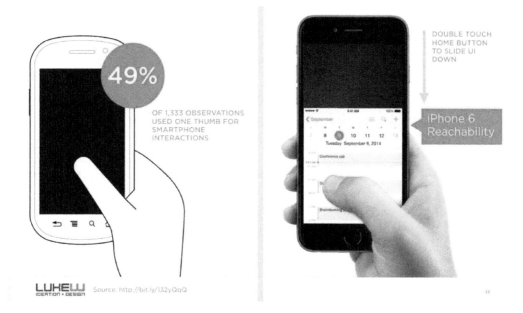

FIGURE 6-34
Steve Hoober's 2013 study found that 49% of those observed used their phone with one thumb.[†]

So it's looking like the 3.5- and 4-inch screens of yore will start their inevitable decline very quickly. That means that those of us who've gotten comfortable building apps, responsive sites, and mobile-optimized web views with the old ways in mind have to learn new tricks.

---

† *https://twitter.com/lukew/status/510442401736187904*

That decline is already in motion. Adobe's 2014 Mobile Benchmark Report claims that mobile browsing among phones with 4-inch screens or smaller was down by 11 percent in May 2014 versus a year earlier (Figure 6-35).[*]

BROWSING SHARE BY PHONE SIZE
(MAY 2013 - MAY 2014)

≤ 4 INCHES   > 4 INCHES

FIGURE 6-35
Adobe reported in May 2014 that phones with "large" screens (defined as being above 4 inches) are driving more Internet traffic than ever.

But this only accounts for phones sold up to May 2014. If you remember, Apple reported the most successful quarter ever of any company well...ever, in January 2015. Almost 75 million iPhones were sold, with the iPhone 6 being its most popular device.[†]

That means that learning how to design for thumbs is now more important than ever. Luckily, it helps that these phone display sizes are going to be practically universal. A cursory examination[‡] of the most popular Android screen sizes points to a range of 5.1 to 5.7 inches.[§]

---

[*] http://www.cmo.com/content/dam/CMO_Other/ADI/ADI_Mobile_Report_2014/2014_US_Mobile_Benchmark_Report.pdf

[†] http://www.slate.com/blogs/moneybox/2015/01/27/iphone_6_shatters_sales_records_apple_has_a_great_first_quarter_in_2015.html

[‡] http://www.forbes.com/sites/gordonkelly/2014/09/04/samsung-galaxy-note-4-vs-galaxy-s5/

[§] http://www.emirates247.com/business/technology/revealed-top-5-most-popular-android-smartphones-of-2014-2014-08-10-1.558896

Apple's changes will make our lives easier as smaller screen sizes die off, since the iPhone 6 and 6+ clock in at 4.7 and 5.5 inches, respectively.

But why do we need to adapt our designs? As Hoober's research showed, people using their phones tend to switch their grip depending on the interface's demands. They seem to do this subconsciously, too, repositioning their hands or setting things down to take an action.

That sends up a red flag for me, though. Why should people adapt to your app? Why is your app special? Why not create app controls that are the most comfortable for most people's grips and thumb arcs?

Designing for Thumbs?

What does it mean to design for thumbs? It means building interfaces that are the most comfortable to use within our thumb's natural, sweeping arc.

But this gets complicated. Take touch screen mobile phones, for example. We unconsciously adjust the way we hold our phones to reach certain controls in various areas of the screen. During any given day, I'll wager that you stretch your grip, choke up on the phone, or angle it in ways that make reaching difficult areas easier.

But we have to start somewhere. Hoober's research suggests that most of us hold our phones in the following way—with the bottom of the thumb anchored on the lower-righthand corner (Figure 6-36).

FIGURE 6-36
Right-handed phone
use means the natural
anchoring of the thumb
in the lower-righthand
corner of the phone.

ENTER THE THUMB ZONE

This leads us to the idea of the Thumb Zone. It's a heat map of sorts—a best guess for how easy it is for our thumbs to tap areas on a touch screen.

Let's use Hoober's research to create a Thumb Zone map representing what seems to be the most common use case for touch screen use:

- One-handed use
- Right thumb on the screen
- Thumb anchored in the lower-righthand corner

Here's the Thumb Zone heat map applied to mobile phone sizes from 4 inches to almost 6 inches, measured diagonally (Figure 6-37).

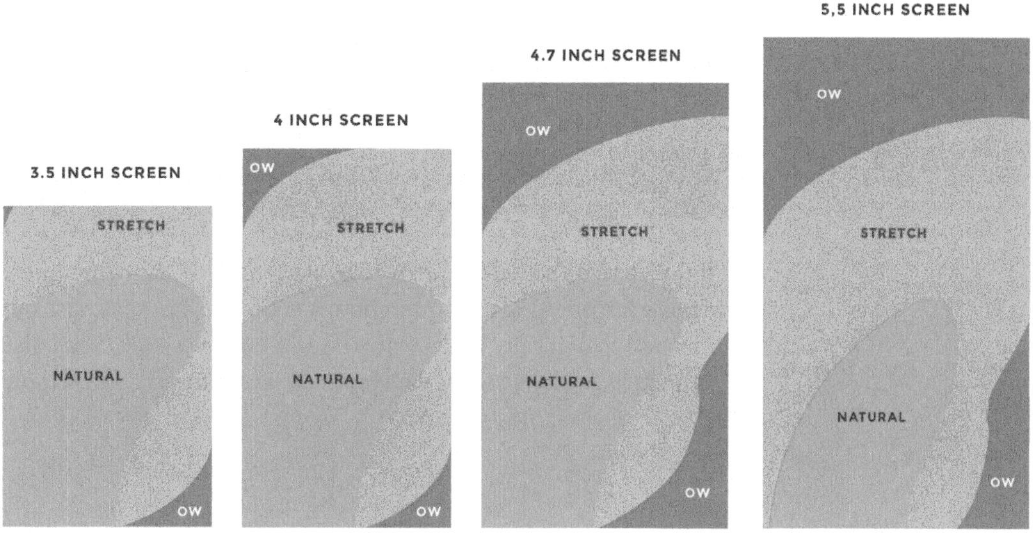

FIGURE 6-37
The Thumb Zone applied to screen sizes from 4 inches up to approximately 6 inches diagonally.

Here's a more direct comparison of large screens next to each other—4.7 inches and 5.5 inches (Figure 6-38).

FIGURE 6-38
4.7- and 5.5-inch
screens with the Thumb
Zone overlaid.

4.7 INCH SCREEN

5.5 INCH SCREEN

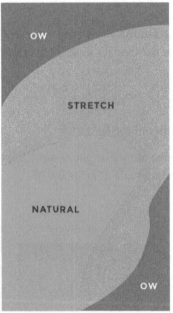

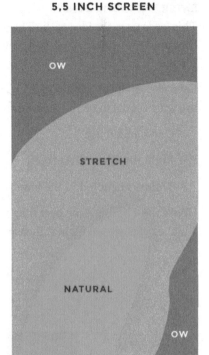

You'll notice that the "safe" green zone stays roughly the same (more on why the largest screen is different in a second). That's because our thumbs don't magically scale with the screen size. And that's also unfortunate, because I loved Dhalsim in *Street Fighter* as a kid (Figure 6-39).

FIGURE 6-39
Our fingers don't magically stretch the way Dhalsim's limbs did in *Street Fighter*.

But what changes is the sheer amount of "Ow" space, which becomes startlingly apparent with the 5.5-inch screen.

Furthermore, you'll notice how the shape of the "Natural" zone changes for the largest screen. That's because it requires a different type of grip due to its size, using your pinkie finger as a stabilizer. It surprises me how different the experience can be with less than an inch of added real estate.

Choking up

Let's analyze how the Thumb Zones change when you shift your grip. Sometimes you might be in a situation where it's easier to tap the phone with your thumb's anchor at the vertical midpoint. This is demarcated by the white dot on the right side of the Thumb Zone mockups.

Here's an illustration of this in action for 4.7- and 5.5-inch screens (Figure 6-40).

FIGURE 6-40
"Choking up" moves
the midpoint of your
hand and significantly
affects your thumb arc.

5.5 INCH SCREEN

4.7 INCH SCREEN

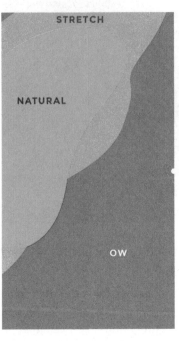

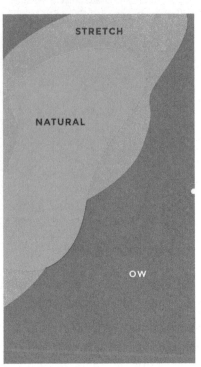

Notice how the larger screen actually gains natural thumb space because of its size. By comparison, the 4.7-inch screen just runs out of real estate.

Thumb-Friendly Interfaces in the Wild

Mobile screen sizes on the whole are becoming more similar, and that's a good thing. But it also means that we can't just treat screens above the 4.7-inch range simply as a scaled-up version of a smaller phone. Grips completely change, and with that, your interface might need to do so as well.

But how would that look? Let's explore a few thumb-friendly interface ideas.

AIRBNB

After Airbnb's rebranding, the home rentals app went through a redesign to place some primary actions near the bottom of the screen. Take a look at the two examples in Figure 6-41.

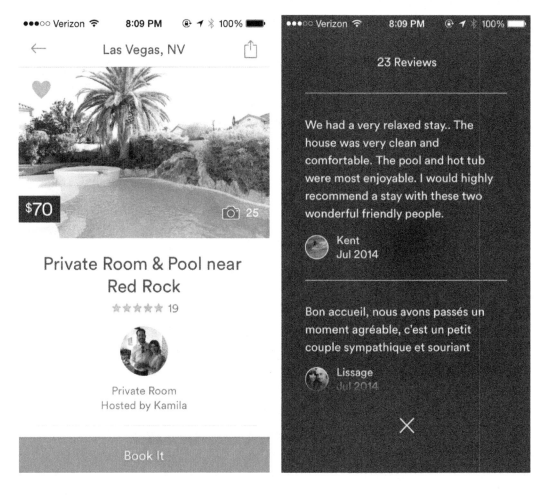

FIGURE 6-41
Airbnb's ergonomic design.

Both screens have obvious primary actions, and they don't depend on obscure gestures or OS-level controls— like Apple's "reachability" feature, which brings the top of the screen down into Thumb Zone green territory with the double tap of the home button.

Airbnb, however, does incorporate Apple's "edge swipe" to prevent needless hand stretching to reach the top back arrow.

TINDER

Tinder's primary controls are nice and obvious at the bottom of the screen, and well in the comfortable realm of the Thumb Zone. But what's even more fantastic is that swiping each card away (both "Like" and "Nope") lives in the green zone as well (Figure 6-42).

FIGURE 6-42

Tinder's a thumb heaven.

Finally, the app's been geared to respond to broader swipes for navigation—so swiping between Settings, Discovery, and your matches can be done with one hand. Beautiful.

In the end, placing controls closer to the bottom of the screen when designing for touch is a wise choice. This way, your controls are in reach of natural thumb arcs. And even if your customer cradles the phone with one hand and uses the other as their primary hand, your product will still be optimized for one-handed use. Don't forget, too, where device manufacturers place *their* primary controls: Apple's home button, Android's navigation controls, and Windows Phone's back, start, and search all rest at the bottom of the device.

Next up: how to design for an unlimited number of devices and their unique screen sizes, capabilities, and contexts.

Cross-Platform Design

There are now more mobile-connected devices than people on our planet.* And each device brings with it a series of constraints: screen sizes, input methods, hardware limitations, and more.

But it gets even more nuanced. We're using a more diverse set of devices on an individual level (Figure 6-43). In the morning, we might use a tablet, a mobile phone, and a TV. During the day, we might use a laptop, our smartwatch, and the onboard computers in our cars. And at night, we might be back to the mobile phone, tablet, and TV combination.

---

* *http://www.cisco.com/c/en/us/solutions/collateral/service-provider/visual-networking-index-vni/white_paper_c11-520862.html*

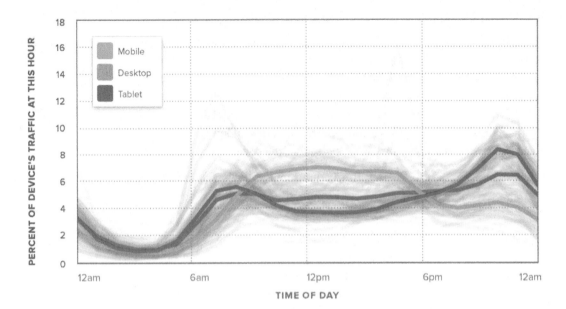

FIGURE 6-43

Charbeat's study of how device usage varies by time of day. Each type of device has a very specific usage pattern.*

With the onset of cheap, networked, and largely touch-driven devices, there's no way that we, as product designers, can predict the future. We live in a world now that already sees networked light bulbs, refrigerators, and toasters. Heck, my electric toothbrush even has a companion app. It tells me when to replace my brush head. Speaking of, I just got a push notification that I'm overdue for a replacement.

So when there's an endless constellation of devices for which we might need to design consistent experiences, how do we cope? How do we create products that are not only future-proof, but can still destroy our customers' pain on any device they decide to use?

This was a big question. And so I turned to Benedikt Lehnert, the chief design officer of successful cross-platform to-do company Wunderlist. Wunderlist spans a slew of platforms from desktop to iOS to Kindle Fire, including iPhone, iPad, Apple Watch, Mac, Android, Windows Phone, Windows, and the Web. Wunderlist was acquired by Microsoft in June 2015.

Lehnert had a few messages for us on this topic.

---

* *Charbeat Quarterly*, vol. 1 (Fall 2014), *http://bit.ly/1GKe9dq*.

What Do Your Customers Need and Expect?

"We want people to feel that Wunderlist helps them get stuff done and keeps their life in sync," Lehnert said in our interview. That's the core task that Lehnert instilled in his product team when setting out to build a cross-platform experience. It's "the most important thing to formulate, communicate, and instill in your team...how it feels for people to interact with your product."

Lehnert's statement reflects the spirit of what we've been talking about from the start in Chapter 1: your product exists to find a customer, and it stays alive by solving their pains. Living on a new platform doesn't change this unbreakable rule.

At Wunderlist, everything flows from here. "From there, you start and go into specific UX definitions and spec for each of the functionalities...we want every interaction to be as lightweight (fast and simple), easy (obvious and clear), and fun (delightful and human) as possible. The values that are formulated in our UX vision for Wunderlist shape every decision we make on flows, colors, language, iconography, etc."

The Berlin-based company—consciously or unconsciously—infuses their product's behavior on every platform with the things that their customers care about. Speed. Clarity. Simplicity. A little humanity. These are the commonalities a customer can expect to encounter when using Wunderlist, from iOS to Kindle Fire.

What's Specific to the Platform?

Just because a customer might expect to have a consistent experience with your product across multiple platforms doesn't mean that you can ignore the specifics of each operating system.

"A cross-platform product experience has to be both consistent with the core product experience as well as the platform paradigms of each operating system," Lehnert said. "So, as a designer your job is to know and understanding those paradigms in order to navigate your way through them." Building a product for multiple platforms means that you have to respect the norms. On Android, for example, system controls are at the bottom of the device, versus a single home button on iOS devices. This significantly affects how you approach a product on mobile phones and tablets.

It's the same with every platform. Designing for set-top boxes? You'll need to know the capabilities of each remote control or controller— Roku, Apple TV, Google Chromecast, Xbox, PS4, and so on—they each have their nuances. Being intimately aware of these nuances and incorporating them into your product is an essential responsibility of a product designer.

But there's a limit. "Knowing when to follow the guidelines of the OS and when to break those guidelines in order to ensure consistency across platforms needs a certain level of experience and design mastery," said Lehnert. Ultimately, we're building a product for our customers. What are their needs? If the guidelines of the platform for which you're building come into conflict with those responsibilities, what should you do?

"Whenever we find conflicting interactions across platforms, we try to come up with a better solution," said Lehnert. "It's easy to follow guidelines. It's harder to know when to break them. We want to encourage all developers and designers to question existing paradigms and push boundaries with the end goal of making products easier and more enjoyable to use."*

One example of this is the pull-to-refresh gesture versus the refresh button introduced by Loren Brichter in Tweetie, and since incorporated into Twitter's app after Tweetie's acquisition (Figure 6-44).

---

* *https://www.wunderlist.com/blog/break-rules-to-design-better-products/*

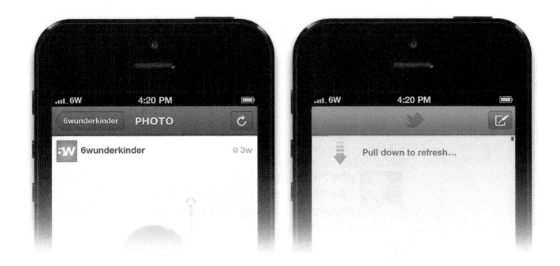

FIGURE 6-44

Lehnert compares the elegance of the pull-to-refresh gesture introduced in Twitter versus the refresh button, seen here in a previous version of Instagram.[†]

This is the perfect example of a UI evolution driven by platform constraints: in Tweetie 1.0, a refresh button would sit at the top of a user's timeline. This was borne of necessity at the time—Brichter couldn't fit a refresh button into the navigation bar. For the next version, he sought to correct this. "Why not just make refreshing part of the scroll gesture itself?" he asked himself. And so pull-to-refresh was born (Figure 6-45).[‡]

---

† https://www.wunderlist.com/blog/break-rules-to-design-better-products/

‡ http://www.macstories.net/news/loren-brichter-talks-about-pull-to-refresh-patent-and-design-process/

FIGURE 6-45

The pull-to-refresh in action in Tweetie.

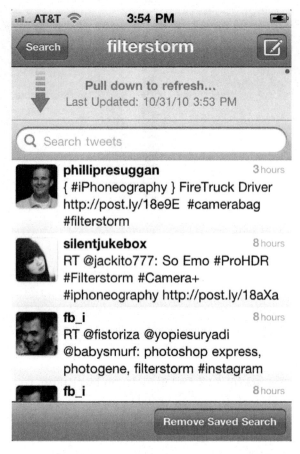

What Are the Use Cases for Each Device?

The same version of your product isn't going to exist on every platform. What are people trying to accomplish on their devices? When are they using them? A product that's tone deaf to these considerations can easily blow it.

I love how Lehnert characterizes this notion. "Wunderlist is a part of our user's life on multiple devices and platforms every day," he said. "Our goal is to escalate Wunderlist from mere software to a character, a helpful friend, that is there when our users need or want it. An authentic character that is opinionated and infused with our values and which evolves over time in the way it looks, works, and speaks. That's what inspires people and makes them fall in love with our Wunderlist."

He knows the expectations that his customers have for Wunderlist in each unique situation, and they build the product on each platform to meet those expectations. "We want to get a deep understanding of what needs and demands people have in certain situations, and how we can cater the product best to their needs."

So that's why, for example, there's not a full-fledged, bloated version of Wunderlist running on the Apple Watch. Instead, it's a stripped-down, lean piece of software that tells someone only what they need to know, when they need to know it (Figure 6-46).

FIGURE 6-46
Wunderlist's contextual Apple Watch app in action.

"One of the most exciting things about Wunderlist for Apple Watch is the hands-free experience in situations where you would have had to juggle your phone," Lehnert wrote. "Whether that's going through the supermarket and checking items off your grocery list or, soon, using smart voice input to add to-dos for tomorrow's meeting."*

---

* *https://www.wunderlist.com/blog/designing-wunderlist-for-apple-watch-from-benedikt-lehnert/*

Remembering what your customer expects, respecting—and breaking, when it matters—a platform's paradigms, and understanding the specific use cases of each platform are principles that are going to benefit any product in the coming years. The number of screens, devices, and contexts is only going to increase.

That concludes our exploration of the mechanics of interface design. Let's review what we've discussed and move onto what goes into the psychology of an experience.

Shareable Notes

- There's a push and a pull between interface copywriting, pixel-perfect mocks, and functioning prototypes. If they were all on a spaceship together, they'd be the directional thrusters responsible for lining up the ship for a clean seal on the airlock.

- Eventually achieving pixel perfection in your mocks—or whatever you call them—is still a requirement. You're still going to need the "hero" version of your product's interface, regardless of the internal living document that is your product plan and milestones—call it a spec, a user story, or whatever buzzword your people use.

- Pixel-perfect mockups are the ultimate communicator, because they can be integrated into your prototypes and filled out with the real copy you've already created. Suddenly, you're fooling everybody that this is a real product. Disbelief is suspended, and true opinions flow out. On top of that, pixel perfection, combined with prototypes, is the ultimate guidebook for engineers. But don't forget: these are most effective after you've written out the user flows and created working prototypes. Otherwise, you heavily risk a flow that falls flat. Too many of these, and you risk a *product* that falls flat.

- "Awkward UI" is a missing loading indicator. It's forgetting to tell your customer where something went wrong (bonus points for doing so with a scary error message). It's a graph that looks weird with only a few data points. It's a linear *snap* into place when a new piece of data is introduced.

- Awkward UI can be alleviated with the UI stack. The UI stack is a combination of five states of interface design—ideal, empty, error, partial, and loading—and how a customer moves seamlessly between each state.

- Design for ergonomics with the Thumb Zone. It's a heat map of sorts—a best guess for how easy it is for our thumbs to tap areas on a touch screen.

Do This Now

- Which pieces of your product's interface are jolting and scary? Apply the principles of the UI stack to every screen of your user flows. See what you're missing, and what you can make more communicative.

- Apply the Thumb Zone overlays to your product's designs. How many of your product's primary controls rest in the easy-to-reach areas?

- Rethink what you know about layouts. Adapt them to the various devices used by your customer base. Refer to Luke Wroblewski's excellent "Responsive Navigation" piece for inspiration.*

- It might be worth conducting your own study of your customer base. How do you observe them holding their phones? What's the context in which they'll be using your product, and what are their hands doing?

---

* *http://www.lukew.com/ff/entry.asp?1649*

Interview: Diogenes Brito

Diogenes Brito is a product designer and a developer who's worked at Slack, LinkedIn, and Squarespace. He can be found at http://uxdiogenes.com and on Twitter at https://twitter.com/uxdiogenes.

I just wanted to start out by talking about a post you wrote awhile ago entitled "On Being a Designer and a Developer: Not Quite Unicorn Rare."[*] You have this very lucid, clear way of breaking down what can be fuzzy, multidisciplinary roles required of a designer and a developer.

Obviously people are very interested in this intersection between design and development. I wanted to ask you what led you to your conclusions, where you talk about how good designers and good developers have a lot in common. I would just love to walk through that thought process.

Sure. It's something that I've been thinking about for a long time, albeit not super clearly, I would say. Partially because I'd always wondered if it was an OK goal, because I was on the fence between design and development. I wanted to do design, but the only way to really accomplish that was to build these things myself.

When you're a freelance web developer and you're a one-stop shop for a client, you have no choice but to do both sides. Once I had that skill set, I was thinking, am I allowed to pitch myself this way? Is that something that even, people will respond to, or they just won't believe me out of hand? It's not a real thing to be both designer and developer.

It's been a struggle, of course, but I think what really cracked it open for me, I'd say, was that Austin Bales talk that I referenced actually in the post.[†]

I had this idea, actually—the diagram came way before the post. The post grew around the original diagram, which is this spectrum.

---

[*] *http://uxdiogenes.com/blog/on-being-a-designer-and-a-developer-not-quite-unicorn-rare*
[†] *https://vimeo.com/61113157*

The Traditional View

LINUS TORVALDS   JONATHAN IVE

WORLD CLASS

WEB DEV "NINJA"   UNICORN   "ROCKSTAR" DESIGNER

PROFESSIONAL

NOOB

DEVELOPER   DESIGNER

I was thinking what is true about the way people consider design and development being diametrically opposed.

I think that it's like he said, that in some cases it is an artist versus, I don't know—I can't come up with a good example. What did he say? He said barista and rocket scientist, I think…

Because all the examples I could come up with actually still had stuff in common. I was about to say an artist or blacksmith or something. That doesn't actually apply, because a blacksmith is both.

After just listening to his talk, I was thinking yeah, the reason you can be both is not because you can be two people—because you can't. There's a limit to how much time you have and how good you can be at anything, really. But because there's so much overlap, and I think of the skills required of making you a good, professional-level designer and developer, because they overlap so much, I think you can do both. It's to your benefit if you can do a little bit of both.

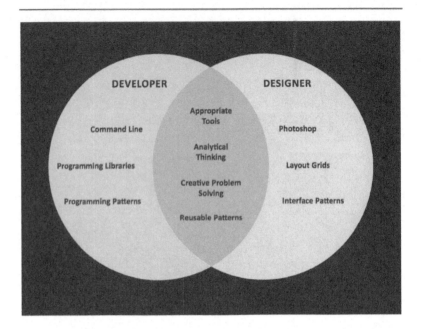

Then I think that leaves the last problem of getting other people to believe, or seeing how that fits in the general marketplace. Because part of the problem is you can only be both of these people when you're in a small development shop, a small startup, a one-man operation.

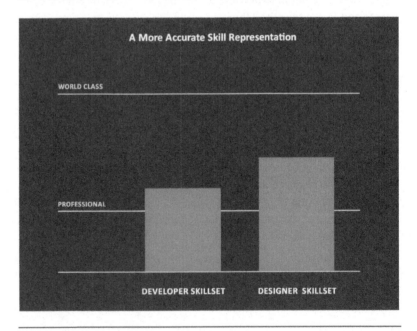

Each person has a certain level of skill in the designer and/or developer subject areas, where many of the skills and habits that would make you excel in either area would help in both. People may have a tendency to lean towards one area over the other, but no one has a "type" that would prevent them from learning and improving as a designer or a developer. What matters is the time and effort put into learning.

Once you get into a larger company where people start to specialize, it's not something you can really pull off successfully as far as selling to other people.

Yeah, and that last point's interesting, because I've always had an urge to be like "Oh wait, no, no, I can do both." Is there a point where you have to be boxed in? How do you deal with that?

See, that's the thing. The way I see it is the reason I put that professional level and that world-class level on there was because I think you can get to a professional level, and you can be really good at both. But if you want to be really world-class, you have to skew in one direction.

That's because world-class musicians, they have one instrument. You know what I mean?

They can play multiple ones, but they're known for this one instrument. I think it's the same deal with being a designer or developer. To really get to a really, really high level, you need to have an in-depth knowledge of your medium.

There's the principles and all that stuff, and a lot of that overlaps, but to be really, really good, you have to know your medium. You have to be in that community. You have to stay up on the latest trends and this, that, and the other. It's pretty difficult to do both of those things at the same time.

You can be professional and you can even do both at work, but I would say I started more as doing frontend stuff actually at Squarespace, and not as much design stuff. Now I've flipped the ratio.

It is difficult to switch modes mentally, from more convergent thinking to divergent thinking. You need time when you're doing design. How do I describe it?

Some things are different enough that it's difficult to switch back and forth or do both simultaneously. Both of these skill sets can be stored in the same person, but you're going to be using each, you're going to be using only one at a time, and then switching back and forth as you go.

The things that'll make you good at one will also make you good at the other. What I mean there is, think of the example of something like staying up late and coding. You can hammer on a problem and just keep going into all hours of the night, and work on this development problem. It's totally the opposite, I think, for design. Where you have to be in a sort of mindset where staying up late or doing any of that isn't really going to help you past a certain point.

I guess the same is true in some respects about development. You're putting yourself in a different place creatively when you're working through a design problem versus working through a development problem.

Switching back and forth between those two kinds of problem solving is, a single person can do it, but in order to do both of those things well—for example, at your job, on a continuing basis, you have to do a couple days of one and then a couple days of the other. Not "I do this for an hour and do that for an hour" kind of thing.

You've definitely got this thirst for research, real raw research, about behavior and the effect of aesthetics on trust and even usability. What are you dialing into these days? Or do you have any authors or professors or thinkers that you like to track? What kind of areas do you spend time investing in and soaking up?

Part of this is a result that psychology was part of the curriculum, but once you know a couple of these basic sorts of heuristics and tendencies that people have, they come up again and again in design. You've got to keep your eyes open for other indications of that same sort of thing happening.

It is a good idea to keep an eye on, I guess, published psychology journals. Really, a good way to get overviews actually of what you might want to read more into is some of those pop psychology books like Malcolm Gladwell.

I think I started back in the day with Don Norman's *Emotional Design*, and that really got me thinking of how some very basic animal tendencies we have should inform the way we design.*

It's like what makes economics interesting. If you make the assumption that humans are rational, there's a bunch of conclusions that follow. Real life will show you, and any economist will tell you, that humans aren't rational. There's loss aversion, and there's all this not mathematical stuff that we do because of how we feel emotionally.

---

* *http://amzn.to/1IViojz*

[I was reading Jim Collins's *Good to Great*, where] he talks about the Hedgehog Concept—which is this one vision to align the company with, but it's not really just the fact that there's a vision to align the company with, but the fact that there's this vision you actually can execute, and you guys are passionate about it and this, that, and the other.

It's easy to see how that idea connects to what you would find in a normal design process when you're searching for insight about what you should do with a particular feature. Like what does the product that this feature's going to be in represent to the user? What can be the best connection between this new feature and what already exists in the product and what people are familiar with?

It all wraps together. It's like different facets of the same idea, trying to figure out what people are about and what they're motivated by. Reading any of those books in general that are informed by—they have good analysis, but they also have good data. That just does, I think, wonders for your ability to think about the craft.

That reminds me of another book. It's a book called *The Humane Interface*, by Jef Raskin.*

What he says, basically—what the whole book is really about—is that an interface should be humane. Humane means that it is considerate of human frailties. It's responsive to human needs and considerate of human frailties.

One thing that he says in the book somewhere, it's like, "consider your users smart but busy." He also says that you should always be focusing your design efforts on intermediates, because everyone goes towards intermediacy. Beginners don't like to feel like beginners. No one likes to feel incompetent, like they don't know what they're doing.

They want to quickly blast by being "noobs" to knowing what's up, being intermediate. Then experts, you need to be able to do expert things, and if you use this thing every day all the time, you need to be able to do things quickly. Really, most people are going to be somewhere in the middle.

Even if you're an expert, the minute you start spending time away from this thing and doing something else, you don't use it for a while, you regress back into being an intermediate. That's where your main design efforts should be.

---

* http://amzn.to/1fjCtWj

He's got so many great things in there, but that is a guiding principle I always think of. Making the interface humane, such that yes, your users are smart, but no, they're not always paying attention. They're not always ready to commit X part of their life to this random application. Maybe they have children, or they have so many more important things in the grand scheme of things.

You need to be OK with that. Sometimes you have to let some decisions that you like go. I don't know what a good example is, but sometimes, you want to make this whole thing a little bit more aesthetically pleasing, so you're going to remove the text and just have this icon that's abstract there.

It'll probably work fine, and people will try it out. They'll figure out what it does. The other option is, don't do that. It may be a little bit more on the interface, but it's perfectly clear; they don't have to think about it. They don't have to wonder what's going on. You don't have to give them that feeling of them not being good at using this interface by just putting this label there, and letting them [flounder].

There's a fine line, I guess, between not patronizing someone, but also real-izing that they're not necessarily a student of interfaces, or interested in learning at all. Because they just want to get X thing done before they move on with their life.

The thing to focus on is that 100 percent of your users are humans. While technology is changing really, really rapidly, human motivations basically haven't at all. Like Maslow's hierarchy of needs, that's still the same.

Designing around that, the closer you are to the base level of what humans desire, the more timeless it'll be. This idea of immediate feedback of some sort with tactility and the idea of affordance where something, while look-ing at it, it tells you what it does, that's so basic that the better it is at doing that, the longer it'll last.

I love that quote: the more you focus on human desire, the more timeless it'll be.

The closer [your product] is to that, fulfilling some sort of basic human need, the longer it'll last. And it's funny, because you see the same design thing happening over and over again in each new technology.

This interview has been edited for length, and you're missing out on thou-sands of words of insights. To read the interview in its entirety, go to http:// scotthurff.com/dppl/interviews.

7

The Psychology of an Experience

Products and Psychology

It is not our intention to make a straight story out of this, we want to gag it in every way we can and make it as funny as possible. These little pigs will be dressed in clothes. They will also have household implements, props, etc., to work with, and not be kept in the natural state. They will be more like human characters.

—WALT DISNEY IN A 1933 MEMO TO HIS STAFF DURING THE PRODUCTION OF THE *THREE LITTLE PIGS* *

"*Mother Mary,*" THE ENGINEER blurted out. The excitement in his voice was palpable. "396 milliseconds."

The temperature in the room instantly increased. His colleagues jumped up from their desks and crowded around him.

"Hot damn!"

"Don't screw with us."

"You sure you ran it right?"

The engineer nodded his head with a smile. "Checked it three times."

The project manager called a company meeting. There was cause for celebration, and the word had to get out.

---

* Bob Thomas, *Walt Disney: An American Original* (New York: Simon and Schuster, 1976), 116.

"When engineers measure the speed of a PC, they talk about something called the Doherty threshold of system response time," he said to the crowded office. "When you ask your computer to do something and hit the Enter key, if it answers you back in less than 400 milliseconds—just under half a second—then you will stay glued to that machine for hours. Your eyes may glaze over, but your productivity will soar. Even a slight deviation back to half-second response time will allow your attention to stray. But under 400 milliseconds, that's the sweet spot. Well, guess what? Our soon-to-be Cardiff PC, though it looks ragtag now, just clocked in at 396 milliseconds. Once assembled, it will not only be faster than all the other PCs on the market, it will also be addictive."

I paused the fourth episode of *Halt and Catch Fire* and looked up from my Netflix stream. *The "Doherty threshold"? Is this a thing?* I thought. *It's probably something made up for the show.*

I was wrong.

The Doherty threshold has its origins in the *IBM Systems Journal* paper "The Economic Value of Rapid Response Time" written by Walter J. Doherty and Ahrvind J. Thadani. Published in 1982, "it was thought that a relatively slow response, up to two seconds, was acceptable because the person was thinking about the next task. Research on rapid response time now indicates that this earlier theory is not borne out by the facts: productivity increases in more than direct proportion to a decrease in response time."[*]

Doherty and Thadani's research had a significant practical finding: the requirement for computer response time was decreased to 400 milliseconds from 2 seconds, which had been the previous standard (Figure 7-1).

The old standard was created in 1968 by Robert B. Miller, who worked in IBM's Poughkeepsie laboratory.[†] He believed that two seconds was more than enough time for a system response because "users were thinking as rapidly as they could, uninfluenced by how long the system took to respond."[‡]

---

[*]   *http://www.vm.ibm.com/devpages/jelliott/evrrt.html*

[†]   *https://www.computer.org/csdl/proceedings/afips/1968/5072/00/50720267.pdf*

[‡]   *http://www.vm.ibm.com/devpages/jelliott/evrrt.html*

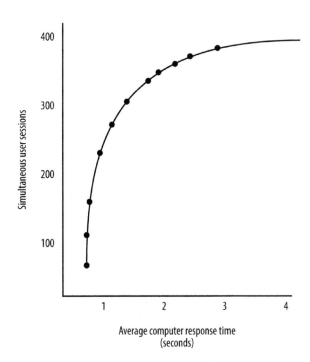

FIGURE 7-1
"Response Time Deterioration with Increasing System Usage at the National Institutes of Health Computer Utility"—in other words, the faster a computer responds, the more people will use it.

Wow. Imagine waiting *two seconds* to get a response for an input.

But Doherty and Thadani disproved that. Humans can hold a series of short-term tasks in their head and are more productive when they aren't hindered by an external delay. Attention spans are preserved on a rotating basis and focus lasts longer. The net result is higher productivity, less time spent working, and a substantial amount of money saved. And, in the end, the product would be given the credit.

This is one of the most fascinating examples I've seen about how the speed of a product—or even the perception of its speed—can significantly affect us whether we know it or not.

Your product's psychology, like speed or response time, is highly dependent on context—how, where, and when a customer is using your product. For example, 400 milliseconds is a *terrible* response time for touch-based interfaces in specific contexts like drawing or painting. Even a 400 percent improvement down to a 100-millisecond response time is a bad experience.

We know this from a Microsoft Applied Sciences Group research study on touch interface latency. With an in-house device, researchers were able to get touch latency *down to 1 ms!* At that speed, the touch response was indistinguishable from pen and paper (Figure 7-2).*

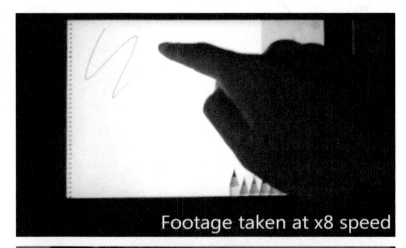

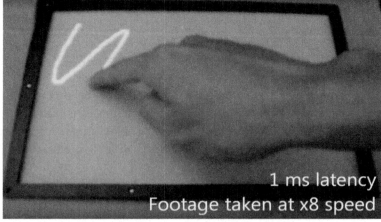

But speed can affect us a whole lot more than someone drawing on their tablet.

Google and Shopzilla are companies that have large enough footprints to test these things at scale.

And wow. Humans are *really* susceptible to latency.

---

* Microsoft Research, "Applied Sciences Group: High Performance Touch," *https://www.youtube.com/watch?v=vOvQCPLkPt4.*

When Marissa Mayer was at Google, for example, she asked the company's users how many search results they wanted to see per page per query. Did they want 10 results per page? 20? 25? 30? The responses to the survey culminated into a "more is better" mentality.

But guess what? After they ran A/B tests on the user segments, "the number of Google searches seen from the users that were in the experiment dropped by 20 percent," Mayer said at a talk in 2010.[†] "When we gave users 30 results per page, they actually searched 1/5 less." What was even more startling was that usage on the first page also dropped 20 percent (Figure 7-3)!

FIGURE 7-3

Marissa Mayer's speed research results at Google (recreated from her original slides).

---

† *https://www.youtube.com/watch?v=BQwAKsFmK_8*

The team was flummoxed. Was it a "paradox of choice" problem? Were people simply being overwhelmed with information?

After poring through the logs, Mayer discovered that it "takes us longer to produce 30 results than 10 results—about twice as long. [This] latency drove this decline. Users really care about speed, and respond to speed. We know as the Web gets faster, people search more. And as it gets slower, people search less."

The team found the same effect on Maps—in this case, when the size of the page was reduced by 30 percent. In return, they got 30 percent more Maps requests! "If you make a product faster, you get that back in terms of increased usage almost right away."

Speed even makes us buy more stuff. Shopzilla redesigned their pages and infrastructure over the course of a year, and the result of a five-second speed increase on page performance (from seven seconds to two) resulted in crazy numbers (Figure 7-4).* It increased revenue 7 to 12 percent and pageviews by 25 percent.†

FIGURE 7-4

Faster products make us buy more stuff.

Performance Summary

Conversion Rate	+7% - 12%
Page View's	+25%
US SEM Sessions	+8%
Bizrate.co.uk SEM Sessions	+120%
Infrastructure Required (US)	-50% (200 vs 402 nodes)
Availability	99.71% → 99.94%
Product Velocity	+225%
Release Cost	$1,000's → $80

Phil Dixon – VP, Engineering | Velocity 2009 | June 23rd, 2009

So if our brains are so sensitive to things like the responsiveness—or the lack thereof—of a product, to what else are we susceptible? And what should we as product designers be doing about these factors?

---

* *http://radar.oreilly.com/2009/07/velocity-making-your-site-fast.html*
† *http://conferences.oreilly.com/velocity/velocity2009/public/schedule/detail/7709*

Transitions and animations. A personality. Positive reinforcement for the key actions of your product. Feedback loops that are thought out. A lack of psychological—or even physical—friction. Heck, even *sound*.

But these attributes are only modifiers for the underlying value of the product. If the product doesn't deliver on the promise to the customer that it's going to solve their problems—well, that's like going to see an action movie that's completely unentertaining.

This is how Jonathan Badeen, cofounder and vice president of product at Tinder, approached the creation of the dating app. He's also the inventor of the swipe right. Yes, *that* swipe right. "You have to be solving a problem," he said in our interview. "That problem might be as simple as alleviating boredom, but it might be as important as finding a soulmate. But from more of a design, animation, and interaction standpoint, I think it's important to simply sweat the details. Insist that things work in a way that feels natural to the user."

We're all human and we're not immune to the effect of these details and the emotions that they surface. So how can your products tap into that emotion? How can emotion be used to create powerful feedback loops that draw your customers into the experience, and keep them coming back for more?

Let's examine these factors now.

Loops

Product loops are ways to get your customers to use a specific flow in your product. Back in Chapter 4, I defined user flows as the way someone moves through your product to complete a specific task.

In almost all cases in product design, there are specific flows you'll want your customer to take at certain times. That's where loops come in.

I was at a friend's wedding on a remote island off the coast of North Carolina, and I inadvertently stumbled upon one of the best loops I've ever seen. The difference was that it was in real life (Figure 7-5).

FIGURE 7-5
A real-life loop that
probably makes life
incredibly easier for
resort staff.

Setting up furniture in a banquet hall for over a hundred people is grunt work. And the last thing anybody wants to do after a night of celebration and revelry is to clean that stuff up and return it to the state you found it.

So the organizers of the banquet hall made it easy. They gave us a template to follow, essentially a paint-by-numbers furniture storage guide.

And, I tell you what, we cleaned that room up in record time. I'm also proud to say that the closet looked *exactly* like that photo when we were done.

For product loops to be effective, they need to incorporate a number of psychological factors. Is it inviting a desirable experience? Is it novel or new? Is it appearing at the correct time?

But these are just traits of a successful loop. For a loop to truly be effective, it needs to take root in your customer's mind that it's worth pursuing because it has payoff.

In other words, successful loops take root in the human mind, effectively incurring some behavioral change.

And loops don't just happen inside of your product. Some of the most effective loops we'll see happen *outside* of the product, with the intention of getting a customer to engage with a specific user flow *inside* of the product. In other words, loops can also be used for activation and retention.

Dr. BJ Fogg, who founded the Persuasive Tech Lab at Stanford University, is an expert on using technology to change behaviors in positive ways. He's also the author of *Persuasive Technology: Using Computers to Change What We Think and Do.*

Fogg invented the "Fogg Behavioral Model" (Figure 7-6) to help designers identify what stops people from performing behaviors that designers seek.[*] For example, if users are not performing a target behavior, such as rating hotels on a travel website, the FBM helps designers see what psychological element is lacking.

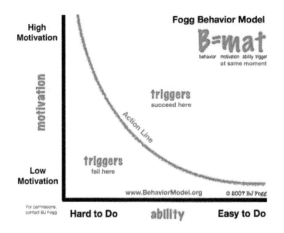

FIGURE 7-6
The Fogg Behavioral Model showing that motivation, ability, and triggers must converge at the same moment for a behavior to occur.

---

[*] *http://www.behaviormodel.org/*

The model shows that three factors must be present at a single moment for a behavior to occur: motivation, ability, and a proper trigger. If the behavior doesn't happen, it means that one of the factors is missing.

"If you plant the right seed in the right spot, it will grow without further coaxing," Fogg wrote in an email. "I believe this is the best metaphor for creating habits."

Fogg's shorthand for this is $B = mat$.

Motivators (Figure 7-7) are defined in three buckets: sensation (pleasure, pain), anticipation (hope, fear), and belonging (social rejection, social acceptance).[*]

Many products try to train or educate people into changing their ability levels to perform an action. But the fact is that we're human, and that means that we're lazy.

"Don't take this route unless you really must," Fogg writes. "Training people is hard work, and most people resist learning new things."

Instead, the Behavior Model advocates making the target behavior easier to perform. Fogg, in fact, sometimes replaces *ability* with *simplicity* because "in practice Simplicity is what persuasion designers should seek."[†] In other words, when we make a behavior simpler to perform, the ability of the person increases—the hurdles to completion are easier to overcome.

---

[*] *http://www.behaviormodel.org/motivation.html*

[†] *http://www.behaviormodel.org/ability.html*

FIGURE 7-7

Fogg's delineation of motivators.

Sensation is a Core Motivator

Anticipation is a Core Motivator

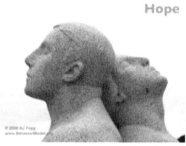 

Belonging is a Core Motivator

The final piece of the Behavior Model is the right trigger to get someone to perform a desired behavior. The goal of the trigger is to also
be simple in its presentation—gently facilitating a customer's pro-
gression through a sequence of events as they gradually perform the
desired behavior.

An example of this can be found in LinkedIn's Groups. After I join a group, this smaller indicator appears in the sidebar with a subtle animation (Figure 7-8).

FIGURE 7-8
LinkedIn's Groups trigger after I join a group for the first time.

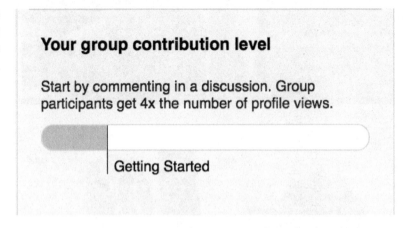

Curiosity drives me to hover over the animation (Figure 7-9). It turns green, as if I've performed the action. But moving my mouse away sets the graph back to yellow.

FIGURE 7-9
Hovering over the graph shows me where I could be, but am not. Also notice the psychologically pleasing shift from yellow to green.

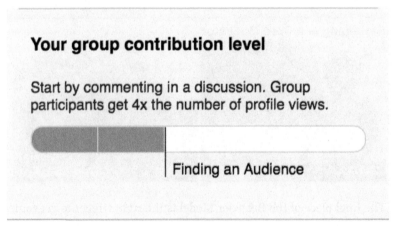

This is a great example of placing the right seed at the right time. The seed compels me to dip my toe into the chain of intended behaviors that the LinkedIn designers have for me—joining a group, then commenting, then getting into a discussion, then posting stories myself.

"The 'right seed' is the tiny behavior that you choose. The 'right spot' is the sequencing—what it comes after," Fogg writes. "The 'coaxing' part is amping up motivation, which I think has nothing to do with creating habits. In fact, focusing on motivation as the key to habits is exactly wrong.

"Let me be more explicit: If you pick the right small behavior and sequence it right, then you won't have to motivate yourself to have it grow. It will just happen naturally, like a good seed planted in a good spot. (Unfortunately, this is also the process for bad habits—they start tiny.)"*

Let's look at some other loops.

ADDITIVE ACTIONS

There will be many occasions that require us as product designers to introduce something new to our customers. (Remember Clippy? See Figure 7-10.) The challenge is twofold: notifying the customer at the correct time, and demonstrating enough value or interest in the moment to encourage use.

---

* *http://tinyhabits.com/sandbox/*

FIGURE 7-10

If only Clippy could
triumphantly return.

When Apple Music launched, for example, the product introduced a rating system to help their underlying algorithms determine what music to recommend. The product designers at Apple extended a "love" system across not only radio tracks, but tracks in a customer's current music library as well.

After tapping the "love" icon, I was presented with a dialog confirming the action while succinctly explaining the value of what I'd just done (Figure 7-11).

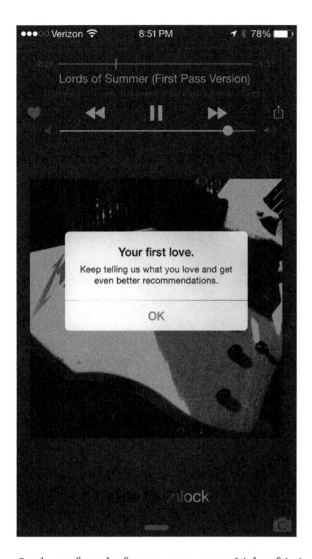

FIGURE 7-11
Apple Music confirming my "love" and encouraging me to continue using the feature, but failing to tell me ahead of time its significance.

On the surface, the feature seems great. It's low friction—it's very simple. It has a potentially huge payoff—I am always listening to music attuned to my tastes. And it'll be forever cemented in the back of my mind that I should tap the icon if I like (sorry, *love*) a song, so I can continue to enjoy the benefits of that payoff.

But the problem with this loop lies in the trigger itself. I had to tap the icon of my own volition. There was no invitation to use it and no indication of its significance.

A better path would be to log how many times I listen to a particular track. On, say, the third or fourth play, pop a subtle toast recognizing that I "love" this song, and suggesting that I tap the heart to indicate that. Imagine the copy:

> *This is the third time you've played this song. You must love it. Why not tap the heart? With just one tap, you'll start hearing more tracks exactly like this one.*

This would check all the boxes—I'm motivated to hear new music, I have the ability because I'm actively listening (since I've sought out the track), and there's a simple path for me to "love" the song.

There are some real-world examples of this pattern at play.

Take Snapchat, for example (Figure 7-12). Anybody moving through the snapping and sending flow would be invited to "Add to Your Story" upon hitting the publish arrow in the lower-righthand corner.

Anybody moving through this flow is in the mindset of getting their Snap published—so, why not just tap the "Add and Don't Show Again" button? After all, Snapchat succinctly pitches me on the value of the feature ("allows your friends to view your Snap an unlimited number of times for 24 hours") and also reassures me that this can be changed ("You can change who can view your Story in Settings").

The payoff of this little dialog has been huge. Stories now account for more views than popular national TV shows.[*]

---

[*] *https://gigaom.com/2015/02/24/snapchats-our-stories-are-generating-tens-of-millions-of-views/*

FIGURE 7-12
Snapchat upsells me
into using their Stories
feature while I'm
performing a similar
action: posting a Snap.

Both Apple and Twitter employed similar techniques for publishing-related features. When Twitter launched Video, for example, they told their users with an unobtrusive tool tip in the Compose view (Figure 7-13).

FIGURE 7-13
Twitter's launch of
Video announced in the
Compose view on their
mobile client.

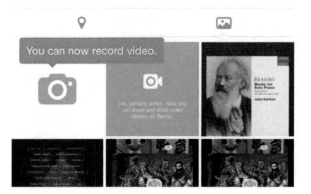

When Apple upgraded their emoji to have more skin tone variations, they took a more aggressive (albeit more educational approach). Upon tapping into the emoji keyboard and onto a variation-enabled icon, I was greeted with a full-keyboard takeover that required tapping "OK" to dismiss (Figure 7-14).

FIGURE 7-14

Apple's introduction of the new emoji skin variations.

The benefit of this was that 1) I was going to use the icon anyway, 2) it demonstrates how to select multiple skin tones, and 3) it only requires one extra tap. Even if I don't read the text, I can tell by the interface element how to use the feature.

GIVING VALUE, THEN ASKING FOR FEEDBACK

For products like Uber, Instacart, and DoorDash to be successful, they need to cultivate an ecosystem of constant feedback. Is my food going to be delivered on time? Where is my car? Was the order correct?

Perfecting these loops is a vital exercise in enacting living versions of the Fogg Behavior Model. How do you communicate progress? When do you ask for feedback on the completed order? What do you do if the transaction was imperfect?

The other challenge is that human memory is complex. Chances are that you can't recall the last Uber ride you took, or how quickly your chicken was delivered. All you know is that it happened, or it didn't.

And that's why the timing and friction of these loops is so important. The key is that the product's customers expect to be receiving some sort of value, and thus they're more willing to provide necessary feedback—*especially* if something goes wrong.

I use Instacart frequently for home grocery delivery. The product makes heavy use of text messages to keep me informed, and to notify me of problems.

I'm glued to these text messages until I receive my groceries, and, after that, I don't really care about them. I'm invested until I get my payoff. Instacart knows this and informs me of order changes by text *and* by phone call, and confirms via text message when the order changes have been made.

Once the order is out for delivery, I'm also informed. I can even watch the driver approach my apartment in real time.

Here's the part of the loop that interests me most: once the driver marks the order as delivered, there's a *very* slight time delay until I'm asked for feedback. Instacart has built in a grace period for me to unpack the groceries, put them in the refrigerator or pantry, and review everything that was delivered.

That takes about 5 to 10 minutes. And that's when Instacart asks me to review the order (Figure 7-15).

This feedback loop enriches Instacart's ecosystem and hits me right at the moment I'm thinking about an action, providing a chance for the product to save me from a poor experience. It increases my trust in the product—and does it in a way that's practically frictionless. I don't have to open the app; I respond to a text message. I don't have to type more than one number; a 1 through 5 will do.

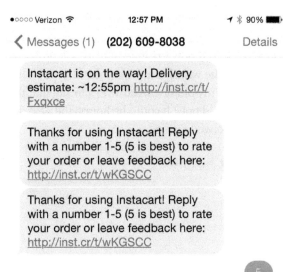

FIGURE 7-15

Instacart reaches me with text messages versus asking me to open up the app and rate my order.

Uber employs a similar model to collect driver ratings (Figure 7-16). The app blocks any other action than a rating once a ride has ended and the app is backgrounded. My only critique with this loop is that it has a tendency to hit you at the wrong time—my mindset is calling a *new* ride, not thinking about my old one. And who's to say that this new ride occurs soon after my old one? It could be hours, the next day, or the next week. This risks skewed ratings.

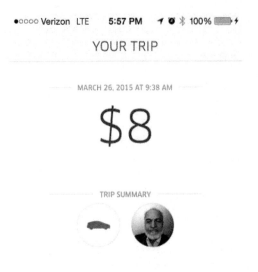

DoorDash, a product that specializes in enabling deliveries from restaurants that don't typically deliver, has combined these two example loops into a superior experience.

The product caters to my combined hunger *and* laziness by providing cues for every step of the food delivery process (Figure 7-17).

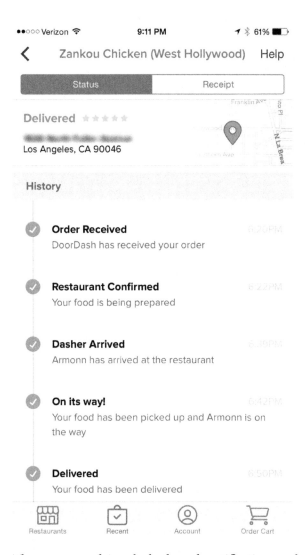

FIGURE 7-17
DoorDash updates
with a push notification
every step of the way.

These cues are driven by both push notifications and within the app—and, I have to say, I am glued to them.

My favorite notification is the one that tells me the driver is approaching my location. It builds anticipation, and has the side effect of getting me ready to meet the driver. This saves both myself and the driver time—I want my food, *now,* and the driver wants to get on with his other deliveries.

And, just like Instacart, the app asks me how the delivery went slightly after I'm handed the glorious bag of food.

But here's where DoorDash differs—they've trained me to *always* respond with that rating. Because after I provide feedback on the order, they inevitably offer a coupon code ranging from $2 to $7 off of my order. And the best part? I have to use it within a few days.

This is an incredible loop. It's one that takes me from an order through the creation and pickup process, builds anticipation for the delivery, encourages me to give order feedback, and, ultimately, makes me want to do it all over again.

VARIABLE REWARDS

Variable rewards, or *variable-ratio schedules* as they're known in psychology circles, are the most powerful reward system known. They're a type of behavioral conditioning that "creates the greatest response to the stimulus, the quickest rate of learning the connection between the reward and the stimulus, and is the least resistant to extinction when the reward is no longer paired with the stimulus."[*]

In other words, positive reinforcement is received after a seemingly unpredictable number of actions by the user. It causes the user to continue usage until receiving positive reinforcement again.

The timeless example of a variable-ratio schedule in action is the slot machine. The user puts the money into the machine, pulls the lever, and may or may not win money. Winning money is simply based upon the number of times the lever is pulled.

I sat down with my colleague Jonathan Badeen, cofounder and vice president of product at Tinder. As mentioned earlier, he invented the swipe right (and left), bringing a game-like experience to finding people to meet.

"While I found my psychology courses in college to be enlightening, I'd never purport to be an expert," Badeen said in our interview. "With Tinder, we were very focused on motivation. We discussed the importance of variable reward schedules. We also knew the sort of weight that introducing yourself to others could carry with it. Putting yourself out there can be scary and intimidating. For this reason we went in the opposite direction for design and interaction. I can only take a small portion of the credit for this, but everything was designed to feel lighthearted, fun, and playful."

---

[*] *http://rationalwiki.org/wiki/Variable_ratio*

Tinder is one of the most addictive experiences, period, with an estimated 50 million people using the product to meet up, date, marry, and more. Since the swiping gesture is so easy and natural to perform, it encourages quick feedback on someone's profile.

But that's not what keeps people swiping. It's the gambling-like reward, that dopamine rush of the "It's a Match" screen that descends upon you without your knowledge (Figure 7-18).

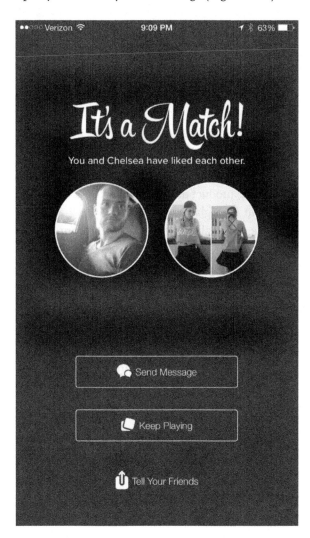

FIGURE 7-18
The "It's a Match" experience on Tinder is a variable reward that encourages continued swiping to experience this again, or to message the person that sent a positive signal of reinforcement.

"I've always felt that software should not only perform a task efficiently, but it should be delightful," Badeen said. "Many lose sight of this, especially when they aren't creating consumer products. Every app has a consumer, though, and every bit of fun you can add to an app makes their day a little bit better, a little more fun. With Tinder, it's been especially fun to make fun. Because we've wanted to keep things lighthearted we took inspiration from games."

Not only does the "It's a Match" experience give you a bit of a rush, it also provides self-reinforcement in the context of a place where people meet. "It's a Match" indicates a signal on the other end of the line, encouraging you to message the person—or to keep swiping for another rush.

Products can also make these sorts of connections with their customers by using unexpected channels, turning what could be a typical or negative experience into something extraordinary.

"I feel more connected with Warby Parker than any other company in the world," said Kurt Varner, product designer at startup Shyp, in our interview. "When I bought [my] glasses from them, they sent me a YouTube video of someone personally thanking me for my purchase. It was a 30-second video. So simple. But they took the time to thank me. Every single interaction I've had with that company, whether it's calling to complain about something, or whatever, it has been an amazing experience, and I feel emotionally connected to that company."

I had a similar experience with Ryan Hoover's Product Hunt. After posting some of my own products there, the team sent me a handwritten note thanking me for sharing my work (Figure 7-19). "Thanks so much for building cool stuff and sharing it with our community."

And they even sent me "meowvelous" stickers to share with my team.

I barely remember giving them my address, and they sure didn't abuse it. But I can't remember the last time I was sent a personal, handwritten note from a team for using their product—*especially* one where I haven't paid them any money (yet).

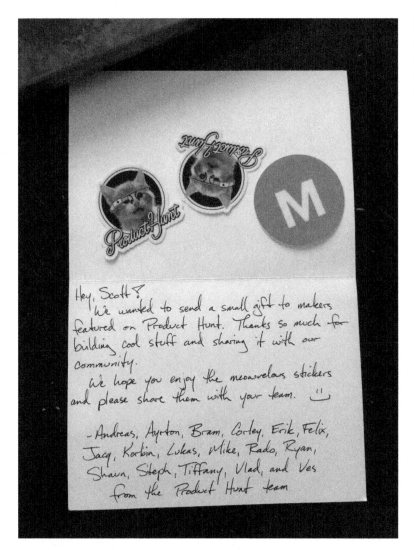

Aesthetics and Personality

Which of these hotel rooms would you trust to be properly cleaned, secure, and more comfortable (Figure 7-20)? In which would you rather stay?

Frankly, if I stepped into the first room, I'd spin on a dime and get the heck out of there.

Multiple studies over the years have confirmed that aesthetics play an important role in shaping responses to products,[*] drawing on "aesthetic factors to judge usability and credibility."[†] A study by Frank Spillers, a usability consultant and user-centered design specialist with Experience Dynamics, went so far as to suggest that product design providing "aesthetic appeal, pleasure and satisfaction can greatly influence the success of a product."[‡]

That's because "attractive interfaces with high aesthetic qualities" arouse "attention, are easier to learn, produce more harmonious results and work better."[§] Pleasant aesthetics stimulate the pleasure centers in our brain, creating emotions that "govern the quality of interaction with a product in the user's environment and relate directly to appraisal of the user experience. Users generate emotion as a way to minimize errors, interpret functionality, or obtain relief from the complexity of a task."

In other words, the right aesthetics in the right product can make us feel good in the context of the product's experience—whether that's feeling secure, cute, or desired ourselves. The aesthetics and the personality of your product go hand-in-hand.

An extreme example of aesthetics and personality blending together to create an emotional connection is the Cockney Cash Machine found in East London (Figure 7-21).

---

[*] Noam Tractinsky, "Aesthetics and Apparent Usability: Empirically Assessing Cultural and Methodological Issues," *http://www.sigchi.org/chi97/proceedings/paper/nt.htm*.

[†] Alicia David and Peyton Glore, "The Impact of Design and Aesthetics on Usability, Credibility, and Learning in an Online Environment," *http://www.westga.edu/~distance/ojdla/winter134/david_glore134.html*.

[‡] Frank Spillers, "Emotion as a Cognitive Artifact and the Design Implications for Products That Are Perceived As Pleasurable," *https://www.experiencedynamics.com/sites/default/files/publications/Emotion-in-Design%20.pdf*.

[§] Ibid., 1.

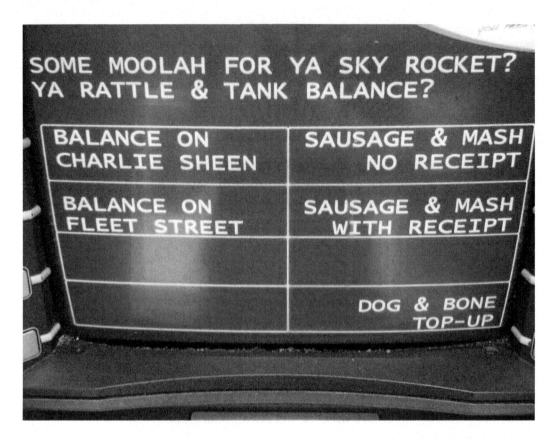

FIGURE 7-21

An ATM that can be used in the Cockney language endears itself to the customer while fulfilling its promise: dispensing cash.

This ATM looks like every other ATM, reflects the history and customs of the locale, and does it while fulfilling its purpose—giving cash to people who need it. And, on top of that, the bank succeeds in creating a conversation piece that'll spread via word of mouth.

"On our cash machines in Wales less than 1% of people opt for the Welsh language, whereas between 15–20% opt for Cockney when given the chance," said Ron Delnevo at the ATM's parent, the Bank Machine Company.[*]

---

[*] *http://www.bbc.com/news/business-17535156*

"Ultimately, you need to deliver on what will make your target audience the happiest and feel a connection to [your product], so that you start to build a relationship," said product design veteran Jeffrey Kalmikoff in our interview. "So it's not just a fleeting one-time thing. Buying the one pair of jeans from the one random brand that you'll never buy from ever again is the same thing as downloading an app and using it once and never opening it up again."

That's the key factor at play here—first having a product that you know solves a problem—*then* doing the work to create a memorable experience that makes a human connection.

"You have to find the mood for your app or service," said Jonathan Badeen in our interview. "The animation and interactions should match those. If you are attempting to impose a sense of fun, then spring animations are probably your best friend. If it's elegance, style, and luxury you are aiming for, then you're going to lean more toward smooth fades and lots of easing animations. Something meant to be very utilitarian might be better served by animations that get right to the point: linear and simple (how boring, though)."

We'll discuss animations and motion more in depth in the next section, but Badeen reinforces the point that deciding a product's mood is a very deliberate process:

> Not all animations should be endearing. For instance, an application focused on home security might not be well served by "fun" and "endearing" animations. Security is serious business. You want your application to pervade that mentality. You might be better served by more mechanical and deliberate animations.

Josh Brewer, former Twitter principal designer, expounded on a similar theme in our interview:

> I think playfulness is super important. But I think it totally depends. If you're building, I don't know, the UI for an air traffic controller, I don't know how much playfulness you need to put in there. But there are a few different ways something can be playful or delightful simply by behaving the way that you expect it to behave.

Brewer focuses on experiences that anticipate a user's behavior in the context of his products.

"It's [the experience] I try to focus on more," he said. "Because some of the other things can be playful, but they get gimmicky or kitschy, and so I tend to fall more towards the 'hey, let me just meet you there and be a step ahead of you' so that when you take that step forward, you were like 'wow, you were there holding my hand the whole way.'"

Let's look at four products on the market and see if we can determine what their designers set out to achieve: Airbnb, Tinder, USAA Bank, and Uber.

AIRBNB

Airbnb—the worldwide community of people that open up their homes for others to rent—is designed with a sense of warmth (Figure 7-22). Its secondary goal is to foster trust, "tapping into the universal human yearning to belong—the desire to feel welcomed, respected, and appreciated for who you are, no matter where you might be. Belonging is the idea that defines Airbnb, but the way we've represented Airbnb to the world until now hasn't fully captured this."*

From the typography (the font is called "LL Circular," by the way)—a geometric, easy-to-read, and, in my opinion, classy font—to the generous whitespace and full-bleed use of high-quality images, Airbnb puts the focus on the space and the people offering it. Soothing colors, fat and appealing tap targets, and clear calls-to-action all come together to make this an extremely appealing experience.

---

* *http://blog.airbnb.com/belong-anywhere/*

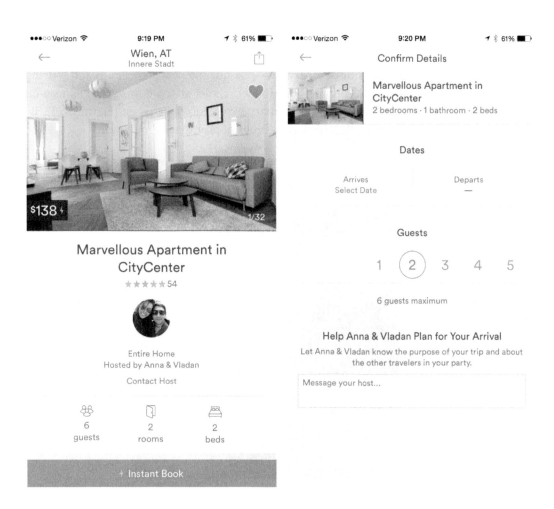

FIGURE 7-22

Airbnb's design imbues the customer with warmth and a feeling of trust.

TINDER

Products meant to facilitate connections between people—whether it be romantic or otherwise—risk hurting people's feelings and souring their perception of the product. Tinder attacked this problem head-on by approaching the primary experience as a game (Figure 7-23). By doing so, they invoked feelings of playfulness and reward.

FIGURE 7-23
Tinder's appealing use of bright colors, large buttons, and a card deck analogy keep the experience of meeting people playful and rewarding when matches occur.

"Humans, like any curious animal, enjoy manipulating their environment," Badeen said in our interview. "They want things to bend to their will. There is emotion in the way that we handle objects. Think of the losing card player who angrily throws down their cards compared to the winner carefully splaying out their cards while taunting 'read them and weep' with pride. I try to add physicality to interactions that provide the same sense of physical manipulation that we are used to in the physical world. Touch screens make this a lot easier than ever before."

This physicality, combined with the bright, almost-primary colors and large "game" buttons, reduced the cognitive overhead of meeting people. It keeps the customer moving through the card deck, taking their mind off of the fact that the person on the other end may not have "liked" them. The playfulness increases the usage velocity and tones down the seriousness level.

But when there's a match, the customer experiences the event like a reward.

USAA BANK

USAA Bank started off as a bank exclusively for U.S. military members and their families. In recent years, the bank's opened its doors to the general public and, in doing so, made *Fortune*'s 2015 Most Admired list at number 28. "It launched a mobile app that allows members to file insurance claims that include video and audio to show the damage. It also was the first bank to offer facial and voice recognition technology for logging into its mobile banking app."[*]

Being a bank, USAA needs to imbue a sense of trust. But USAA's also got a unique history with its association with the U.S. military. USAA blends these two worlds with hard corners, the use of blues, red, and white, and no-nonsense navigation (Figure 7-24). The customer is left with an experience that constantly reminds them of the military values of service, honor, and valor.

---

[*] *http://fortune.com/worlds-most-admired-companies/usaa-28/*

FIGURE 7-24
USAA Bank's mobile
app exudes security
and honor.

UBER

Uber is the ultimate example of the intersection of luxury and efficiency.

Black is used everywhere, and the app opens directly to a map where you can set your pickup location.

And that's it. There really isn't much to *do* in the app, as the product really is the car that picks you up at the push of a button (Figure 7-25).

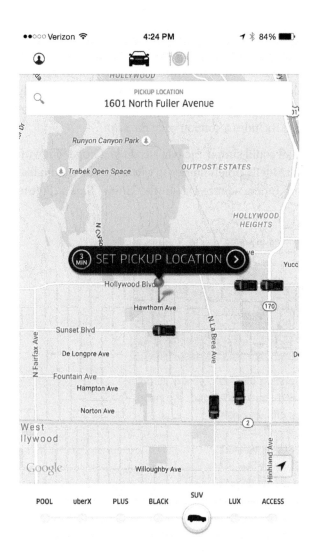

FIGURE 7-25
Uber's intersection of
luxury and efficiency.

What Uber is saying is that the mobile app doesn't need to say much. Rather, it's the superpower that it grants to every customer that's unique—the power to summon a car on demand to take you wherever you desire.

Believe me. Once this superpower is taken away, you realize how powerful it truly is.

EAT24

This food delivery product—beyond the typical red color seemingly associated with all food-related apps—infuses a sense of directness and humor that helps it stand out from the pack. It does this primarily through copywriting and storytelling—for example, in its weekly marketing email where it includes a coupon code for $2 off.

While a coupon email could simply include a code in a huge font with a link to the app, Eat24 tells timely stories to catch your attention, like this one right before Independence Day in the United States (Figure 7-26).

FIGURE 7-26
Eat24's hilarious coupon-code-delivering newsletters.

Hey, is anyone reading this? Oh, you're all out celebrating jello and sparklers? Good. We need to get a few things off our chest:

- Our British accent is fake.
- We've never seen Star Wars.
- Sometimes we eat broccoli.
- Sometimes we wear pants.
- We started the chia seed fad.
- Kale? Love it.
- We also love Nickelback and Creed.
- We're responsible for that nacho stain on your couch.
- We cried about Jennifer and Ben.

Whew. Felt good to get that out. Anyway, even though no one is reading emails this weekend, we're still giving you a coupon to order something covered in America (cheese)*, and also here's a link to our deep fried app.

The tone of this personality is consistent throughout the app, working its way into mundane dialogs such as "Empty Cart" notifications (Figure 7-27).

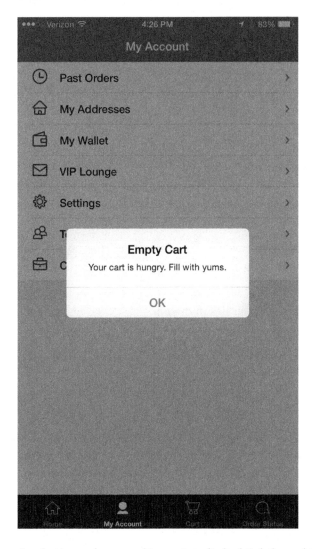

FIGURE 7-27

Eat24's tone is consistent, even with messages that could be mundane.

Aesthetics and personality are interlinked tightly, and take into account the audience for your product. These traits build trust, increase loyalty, and make your products easier to use.

"I've always felt that software should not only perform a task efficiently, but it should be delightful," Tinder's Badeen said in our interview. "Many lose sight of this, especially when they aren't creating consumer products. Every app has a consumer, though, and every bit of fun you can add to an app makes their day a little bit better, a little more fun."

Speaking of ease of use, let's segue into discussing animation and motion, and how they can significantly affect engagement and understanding.

Animation and Motion

The states of a user interface work together to communicate to your customer what they should be doing next, what their expectations should be at a given moment, and how they should be using a screen at any given time.

But how do you effectively travel between each state? How do you communicate what's happening without displaying each event like some logfile?

I'll give you a hint: the answer lies in motion.

Motion is humanizing. It's a reflection of how the real world operates. But, more specifically to our realm as product designers, if we assume that the world moves in 60 fps, "there's 58 frames you need to design between Mock A and Mock B," as Paul Stamatiou of Twitter reminds us.[*]

Josh Brewer, formerly of Twitter, echoes this notion. "As a product designer, you're responsible for every one of those moments in between every one of those screens just as much as those screens themselves," he said in our interview. Brewer calls this the "in-between states."

We're nearing a time in product design where creating mockups or stripped-down prototypes isn't going to be good enough. We have to be the arbiters of motion, interjecting it into transitions and personality-infusing animations that make their way into the products we build.

Because motion is more than cute; it's functional. It accounts for the passage of time, and helps your customer follow what happens after they take an action. Even better, you communicate in a visual way how they got from point A to point B.

---

[*]   *http://paulstamatiou.com/design-provide-meaning-with-motion/*

After all, we *live* in a world of motion. Motion is the story of how things exist, how they move, how they go from one place to another.

"Animations tell a story," said Jonathan Badeen of Tinder in our interview. "That story might be why and how an element appeared or disappeared or how you got from one screen to another. Stories at their core stir up emotion, so I believe trying to tell a good story will automatically do this. Each story has an assortment of actors and we like to be introduced and we want to know what happens to them. Thinking this way about the elements on your screen helps to transition elements in and out as well as the transition between screens. When it makes sense I try to incorporate an actor between scenes. In Tinder this is most easily visible in our transitions between the card stack and the profile, where we attempt to make the card at least partially transform into the profile (Figure 7-28). The photo transitioning hopefully lets the user know that if they perform the same tap action on the photo to open the profile, it might do the reverse and close the profile."

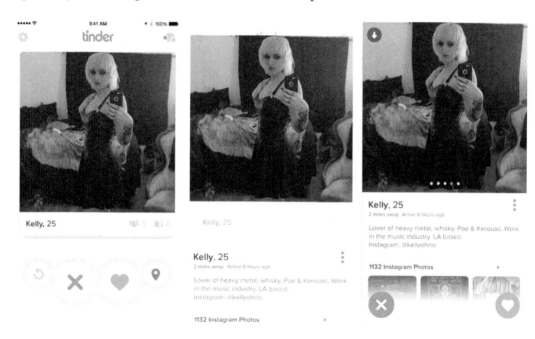

FIGURE 7-28

Tinder's open and close animation on the profile card transforms the photo on the card into the full-bleed profile, communicating that the two views are connected by a single tap.

Check out this example from Pasquale D'Silva of Elepath, from an insanely excellent piece called "Transitional Interfaces" (Figure 7-29).

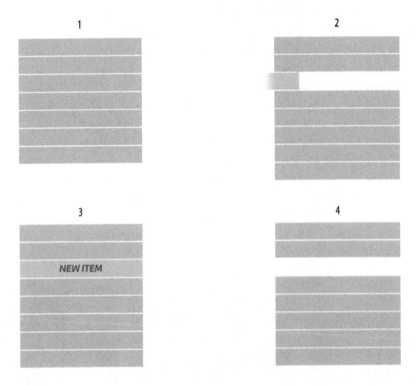

FIGURE 7-29
Pasquale D'Silva of Elepath illustrates how animation can mimic real life, and help one understand what's happening better onscreen.

D'Silva shows us how "for a new item to be added, the list needs to make room for the item, and then the new item (which came from somewhere) fills in the space. Much less jarring. There's easing in & out of states to soften the change. It feels more natural, because we have the contextual hook of space—mirroring the way you'd add something to a stack of things in real life!"*

It's simple, really. Mimicking real life helps our brains better understand what's happening. It's an "illusion of life."

---

* *https://medium.com/@pasql/transitional-interfaces-926eb80d64e3*

This just so happens to be the title of the greatest book on animation of all time: *The Illusion of Life: Disney Animation*, published in 1981 by Disney animators Ollie Johnston and Frank Thomas.[†]

These two guys are legends. Thomas joined Disney in 1934 and Johnston in 1935. They worked with Walt himself and animated characters from Snow White to the Rescuers.

Their book distilled 50 years of Disney animation into what's now known as the "12 principles of animation."[‡] Painstakingly created out of necessity over the course of 23 animated feature films, these principles were used to mimic the basic laws of physics. And their goal? To express emotional timing and emphasize a character's personality.

The result? Believable on-screen motion and characters that seemed real and became, as a result, memorable (Figure 7-30).

FIGURE 7-30
Snow White comes alive with these innocent, cheerful movements.

Motion within product design can accomplish two things for us: making our products memorable and more usable. That's a pretty amazing one-two punch.

Let's explore a few animation principles and see how they fit into the realm of product design.

SLOW IN, SLOW OUT

Johnston and Thomas described the value of replicating lifelike motion with the principle of "slow in and slow out," which is a less computer-like term for "ease in and ease out." When humans move in Earth's gravity, there's a necessary period of acceleration and deceleration. The implication for animation is that there will be more frames near the

---

† *http://amzn.to/1fjpB2k*
‡ *https://en.wikipedia.org/wiki/12_basic_principles_of_animation*

starting and ending positions as a result, and fewer frames in the middle of the animation arc. These extra frames soften the action at the beginning and the ending to simulate lifelike movements.

This principle can be modified to communicate different emotions—for comedic effect, for example, the slow in or slow out could be shortened to create an element of surprise, making the action snappier.

Check out this real-life example from Skype's Qik app (Figure 7-31).

FIGURE 7-31
Skype's Qik app in motion.

This is a great example of giving a user interface component a simulated mass. With this simulated drag comes an understandable heft that doesn't surprise the person using it when the menu appears. We know from the motion's vector, as well, where it originated.

Also, notice what happens at the end of the menu's introductory animation: a slight overlap and retraction.

This added animation element is called *follow through and overlap*. It was created to reflect the fact that a character can change direction, but nothing stops at once. Hair, clothing, arms, even oversized ears continue with some inertia in the direction the character was originally heading.

In product design, we can use this technique to add a little personality while emphasizing the direction from which a UI element originated. But, most importantly, we can use it to *train our customers* to anticipate the arrival of a new button or menu over time.

I love how Keezy's menu uses this principle (Figure 7-32).

FIGURE 7-32
Keezy using "follow through and overlap."

STAGING

Staging is an animation principle that communicates to the audience what's the most important part of the story in any given scene. In explaining this principle, Johnston and Thomas emphasize that films have a finite amount of time to communicate what's worthy of an audience's attention. So staging is used as a tool to direct an audience's attention to the main story or idea being conveyed.

In our world, I interpret this principle in two ways:

- First, get to the point. Don't spend an excessive amount of time animating UI elements into view. In my own experience, anything that's over .2 seconds feels way too long.

- Second, confine motion to what matters. Distracting a customer with too many elements flying into view just detracts from the experience.

There's a great example over at Google's Material Design guidelines under the "Hierarchical timing" header that embodies this principle.* Here's the live example (Figure 7-33).

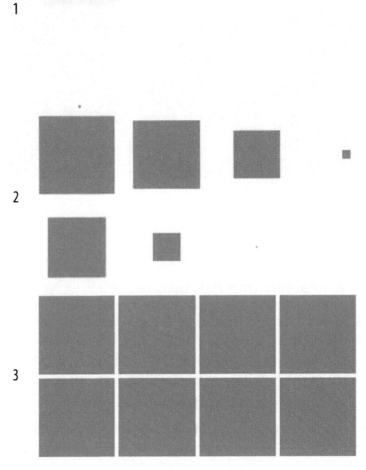

* *http://www.google.com/design/spec/animation/meaningful-transitions.html*

This is a great example of how motion can be used as a tool to emphasize what the most important elements on the screen are. Secondary and tertiary options reside on the screen, but are brought in later. Your eye is already resting on what the animation determines will be the most actionable item in the grid.

Motion in products is a pretty damn exciting prospect. I think what makes it more exciting than it should be is the state of our tools—even with Quartz Composer, Framer.js, InVision, or Keynote, it's still a difficult path (no pun intended) to create wholly original animations and transitions that support the purpose of your product.

In other words, it's still difficult to create original animations that don't interfere with your product's flows. That's why sticking to the 12 principles of animation can reduce your time spent in trial and error and can instead focus your efforts on the motion that matters.

"I think it's important to simply sweat the details. Insist that things work in a way that feels natural to the user," says Tinder's Badeen. "The past couple years, like many others, I've been referencing Disney's 12 principles of animation. I don't pretend to be an expert, but it's a great thing to keep in the back of your mind as you animate and design interactions. It doesn't hurt that I love Disney."

Shareable Notes

- We're all human and we're not immune to the effect of speed, behavioral triggers, aesthetics, personality, and motion. The best products nail the problem they set out to solve for their customers, then laid these traits on top to make flow-inducing and memorable experiences.

- Speed and responsiveness have significant effects on product usage, but required response times are highly dependent upon context. Acceptable response times differ from desktop to mobile to wearable, and from console-driven to touch-driven interfaces.

- In almost all cases in product design, there are specific flows you'll want your customer to take at certain times. That's where loops come in. For a loop to truly be effective, it needs to take root in your customer's mind that it's worth pursuing because it has payoff.

- Aesthetics and personality are tightly interlinked, and take into account the audience for your product. When you nail these traits, they can build trust, increase loyalty, and make your products easier to use.

- Motion is humanizing. It's a reflection of how the real world operates. As a product designer, you're responsible for every one of your product's screens, as well as what's in between them.

Do This Now

- Make speed work for you. Ensure that your product is responsive in key areas, and reference Chapter 6 for help with friendly loading states.

- Audit your product's loops. Are they taking into account the Fogg Behavioral Model? If not, what pieces—motivation, ability, or triggers—are you missing?

- Ensure that your product's aesthetic and copywriting choices reflect your audience.

- Study up on the 12 principles of animation and, if you can, score a copy of the book *The Illusion of Life*.*

- Visit capptivate.co for animation inspiration (disclaimer: it's tough to judge an animation's value in isolation; studying in the context of the application is a much more productive endeavor).

- Study up on Google's Material Design animation guidelines. There's a lot of good thinking here.

- Take up a tool like InVision, Origami, or Framer.js so you can start crafting your own original animations that serve your product and your customers.

---

* *http://amzn.to/1G71VZ1*

Interview: Jonathan Badeen

Jonathan Badeen is the cofounder and senior vice president of product at Tinder. The actor-turned-developer-designer helped invent Tinder, its concept of a card stack, and the swipe right. He can be found at http://badeen.com.

What are some general human/psychological principles that you try and weave into your work?

While I found my psychology courses in college to be enlightening, I'd never purport to be an expert. With Tinder, we were very focused on motivation. We discussed the importance of variable reward schedules. We also knew the sort of weight that introducing yourself to others could carry with it. Putting yourself out there can be scary and intimidating. For this reason we went in the opposite direction for design and interaction. I can only take a small portion of the credit for this, but everything was designed to feel light-hearted, fun, and playful.

Humans, like any curious animal, enjoy manipulating their environment. They want things to bend to their will. There is emotion in the way that we handle objects. Think of the losing card player who angrily throws down their cards compared to the winner carefully splaying out their cards while taunting "read them and weep" with pride. I try to add physicality to interactions that provide the same sense of physical manipulation that we are used to in the physical world. Touch screens make this a lot easier than ever before.

What have you found that helps to make a design more emotional?

I believe animation and physicality is key to making a design more emotional. It makes the design relatable. Elements that move with your touch allow you to connect with the interface on an emotional level that a static screen never could. They involve the user.

How do you use motion and animation to build memorable, unique experiences? Is it your goal to make products endearing with animation, or is that a byproduct?

Not all animations should be endearing. For instance, an application focused on home security might not be well served by "fun" and "endearing" animations. Security is serious business. You want your application to pervade that mentality. You might be better served by more mechanical and deliberate animations.

You have to find the mood for your app or service. The animation and interactions should match those. If you are attempting to impose a sense of fun, then spring animations are probably your best friend. If it's elegance, style, and luxury you are aiming for, then you're going to lean more toward smooth fades and lots of easing animations. Something meant to be very utilitarian might be better served by animations that get right to the point: linear and simple (how boring, though).

I think I prefer working in the realm of fun. I'm constantly thinking about how to make an element feel a bit more alive. This might require an element to move in a slightly unpredictable manner, or it might mean imitating the exaggerated physics of children's cartoons.

Animations tell a story. That story might be why and how an element appeared or disappeared or how you got from one screen to another. Stories at their core stir up emotion, so I believe trying to tell a good story will automatically do this. Each story has an assortment of actors and we like to be introduced and we want to know what happens to them. Thinking this way about the elements on your screen helps to transition elements in and out as well as the transition between screens. When it makes sense I try to incorporate an actor between scenes. In Tinder this is most easily visible in our transitions between the card stack and the profile, where we attempt to make the card at least partially transform into the profile. The photo transitioning hopefully lets the user know that if they perform the same tap action on the photo to open the profile, it might do the reverse and close the profile.

What are the necessary ingredients that make products addicting and magnetic for people? What makes them want to use a product?

First off, you have to be solving a problem. That problem might be as simple as alleviating boredom, but it might be as important as finding a soulmate. From more of a design, animation, and interaction standpoint, I think it's important to simply sweat the details. Insist that things work in a way that feels natural to the user.

Your designs have an inherently playful quality. What are the inspirations for this?

I've always felt that software should not only perform a task efficiently, but it should be delightful. Many lose sight of this, especially when they aren't creating consumer products. Every app has a consumer, though, and every bit of fun you can add to an app makes their day a little bit better, a little more fun.

With Tinder, it's been especially fun to make fun. Because we've wanted to keep things lighthearted, we took inspiration from games. The past couple years, like many others, I've been referencing Disney's 12 principles of animation. I don't pretend to be an expert, but it's a great thing to keep in the back of your mind as you animate and design interactions. It doesn't hurt that I love Disney.

Who are your design heroes?

Loren Brichter. I'm not sure he's exactly a designer in the normal sense, but he is a god to me.

Mike Matas. His work at Apple, Push Pop Press, and currently Facebook inspires me and makes me feel very inadequate.

Louie Mantia mainly because of his Disney and geek culture wallpaper goodies.

Bret Victor is not a designer but more of a developer who believes in enabling the creative process in software development. His talk "Stop Drawing Dead Fish" is pretty inspiring.

Interview: Josh Brewer

Josh Brewer is the founder of Habitat; the former principal designer at Twitter; cocreator of 52 Weeks of UX, FFFFallback, and the Shares app; and the former director of user experience at Socialcast. He can be found at http://jbrewer.me *and on Twitter at* https://twitter.com/jbrewer.

What are the things you keep in mind when you're building stuff?

Oh man. Users, users, users. People. That's probably first and foremost and always ever present. When I say "people," that can mean all kinds of things. It can be something small that I'm building and it's for me and anybody else who fits in. FFFFallback (*http://ffffallback.com*) is a great example [a tool by Brewer to test fallback font choices on the Web]. Web fonts were just becoming a thing. I'm sitting there realizing "hey, if these don't load, your stuff looks horrible, and it's not just like 'oh, stick this in and then there goes my normal font stack.'" So it was born really genuinely out of my concern that my work was going to look terrible if the web fonts didn't load and come through. So, building a little thing in order to scratch that itch. I was thinking about me and all the other designers out there that were about to get caught with their pants down, you know, if JavaScript didn't load.

But you can take Socialcast or Twitter or any of the stuff that I've worked on, honestly—it's keeping the users in the forefront of your mind and trying to understand at every step. Either anecdotally or if you can with research.

What are the motivations, what are they thinking, how might they want to accomplish this, what's the end objective, task-wise—but then, also, what's the feeling I want to leave them with? I don't know. For every project I've worked on, I'd say there's probably a small subset of principles I work against. But I don't know that any of them are universally "OK, I'm working on this project now, check check."

But working as quickly as possible to get something of a decent fidelity so I can put it in front of a few people or even use it myself—I'm a huge proponent, and you can ask anybody I work with—they probably would agree that you've got to build it, like static comps just do not work in this era. They don't communicate enough. There's too many holes and gaps in between all of the states that get left open to interpretation. As a designer, and especially as a product designer, you're responsible for every one of those moments in between every one of those screens just as much as those screens themselves.

So build it as quickly as you can, because it's going to change. I guarantee it. And until you're using it, and you're going to take it outside on your phone in the sunlight, or you're going to sit in a dark room. You're going to use it with one hand and you're testing it with a thumb or you're going to sit on a laptop on a 27-inch screen or an 11-inch screen. You know what I mean, actually using the thing. I find it's really hard to say I'm done [until I do that].

That's a good segue because I'd love to know how you work. Can you walk me through the process? And I'm sure it's been different from Socialcast to Twitter to your own stuff too.

Yeah, I would definitely say it's been very different in each of those cases. If I were to try to paint an overarching picture, it would look something like sitting down to do a lot of just basic requirements. Like what am I working with, what kind of data do I have, what do I know about this thing already?

OK, so let me backpedal. A brand new feature is different from improving an existing feature. So a brand new feature that data might not exist for yet— so, at that point, you're going to have to start thinking about "what kind of data do I need, what kind of things to I need to go talk to engineers about?" I try and just understand the technical constraints of what I'm tackling as much as I can.

Then, especially at Twitter, working closely with a product manager, or even with Mike Davidson, someone to identify what is the problem we're trying to solve.

That is the most important thing. It's not "we need a new feature" or "we need something that will accomplish x." It's actually "what problem are we solving for these people?" and then asking really hard questions like "OK, why is this a problem? "What do we know about this?" "Do we have data about this in our logs, do we have things that confirm or deny this, is the picture fuzzy?"

So using all the tools that I've got to paint as clear of a picture or at least of the pieces that I want to start working with up front. I was super fortunate at Twitter. We had an incredible research team, and working with those guys has been fantastic. I'll start making progress on stuff like this— I'm white-boarding, I'm putting sticky notes up, and just grouping things together trying to paint a picture before a pixel ever gets pushed.

One of my favorite things is being able to grab one of the researchers and say "Hey, knowing what you know and given what we've done research on and whatnot, let's walk through this together" and really being able to push it and poke holes in it and spin it around a couple times and look at it from different angles. And, at that point, then I begin to start diving into an actual solution to the problem.

I'll usually sketch; sometimes I'll jump from sketch to code and just start cranking out an HTML prototype. Other times I'll jump right into Photoshop because I know that there's a certain level of fidelity I need to feel confident that this is actually articulating what I want it to articulate.

And even then whenever I'm in Photoshop mode, it's still getting out of that into code as quickly as possible to try and get something going. It's either me—or, if I'm lucky, getting one of the native iOS or Android engineers to actually prototype with me. So that we can get something really real and native as fast as possible.

From there, it's a process of refinement. You go in—you bring some other people in to sit and work with you, and talk through it and poke holes in and review it, and critique it, you know, run it through all of our design principles, and you know, go back to the drawing board if you need to. Or go and subtly refine things and just kind of keep iterating that process until that thing seems as tight as possible—until you've addressed all the states and all of the transitions and the interactions and the way the thing fits within the context of the existing system. That's a broad overarching way that I work.

Of course, I have to caveat it with "it totally depends." Sometimes it's Keynote, you know what I mean, and sometimes it's Photoshop. And sometimes it's a napkin sketch, and other times it's really high-fidelity HTML and CSS and JavaScript.

It just depends on what the thing is. What the time constraints are, and what level of fidelity I need to deliver in order for the rest of the folks to be able to move forward.

You mentioned designing the in-between states—the transitions and animations—and that's something that I think a lot of people are struggling with. How do you personally do that?

It's hard. Quartz Composer is like a giant wall. But some things just have a learning curve—[Quartz Composer] has a learning wall—and I haven't gotten over it yet. I definitely played with it a bit, and some of the patches that people have been putting out recently definitely help a lot.

I think we're really fortunate at Twitter that we had a couple guys that were pretty good at [Adobe] AfterEffects and motion design. It was something that we specifically hired a couple of people for that had proficiency in that, so they could really dial in those things. So that when we handed it to the engineers, the engineers were like "yes, awesome, I got it done." And we didn't have the back and forth and back and forth and back and forth and back and forth.

But when you can't do that, I think you fall back into things. I fall back to both JavaScript, and trying to use some easing functions and try and dial it in as close as I can.

Or I jump into Keynote and get as close of an approximation as you can get it and then you and I go back and forth with the developer to tighten it up.

But at this point, again, it's like anything: do whatever you possibly can. But I personally feel like the one thing that's missing more than anything else is the motion and interaction component in our design process. And it's super weird, to be totally honest with you, it's almost like we need Flash—I can't believe I'm saying that. We need something like that that says like "great, here's my stuff and here's how it needs to move and behave right."

And if somebody out there is going to be working on this sooner than later, then God bless them for it. But I just want to be able to identify components and all this stuff and then assign interaction to those components. Who knows, it might be that one of these days somebody just basically figures out how to do a more simple GUI on top of Xcode. Or Xcode Storyboarding gets easier to use or something, I don't know. I would imagine that Android and some of the others coming along will continue to push us into this realm of really, really having to own the interactions and the in-between.

This interview has been edited for length, and you're missing out on thousands of words of insights. To read the interview in its entirety, go to http:// scotthurff.com/dppl/interviews.

8

Interpreting Feedback and "Leveling Up" Your Product

It's a Creative Journey, After All

One thing that comes out in myths is that at the bottom of the abyss comes the voice of salvation. The black moment is the moment when the real message of transformation is going to come. At the darkest moment comes the light.

—JOSEPH CAMPBELL, *THE POWER OF MYTH*

BUILDING A PRODUCT IS MESSY. Just ask game designer Jake Solomon, lead designer of the critically acclaimed *XCOM: Enemy Unknown*.

After growing up obsessed with video games, he turned that fixation into a gig with famed game designer Sid Meier at his company Firaxis. Meier is the mastermind behind legendary classics like *Pirates!* and the *Civilization* series.

Solomon moved up within the ranks quickly, becoming a "trusted member of Sid Meier's team, helping solve complicated problems and interfacing between Meier and other members of the staff."

There was one game in particular that captured Solomon's interest as a kid: 1994's *XCOM: UFO Defense*. And from the earliest days at Firaxis, Solomon lobbied the team to make a modern version of *XCOM*. As *Polygon* reported, he believed so much in the dream that it even became a running joke.

Yet it paid off, and Solomon got a small team and a few months to come up with a prototype for how the new *XCOM* would work.

But Solomon screwed it up. Over and over again. For almost half a decade.

"Our job is to make a fun *XCOM* and we've completely failed at it," he said in an interview. "It was a really hard moment, because up until that point, I had probably not had any real stress. When the feedback started coming back, I was thinking, 'Holy shit. Here I am. I'm the designer. I have this vision, and almost unequivocally, everyone thinks it's not fun.' That's when, as a designer, you start to think, 'OK...I have no answers.'"

After designing dozens of successful games, Meier knows this phase of the development process well. He calls it the "Valley of Despair."

"You start a project with very high hopes and expectations and visions of what the game is going to be and how awesome it's going to be," Meier said. "Some of those are realized and some of those are not. In the middle of the game, not everything works, not everything looks as good as it should and you're a little burnt out. You've seen it a hundred times. You're maybe wondering whether you're the only one that's having fun, the only one that likes this game, the only one that believes in it. You have to push through that with a little bit of faith. That's the Valley of Despair."

The Valley of Despair. We all know that feeling as product designers. We all have hit that moment where we think our product won't work, that nobody is going to use it. That's the fear taking hold—the fear that all of your research and work has been wrong.

But the only way to plow through the Valley is to keep going. Sometimes, it's a return to the basics that can illuminate the path forward. And that's what Solomon did. After scrapping years of work and multiple attempts to get *XCOM*'s gameplay right, Solomon and Meier returned to the most basic, stripped-down form of a game that you could get: a board game.

Requisitioning pieces like model tanks and the cards from *Risk*, Meier and Solomon created a prototype *XCOM* strategy game. They spent two weeks playing the homemade strategy game. It helped them to refine the rules and solve the most glaring gameplay problems.

"We'd draw the earth and we'd say, 'OK. Alien invasion strategy game. This is how it works,'" Solomon said. "From a very high level, which is where you have to start. You have to say, 'What are the big choices? What's the player doing every turn?' That can be real time, but there are these discrete moments where the players are making choices. What are those choices? What is the player weighing? What are they doing?'"*

XCOM: Enemy Unknown would go on to become an immense success, earning a score of 89 from Metacritic and becoming one of the top-selling titles of 2013 across PC, Xbox, and Playstation. That's quite an achievement for a non-AAA game title.[†]

We see this pattern all throughout creative work.

Take one of science fiction's greatest characters, for example: Chewbacca from *Star Wars*.

The design of the iconic walking carpet didn't just spring to life from the mind of George Lucas or legendary conceptual designer Ralph McQuarrie (Figure 8-1).

Ralph McQuarrie
Circa March/April, 1975

FIGURE 8-1

Michael Heilemann's excellent Kitbashed.com, which chronicles the creation of *Star Wars*, highlights the earliest concepts of McQuarrie's Chewbacca. They certainly changed.

"Chewbacca didn't spring to life out of nowhere, fully formed when Lucas saw his dog in the passenger seat of his car," Heilemann writes. "That's the soundbite. A single step. The reality is complex and human.

---

* All *XCOM*-related quotes from *http://www.polygon.com/features/2013/1/31/3928710/making-of-xcoms-jake-solomon-firaxis-sid-meier*

† *http://www.vgchartz.com/game/70978/xcom-enemy-unknown/*

From vague names floating around, the kernel of an idea, changing purposes and roles of characters, major restructuring, the design hopping from person to person, scrapping the existing concept and going down a different path, seeing existing things in a different light and having to conform a range of ideas to complement and enrich one another... It makes one breathe a sigh of relief; *Star Wars* wasn't a mystical, muse-favored event; an all-powerful force of unbridled inspiration. It puts its pants on one leg at a time, just like everyone else."*

For any creative endeavor—including the act of building a product—the process is roughly the same (Figure 8-2). It's a stream of refinement before each release.

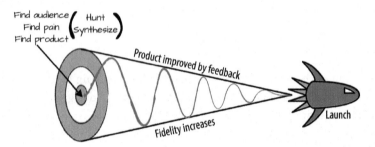

But where does this refinement come from? Feedback or critiques from your team, friends, family, outside beta testers, or, hopefully, customers?

If so, how do you collect effective feedback? What structures should be in place? Who gives the feedback? And how do you know which feedback is worthy of *leveling up* your product?

We'll discuss this next.

Leveling Up

We spoke a lot in Chapter 5 about the value of getting your product's ideas into prototype form as quickly as possible. That's because it begins the process of gathering feedback. And we all know that products created in a vacuum—without the oxygen that is feedback —lead to, at best, vaporware, and, at worst, complete failures.

---

* *http://kitbashed.com/blog/chewbacca*

There's a theory in game design called *acceleration flow*. It's a very unique state of flow—not unlike a traditional *flow state*, where you're not thinking about what you're doing but are acting almost hypnotically. The difference between traditional flow and acceleration flow, though, is the feeling of accelerated power. Players get caught up in a future where they can see their characters becoming more powerful, but the catch is that they don't quite know yet what exactly that'll look like.

This state is quite prevalent in role-playing games like *World of Warcraft*, *Mass Effect*, or, my all-time favorite, *Knights of the Old Republic II* (Figure 8-3).

FIGURE 8-3

A skills screen from *Knights of the Old Republic II*, which shows what a player needs to do to level up their character.

The secret behind the allure of this endless loop is the possibility of the acceleration of power. For each piece of gear that a WoW player gets from a raid, the game becomes a little bit easier. The bosses that drop the next piece of gear fall a little bit faster. Not only is the player character getting progressively more powerful with each piece of gear, but that gear is helping them to grow more powerful, faster. The rate itself at which the player character grows more powerful increases. A positive feedback loop is in effect, heading toward what the player infers to be a singularity: the point they become an ever-growing unstoppable force.[†]

---

† *http://thegamedesignforum.com/features/acceleration_flow_1.html*

Acceleration flow follows a specific curve—great strides early on, then a long period of gradual growth. At the end, though, there's an acceleration of level-ups as the player approaches the endgame (Figure 8-4).

Rather, those players are caught up in a future in which their character(s) will be powerful in a way they can't even understand yet. To put it more technically, they're inferring an exponentially increasing power structure that vanishes beyond their player prediction horizon.

FIGURE 8-4
The acceleration flow curve in role-playing games.

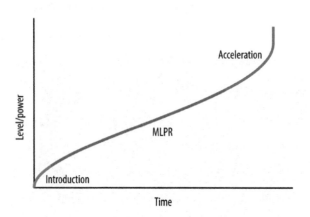

A product levels up in much the same way. We make great strides early on as we're exploring broad concepts and nailing down what it is we're dealing with. Then, there's a long process of refinement, and, finally, as cumulative feedback rolls in, we shift the product into a state that's even more powerful than we imagined.

It's worth mentioning something quickly before we dive into gathering and interpreting different sources of feedback. Feedback can be tough. We, as product designers, throw ourselves into our work. So don't take negative feedback personally. Creative work naturally reflects the individual that created it, but that doesn't mean that any negativity is directed toward you personally.

So, with that in mind, there are three potential sources of feedback that'll help to level up your product and get it ready to ship. Feedback from:

- Your team

- Current customers and/or clients

- Potential customers and/or clients

Let's take a deeper look into each source, and discuss effective ways to gather and incorporate the feedback you receive.

Team Critiques

There are two variants of team product critiques: the informal, more intimate kind, and a larger-scale, more structured variant.

START WITH WHO HELPED TO DEFINE THE PRODUCT

Way back in Chapter 3, we talked about who was in the room defining the product you'd end up building. Soliciting face-to-face feedback from these individuals on an informal, one-on-one basis is an incredible way to get early feedback and spot problems. Ideally, these people are from a number of different teams—product, engineering, marketing, sales, you get it. Get whatever you can in their hands, as early as possible. Ask for direct, targeted, actionable feedback. This is why getting to a prototype quickly is valuable. And the side effect? These individuals feel more invested because their voice is being heard, considered, and directly affecting the product's trajectory.

"You bring some other people in to sit and work with you, and talk through [the product] and poke holes in and review it, and critique it," Josh Brewer, formerly principal designer at Twitter, said in our interview. "You run it through all of our design principles and you go back to the drawing board if you need to—or go and subtly refine things. You keep iterating that process until that thing is as tight as possible. And after you've addressed all the states and all of the transitions and the interactions—[you address] how the thing fits within the context of the existing system."

This is a similar concept to a process used at Pixar. Called the Braintrust, it's a "primary delivery system for straight talk. The Braintrust meets every few months or so to assess each movie we're making. Its premise is simple: Put smart, passionate people in a room together, charge them with identifying and solving problems, and encourage them to be candid."*

---

* *http://www.fastcompany.com/3027135/lessons-learned/inside-the-pixar-braintrust*

Pixar's managed to harness creativity to the tune of a total box office run of almost $10 billion worldwide.* That's 14 movies and 14 number-one box office hits. The Braintrust is a central part of driving that creativity to the best possible place, with the right balance of candor and constructive feedback.

> *People who take on complicated creative projects become lost at some point in the process. It is the nature of things—in order to create, you must internalize and almost become the project for a while, and that near-fusing with the project is an essential part of its emergence. But it is also confusing. Where once a movie's writer/director had perspective, he or she loses it. Where once he or she could see a forest, now there are only trees.*

BREAK DOWN COMPANY SILOS BY OPENING UP DESIGN REVIEWS

"It's a common practice in design teams to have frequent collective reviews of their work," Benedikt Lehnert of Wunderlist wrote. "Design reviews create a space for designers to show and constructively critique each other's work throughout the design process with the goal to increase the overall quality of the final product. Ultimately, as most of you know, the goal of giving feedback to fellow designers is to help them succeed with their work.

"So, what happens if you break down the silo and open up the design review sessions to your entire company?"†

Structured design reviews are essential for design teams, but they risk becoming too insular as time goes on. Lehnert's innovation at Wunderlist is a wonderful template for product designers to stay on their toes and face tougher internal feedback.

As chief design officer, Lehnert created a biweekly "Open Design Review" at Wunderlist, where product designers shared what they were working on, explained the rationale behind their progress, and prepared specific questions to ask the group.

I love this innovative spin on the design review for a number of reasons:

---

* *http://www.boxofficemojo.com/franchises/chart/?id=pixar.htm*

† *http://www.benedikt-lehnert.de/blog/open-design-reviews-as-a-tool-to-establish-a-company-wide-design-culture*

- The Open Design Review creates natural internal checkpoints for feedback, and ensures a constant communication to the team about progress.

- It sets clear expectations for all parties: who needs to be prepared, and when, and with what.

- Designers can't hide. If internal opinion is low, this becomes obvious through constructive, structured means. It also allows the designer to explain the thought process and rationale of every decision to see if this affects opinions.

Lehnert recommends having a facilitator in every session to take notes and moderate, and adds that the individuals in the company need to make an effort to be thoughtful and customer-focused, and approach the feedback from a position that fits within their expertise.

OPEN UP TO A PRIVATE, INTERNAL BETA

"If the team starts building it and everybody's like, 'this sucks,' [that's a warning sign]," said venture investor Josh Elman, a veteran of Facebook, LinkedIn, Zazzle, and many more companies. "You trust the resonance of the team. But sometimes you've got to fight through that because people are just bogged down, or because it's harder than they thought or whatever. But if you still think it's right, you still think it's right."

The evolution of Lehnert's Open Design Review is putting the product in the hands of your team. Distribute beta builds internally—and, by the way, watch that download percentage; I'd try to get at least 40 percent of your team on a build—so you can get real-world usage. Not only will you be able to identify places that are especially crash-prone, but you can also look at usage analytics and see where your team members drop off or abandon a user flow.

Finally, though, it's tough to really grasp a product until you make it part of your routine. An internal beta test eases that burden for all the members of your team. They can use your product under real live conditions, in multiple places and scenarios that might not be immediately obvious to the intention of the product. They can use it when they can't sleep. They can use it in a moment of inspiration.

Because one never knows from where ideas can come.

ENCOURAGE BUG FILINGS

One of my favorite experiments is encouraging my team to file bugs, and then seeing what people think are bugs versus designed behavior. Don't get me wrong: this isn't a sick social experiment, but it's an inadvertent commentary on what might be an incredibly obscure or confusing flow or action in an early product. Yes, you will get a lot of false positives in this phase, and a number of irrelevant things will be pointed out that you've already fixed in an unreleased build, but if something in a primary flow or action is reported as a bug, it can give you focus.

COMMUNICATE UPDATES OFTEN

"Iterating design is hard," said Wells Riley, an experienced product designer who's currently at startup Envoy. "People don't want to change something that they worked so hard to make perfect. So I don't try to make things perfect. I try to make them good and let them get better over time."

This is part detaching yourself from what you've created, and part being open about what's changed. As we've seen over and over again, the process of creating a product is one steeped in persistent change. So communicate that. Make it obvious what's new. What's been struck. What's been reconfigured.

Humans are drawn to newness; there's a "thrill associated with a new possession."[*] By updating the team about exciting new developments once or twice a week, you'll maintain attention and that all-important feedback loop.

"I consider communication one of the biggest parts of my role—and this includes anything I find out about our concept or competition," said Ruby Anaya, currently director of social products at WeWork. "As soon as I find something that I think is impactful, I message my team to get their thoughts and perspective. I follow up with a more detailed analysis of what I've learned, but I love dropping quick bits of info to keep them in the loop of what people are thinking/doing. With every team I've worked with the first thing I do is set up an IM group (more often than not named some variation of the name 'Peons') where we keep in touch constantly about what we're working on and of course many, many cat GIFs."

---

[*] *http://www.acrwebsite.org/volumes/14483/volumes/v36/NA-36*

ADDRESS THE TOUGHEST FIRST

It's going to be tempting to focus on fixing the easy stuff—the font mismatches, the pixel misalignments, and the incorrect colors. But all of these things are secondary. Putting off the big worry-points means you'll have little time to make essential product course corrections down the road.

That's why fine-tuning and iterating on feedback is so important before the final polish goes into the product. Get the core right—be true to the story your product is telling—and *then* move forward.

Eventually, you'll reach a minimum level of quality that adequately solves your customer's pain. It won't be perfect, nor should it be. But it'll have enough polish that you can ship small improvements every week, learn from those releases, and be in a far better place than if you hadn't launched it at all.

TRUST IN THE RESEARCH

Feedback has a tendency to stir up even the most well-formed plans. If you get lost, refer back to the customer research you originally performed. Why are you building this product? What are the key pains you're obsessed with eliminating? Is what you're building the best vehicle to do this? Your primary research is the guiding compass for all of this effort. Don't forget the conclusions you drew from it at the beginning of the process.

All this focus on feedback has only been about your team. Let's talk next about gathering feedback from customers—both current and potential.

Customer Feedback

Products live and die at the hands of their customers. So why wouldn't you get a product in front of your customers as early as possible to gather their feedback?

But getting customer feedback is an entirely different animal than getting critiques from your team.

You have to find the right customers. And then you have to parse the feedback and act on it.

It's a tricky tightrope to walk, and you risk defeating the entire purpose of your initial research if you muddy the pond by letting your own bias creep into the feedback you receive.

Then again, you've done the research. And you also know how to build products. You're here because the research has given you an intuition. So how do you know when to make a bet and when to stay true to your analysis?

I'm glad you asked. So let's start with the *who*, and then we'll move to the *how*.

IDENTIFY THE RIGHT CUSTOMERS

You're either building a product with existing customers, or one that has no existing user base.

Existing customers

There are so many ways to slice up your existing customer base. Many of them will be wrong. In the case of asking for feedback on a new piece of your product, focusing on *every single customer* is a big mistake. Not only is it going to overwhelm you, but it's going to pull your focus away from areas that are relevant only to the portion of the product you're improving.

Would you ask a luggage handler at an airport to test new controls for an air traffic controller? Or, better yet, would you ask the entire airport staff to weigh in on the benefits or challenges of a new feature for people *pushing tin* (yes, I just referred to a terrible 90s movie)?

No. Because your results would be incredibly skewed. At best, they'd be ill-informed opinions, and at worst, you'd implement changes based upon completely biased experiences.

When it comes to your product, you can't treat your customers as existing on an equal playing field. Not every customer is as valuable as the next one. Some have experienced parts of your product that others haven't. Some pay you money. Some don't. Some are new; some are old. Some have just signed up and are incredibly active. Some are inactive, and might also be new.

My point here is that you need to match the customer set to the problem you're solving.

Are you building a new feature that allows media sharing? Great. You should be talking to people who've recently sent text messages and uploaded new profile photos.

Are you trying to enhance your signup process? Great. Find all the people who've just recently started the signup process—*especially* the ones that didn't complete the flow—and talk with them about their experience.

Are you trying to increase your product's revenue? Find your customers on the free plan that went to upgrade, but didn't. Then find the customers who've been paying for the most amount of time. What makes them different?

When he was at KISSmetrics, Hiten Shah, for example, gave existing choice customers a sense of context and comfort when looking at new features he released.

"Once a clickable prototype is done, we spend a lot of time doing usability testing, if you want to call it that, or early testing with actual users/customers on those flows to make sure that we are not missing anything," he said in our interview. "We like to get something that works, especially with the analytics tool at KISSmetrics, to a customer as fast as possible using their own data—because an analytics tool is really about your own data."

Shah stressed that gathering feedback from a limited set of existing customers can help, rather than hurt, the process of collecting feedback.

"Sometimes in the prototyping phase, there's more crap on the screen than when we actually release it for the first time for a lot of customers," he said. "The scope has to flex, and it has to be based as early on as possible on feedback from the customer. The earlier you can get the prototype in the customers' hands, the better off you are in most cases, in my experience."

Potential customers

What do you do if you're creating a product from scratch, and are either a startup or a company looking to expand into a new category?

One angle is to recruit potential customers from the research you've performed. But this is risky.

That's because the whole point of the intense, ethnographic research we examined in Chapter 2—called Sales Safari, and invented by Amy Hoy, remember?—is that *you shouldn't be asking random people what they think*. People don't know what they want. And, unless you're an expert at excluding bias from your questions, there's a high probability that you're going to do it wrong and end up like Donald on the show *Silicon Valley*, wandering around San Francisco and harassing people with crazy-sounding pitches like:

"Interested? Very interested? Or interested?"*

History is littered with thousands of corpses of technology startups that approached random people at Starbucks to ask them what they thought of their product.

Even Intuit, which was one of the first technology companies to take an ethnographically driven approach to product design, lost its way. The company risked being a one-product wonder, with all other efforts to expand into new categories looking like they'd be permanently relegated to "shelfware."

"[Scott] Cook reembraced a P&G fundamental—that new products should be based on actual customer behaviors, not on what customers *said* they wanted to do," recount the authors of the book *Inside Intuit*. "Many customers said that they should do a better job of retirement planning and told the company that they would purchase Intuit's product to do so. However, since customers by and large did no financial planning before Intuit's product came to the market, Intuit's product could not persuade them to start."†

Recruit potential customers by approaching them individually, or by openly inviting a set of customers to a private build.

The former—recruiting potential customers by approaching them individually with a prototype or barely functional version—is how Ryan Hoover learned what it'd take to make Product Hunt viable.

---

* *http://www.imdb.com/title/tt3557358/*

† Suzanne Taylor and Kathy Schroeder, *Inside Intuit: How the Makers of Quicken Beat Microsoft and Revolutionized an Entire Industry* (Boston: Harvard Business Review Press, 2003), 221.

Years of blogging, relationship building, and projects like Startup Edition have given me an audience and network of supporters. The term "startup" is deceiving. Successful companies don't start up overnight; they are founded upon years of experience and help from others that must be earned.[‡]

The individual approach can be really useful for highlighting problems with your pitch. Josh Elman of Greylock, Twitter, Facebook, LinkedIn, and Zazzle (whew!) describes this more in detail:

"When [your product] can't be succinctly described—or you tell it to other people and they completely don't get it and they tell it back some other crazy way—I think those are really the two that concern me," he said in our interview. "I think that's what's most important. You either can't describe it or when you describe it, people just go, 'Meh.' But even on that, if you really believe it's right, I'm OK with that as long as they aren't completely misunderstanding it. Because that just means you need to describe it better," he said.

The latter approach—openly inviting a set of customers from your community to a private build—is how Dropbox first launched (Figure 8-5).[§] This approach, however, requires a little more preparation. You'll need to have a rough pitch, a functioning registration and login system, and a way to distribute your logins or builds in a controlled fashion so others can't get in. Finally, you'll need a way to track product usage so you can monitor activity without biasing results.

[‡] *http://www.fastcolabs.com/3023152/open-company/the-wisdom-of-the-20-minute-startup*
[§] *http://techcrunch.com/2011/10/19/dropbox-minimal-viable-product*

FIGURE 8-5
A slide from an early
presentation by Drew
Houston.

What we learned

- Biggest risk: making something no one wants
- Not launching → painful, but not learning → fatal
- Put something in users hands (doesn't have to be code) and get real feedback ASAP
- Know where your target audience hangs out & speak to them in an authentic way

If you choose this method, keep releases tight and consistently ship iterations to show progress. Let the support emails and the usage patterns speak for themselves.

But analysis is an entirely different topic. So, how do you analyze customer feedback?

HOW TO ANALYZE CUSTOMER FEEDBACK

Analyzing customer feedback is really a version of Sales Safari at a different scale. We went through the specifics of this in Chapter 2—Sales Safari is "'net ethnography,' combined with some close reading and empathy," Amy Hoy said in our interview. "[It's] step-by-step empathizing with your customer to understand them."

Getting negative or contradictory feedback at this stage doesn't necessarily mean that you're on the wrong path or that you have to change everything. And just because someone does something or says something doesn't mean that it's worth listening to.

This process requires *close reading*, a study technique that's meant to uncover layers of meaning in text. When you close read, you're focusing on the way the person communicates, how they see the world, or how they argue a particular point.* We're doing this to understand

---

* *http://writingcenter.fas.harvard.edu/pages/how-do-close-reading*

what people want. That's because close reading, when used to understand an *audience*, uncovers a series of data points that will begin to form patterns.

"[People] get one data point or they get one potential client or customer, and they think, 'All right. This is it. I'm going to [make this product].' That's really a recipe for failure," Hoy said.

Remember, your potential customers have no allegiance to you. They don't know what you're capable of building. And they probably don't know how to identify their own pains. It's your job as a product designer to lead your team through that analysis and to extract the most relevant bits for your product's improvement.

For example, let's say that you're building a dating app. Early feedback shows that two interested parties have no problem showing mutual interest, but that's where the interaction stalls. The feedback is that people think that the profiles are fake—the people on the app seem too attractive and their bios aren't filled out.

There might be a couple of problems here.

Nobody knows how to make the first move, and a little help might be in order. And perhaps your early, potential customers aren't filling out their bios because it's too hard.

Notice how there are two possible problems, with a similar theme: pressure. People feel pressure to do something, and they don't quite know how to react.

Don't Squander Your Gains

You can get a *lot* of fresh research to sift through when you put a product in the hands of your colleagues, customers, and potential customers.

Don't squander it. Sweat equity is expendable, but real, raw, proprietary data isn't. Take the time to parse it, understand it, and interpret back into your product.

The biggest benefit of this process is that you don't end up building the wrong thing. While it's a grueling experience to interpret what current or potential customers are really trying to say, it's significantly *less* painful than building the wrong thing and launching to crickets.

"The only way to create good product is to fall in love with the problem and really internalize it and understand it," Jon Crawford, CEO and founder of ecommerce company Storenvy, said in our interview. "I would say the only way to create good product is to spend more time understanding the problem than creating the solution...most designers, they're so excited to solve the problem that it's really easy to skip over understanding the problem really well first. It's so exciting to solve the problem, [but] it's not very exciting to learn and understand the problem."

What *is* exciting are the benefits of getting customer input early. Assuming that you've interpreted your early Sales Safari data correctly, the benefits to your marketing and sales efforts can't be overstated.

You'll have access to testimonials, early success statistics, and possibly even evangelists before you launch. That means you can weave this into your product pages, sales pitches, and, if you're *really* lucky, have alpha customers selling *for you* before you launch.

Shareable Notes

- The Valley of Despair: we all know that feeling as product designers. We all have hit that moment where we think our product won't work, that nobody is going to use it. That's the fear taking hold—the fear that all of your research and work has been wrong.

- For any creative endeavor—including the act of building a product—the creative process is roughly the same. It's a stream of refinement before each release.

- Feedback levels up your product, much like a character does in a role-playing game. We make great strides early on as we're exploring broad concepts and nailing down what it is we're dealing with. Then, there's a long process of refinement, and, finally, as cumulative feedback rolls in, we shift the product into a state that's even more powerful than we imagined.

- Feedback can be tough. We, as product designers, throw ourselves into our work. So don't take negative feedback personally. Creative work naturally reflects the individual that created it, but that doesn't mean that any negativity is directed toward you personally.

- Team critiques can range from the Pixar-style "Braintrust" meetings, Wunderlist-like "Open Design Reviews," or internal beta tests.

- Customer feedback begins and ends with identifying the right customers for the type of feedback you need, getting feedback in a nonbiased manner, and analyzing it in the same way as you would Sales Safari data (found in Chapter 2).

Do This Now

- Get at least your prototypes done. And at least get them in front of your "Braintrust." They were aware of the research, and know the basis of the product you're trying to build.

- Don't take feedback personally. Creative work bleeds from our souls, but it doesn't mean that it's sacred just because we made it.

- Don't build the wrong thing. Take feedback seriously after you've parsed its meaning. This is your chance to course-correct if the overwhelming response is paltry and underwhelmed.

Interview: Ruby Anaya

Ruby Anaya is an experienced product executive. She's currently direc-
tor of product management at WeWork, and previously worked at Yahoo!,
Tomfoolery, and AOL.

How do you define and decide what you're building? Who's involved in this process?

Creative people who ask questions. When we're starting the definition process of a new product or feature, it usually involves a lot of what ifs, sketching, and joking around. The most effective teams I've worked on are ones where everyone feels a similar sense of ownership over the idea/problem at hand, so I try to capture everyone's perspective.

What do these discussions look like?

I'm a very visual person; I like to draw out solutions. Almost all product ideation discussions start with wireframing the main interaction flow(s), coupled with listing out open-ended questions that we encounter through the process. There's always a back-and-forth with examples from competitors or best practices, but I try to focus a lot of the initial stages more on instinct and aspiration. The discussion ends with ensuring that everyone agrees on and understands a value statement for the product to ensure that moving forward we're all working towards the same goal/understanding.

What's the takeaway from this meeting—a document? A plan? A calendar? How do you communicate this?

Action items—what can everyone do right now to make this happen, or, more specifically, what do we need to do next to test our idea? Our product plan is communicated with basic wireframes to kick off both a visual and technical foundation of our MVP and research (if available; if not, that's my next action item to bring to the team). This is followed by open-ended questions like who is our biggest competition, who is our target market, what's the history of this concept/product (if available), etc. I try to answer these questions and become an expert at whatever it is we're trying to accomplish.

What sort of competitive analysis do you and others perform? When researching competition, what are you looking to absorb? Product flows? UI conventions? What's done right or wrong?

All of the above. I try to immerse myself in any product or company that is in a similar space or trying to solve the same problem we are. I usually start with looking at flows on sites like UXarchive.com which I find super helpful to get an overview of how people are tackling the same problem we are. I just looked it up and I have 225 apps on my phone, many of which are in folders named "Design" or "Testing Out."

Do you use forums, app reviews, or customer "watering holes" to analyze the pain points and/or potential opportunities of customers? If so, what does that research look like?

I definitely look into app reviews and tech article comments reacting to any competition, but I also like to spend time asking the people around me (and myself) why they use one product over another, what drew them to it, why they talk about it, etc.

How do you communicate the pros and cons of what others are doing in the space to your team, if this is your role?

I consider communication one of the biggest parts of my role—and this includes anything I find out about our concept or competition. As soon as I find something that I think is impactful, I message my team to get their thoughts and perspective. I follow up with a more detailed analysis of what I've learned, but I love dropping quick bits of info to keep them in the loop of what people are thinking/doing. With every team I've worked with, the first thing I do is set up an IM group (more often than not named some variation of the name "Peons") where we keep in touch constantly about what we're working on and of course many, many cat gifs.

If there are no direct competitors to what you're building, what do you seek out for inspiration?

I seek out people who would be impacted by what we're building. Ask them questions, show them what we're working on, and find out as much as I can about them. Then I try to find common themes among them.

How do you identify edge cases, data requirements, and other potential challenges before you start building?

Edge cases and challenges are something I find best to work with our engineering team—I always start defining it, but I lean on them a lot for filling in gaps I might have missed. I think because they are so much closer to the inner workings of the product they have a much better sense of when something is going to be in an empty state or error.

Whether it's you doing the design or someone else, what does this give-and-take look like? How far do you go with your designs before prototyping?

I kick off the process with handing our design team initial wireframes where I try to show all possible states and a high-level flow of the main features of the product. I let them take it to the next level. Most of the time it's a frequent back-and-forth with feedback—and by "frequent" I mean as frequent as every hour or so. I love it when something I did inspired them to take it somewhere else, or vice versa. Like I said before, I'm really visual, and although I don't consider myself an artist by any means, I appreciate great design and fight for it.

How do you account for the different states in your product?

This is where I like to look at best practices and other products for inspiration. Onboarding is almost always one of the biggest challenges, but I appreciate how I've evolved at approaching it over the years. I remember when I first started working on building products I was actually quite paranoid about onboarding—in the sense that I wanted to make sure I covered every possibility and that everyone knew what they were getting themselves into. I think I was scared to mess something up. But as I've grown, I've learned to give people more credit for knowing what to do, and thinking about how I can both simplify the process and make it as familiar to the actual product itself.

For example—in a messaging app I worked on at my last startup (we were acquired before it launched), my concept for onboarding was to have it start off like you were messaging with the app to get your name and phone number. [It's as if the] input fields were [filled in] like you were just chatting.

For error states, I like to take advantage of blank or error states with something fun or visually interesting (sometimes I even throw a picture of my cat in there).

When do you know something is "good enough" to move onto the next phase? Do you test internally and "dog food" a product, or do you test with potential customers?

I do both—dog food and testing. I know something is good enough when it's not a job for me to use it, and when I see similar usage trends from our test cases. It's easy to fall in love with what you build even if it doesn't make sense or your timing is off—it's your baby. Being objective isn't easy, but when you take a step back and realize that if you're not objective/realistic you're potentially hurting yourself and your team, it comes more naturally.

What do you look out for when your product is launched? How do you gather feedback to know whether or not it's working?

Analyzing usage is key. Looking deep into how the people are using it IRL versus how our team uses it or our assumptions of how we think the market will use it. We look into who is using it—is it the market we designed it for? How often are they using it? Is it solving the problem we outlined, or perhaps something else? When are they using it? Where are they when they are using it? All these things you can't tell until you get it in the hands of others. And this is going to dictate next priorities—are you on the right track? Do you need to pivot? Do you need to rethink things entirely?

Take ownership of everything. You're the CEO of your product. You need to know how it works, what stage it's in, what issues are open, and what's next at all times. I recently was at a product off-site and our SVP Jeff Bonforte gave some great advice: always have a 10-page deck for your product. Whether you work at a big company like Yahoo! or a tiny startup, you need to be always ready to defend and own your ideas. Keep evolving on your deck as you learn more about the space or your target market.

Staying positive is something that I think is needed to keep momentum. If you're the go-to for the product vision and strategy and you're a bummer to be around, what does that say about the vision? Is something wrong with it? I think as a product manager part of my job is to be a representative of the product at all times—and that applies to both being prepared to present your product but also being able to represent the team building it.

What tools or skills are you actively trying to learn related to building products?

I just started taking an iOS class—coming from a nonengineering background, I'm trying to learn more about the development process. I also just started using Sketch to wireframe.

I'm also trying to get better at being a salesperson for my product. It's not something that has come that naturally to me, so I try to watch and learn from people that I think are good at it. And something I've learned regarding this is to not let people's doubtful questions get you down. A few years ago I had a VP ask me about a redesign I was doing. He asked, "What new features are you putting in?" My response was "None."

He questioned how we could "get away" with that. I think a lot of people might freak out and think "what new features can I get in there, too?" But instead I stood my ground—"this project is focused on redesigning our visual and structural hierarchy to make it a better and more familiar experience for our users, as well as create better ad opportunities. I don't want to overwhelm people with new functionality at this stage." And he was OK with that. Stick by your guns and don't be afraid to say, "I didn't think of that" if you didn't. Just go and take a note to think about it later. Or if you did and decided it wasn't the right time, stick to it. There's always the possibility that we'll make mistakes, but there will be regardless of whether you stick to your ideas or just blindly follow people above you. At least they'll be your mistakes/wins to take credit for, not someone else's.

How do you stay creatively inspired?

Constantly playing with new products and talking about them. I think Ryan Hoover's Product Hunt is so awesome for this—it's great to see a community around new ideas. I also love living here in the Valley. I know a lot of people complain about how all everyone talks about is tech, but I love it. I love what I do and I love talking about it and hearing how other people solve problems. I think it's a tribute to the fact that the tech community really enjoys their professions that we talk about it all the time, and I appreciate that. Talking about what you like about a product or a feature you would do differently helps me stay inspired with solving my own product problems or coming up with new ideas.

9

Shipping Is an Art—and a Science

The Invention Versus the Manufactured Article

It's traditional to work until someone just takes it away from you.
Films are not released. They escape.

—BEN BURTT, SOUND DESIGNER, FILM EDITOR, AND
DIRECTOR FOR THE *STAR WARS* FILMS[*]

Thomas Edison was under the gun.

It was 1882. He was years removed from the dazzling display of light he'd exhibited to the public on New Year's Eve in 1880 when he'd opened the gates to his secretive Menlo Park lab. It was the first time that the world had seen the power of electric light in one place. Edison even went as far to invent Christmas lights for the occasion.[†]

About 3,000 unsuspecting, perhaps skeptical, pilgrims had arrived at night onto the train platform of sleepy Menlo Park. What they saw rivaled anything they could see even in Manhattan, which was 20 miles away: the village was bathed with the non-flickering light of electric bulbs.[‡]

---

[*] *https://www.youtube.com/watch?v=FM_V9dqtBug*
[†] Neil Baldwin, *Edison: Inventing the Century* (New York: Hyperion, 1995).
[‡] *http://www.pbs.org/wgbh/americanexperience/features/introduction/light-introduction/*

The crowd's energy—no pun intended—must have rubbed off on him. Because Edison then publicly promised to bring the technology to an urban site: New York's Pearl Street. The road to bringing electricity out of the labs was wrought with pitfalls. Not only did he have to recreate what he did in a lab in the real world, but he and his team had to design all of the components of an electrical system (switches, sockets, generators, etc.), and had to find a proper site while lining up early customers. Wow.*

On top of that, Edison didn't have a pricing model worked out yet. So he sent survey teams into the field to conduct market research. What were people paying for gas? What would they be willing to pay for electricity and equipment?

Despite his promises, Edison wasn't producing. Critics were spreading. Was this all vaporware?

> There's a wide difference between completing an invention and putting the manufactured article on the market...It was years after photography was invented before the first photograph was taken; years after the steamboat and telegraph were invented before they were actually set going.†

It's not that different for digital products. You create the prototypes, design the mockups, and get something sort of working. You fake out user testers with just enough of the experience intact that they think it's real. You get feedback, gather critiques, and iterate until the fidelity increases.

Making the leap from these iterations and onto something that can support real customers and real data is a huge one. And while the stakes might not be quite as high as they were for Edison when it comes to the product you're launching (creating a power grid is, you know, kind of a big deal), it's still your life we're talking about here. If you've taken the time to create a product that you know will improve the life of the person using it, then it's worth taking the time to make sure your product's ready to get out in the wild.

But what defines "ready"? And if it's ready, how do you get it out into the world?

---

* James Tobin, *Great Projects: The Epic Story of the Building of America, from the Taming of the Mississippi to the Invention of the Internet* (New York: Free Press, 2001).

† *http://www.history.com/topics/inventions/thomas-edison*

It's Ready When It's Ready

The simple answer is...when it's ready.

I'm not trying to be smug. And no, I'm not trying to create a phrase that you'll tweet to your billion followers with two clicks.

The simple fact is that launching a product has become a buzzword.

Burn the ships.

F* it. Ship it.

Stay focused and keep shipping.

And it's not that these motivations aren't rooted in a good place. A product in motion—refining and learning about its customers—is a product that's evolving and, potentially, improving.

But shipping for the sake of shipping helps nobody. And it's become an obsession in our insular culture of technology. The phenomenon is leading to lots of bad work—with individuals in our community being more proud of how quickly they produced something than of how effective their product is at what it set out to do.

I love how Cat Noone, an experienced entrepreneur and product designer, puts this:

> *It's called "ship," not "shit."*

She continues:

> *It's all about shipping.*
>
> *Except it's not. Don't get me wrong, I'm an advocate for getting a product out there and continually iterating based on user testing, gut feeling, feedback, etc. There are going to be bugs, things are going to flat out break sometimes, some things might not look as visually appealing—and that's okay. However, there is a fine line between shipping for the sake of putting anything out there and shipping a product that is of quality.*
>
> *It is forgotten all too easily that there is a responsibility that comes with pushing a product out into the world that individuals will use. It is your job to ensure the problem is solved.‡*

---

‡ *http://blog.heyimcat.com/its-called-ship-not-shit/*

In my experience, organizations overly focused on shipping for the sake of shipping are doing so because they don't know what else to do. They don't know what their customers need. They may not even know who their customers are.

Sadly, shipping for the sake of shipping won't change that.

So if that's where you are, take a step back. "Don't mistake speed for precocity: the world doesn't need wrong answers in record time," as Cennydd Bowles, former design manager at Twitter, wrote. Get the right answers.

And that's even what Facebook realized. In 2014, Mark Zuckerberg made a public declaration that they were changing their famous "move fast and break things" philosophy—the one they'd emblazoned on walls and in their IPO prospectus.

"In the past we've done more stuff to just ship things quickly and see what happens in the market," Brian Boland of Facebook clarified. "Now, instead of just throwing something out there, we're making sure that we're getting it right first." The time and effort it took to repaint the walls and shred the IPO prospectus has been more than made up for with the rise in their stock price.

While we're talking about tech giants, we might as well talk about Apple. From the outside, it looks like Tim Cook and Jony Ive only ship products when they're "magical" enough. After all, they've got more cash on hand than the U.S. Treasury has on hand. So who needs deadlines with friends like that?

But that's actually not the case. "Not only does the company set internal deadlines, it also creates deadlines for deadlines that have their own deadlines," wrote former Apple Senior Designer Mark Kawano (now CEO of photo storage company Storehouse). "Every aspect of the company's production cycle, from conception to ship date, is calculated."[*]

But wait a minute, you faceless author, you're probably thinking. You just said that you should ship a product when it's ready. You're not making sense.

Well, how about this plot twist? Kawano continues:

---

[*] *http://www.inc.com/mark-kawano/lessons-from-my-time-at-apple-ship-something-you-re-proud-of.html*

But—and this is a big "but"—what makes Apple different is that it is a company that is willing to move those deadlines. If a product in development isn't ready to be released, the deadline is pushed back. If an idea isn't perfect, or isn't considered truly magical and delightful internally, it's held back, revised, and the product given an entirely new launch date.

Now, all magical fairy dust aside, we can learn from these examples. Shipping alone is not the end goal. Shipping alone will not make your product great.

Shipping is about creating a "minimum lovable product." Coined by Noone, this term encompasses the struggles we face as product designers creating pixels—a product that solves a problem, but also creates an emotional connection and leaves an impact on the person who used it.

She writes:

So what if we started pushing "Minimum Lovable Products" into the world? The lowest form that is capable of being loved, accepted and a problem solver; with an understanding that it is not flawless.

This doesn't mean monolithic product releases, or taking years to release something until it's just right. Release something every day if you want.

But as Ben Burtt, the famous sound designer of the *Star Wars* films, said of the filmmaking process: "Films aren't released, they escape."

A focus on your audience's problems. Self-imposed deadlines. And a threshold for quality. These are natural forcing functions that push you to create and iterate until the product just has to escape when it's ready. That's why the "minimum lovable product" rocks.

Being "Chief of Everything"

Shipping your product means you take ownership of everything. You're the "COE" of your product. You need to know how it works, what stage it's in, what issues are open, and what's next at all times. Your responsibility doesn't end once the product is ready to ship or has shipped.

Everybody tracks what they need to do differently. Trello boards. Post-it notes. Wikis. It doesn't matter which tools you use. Just be clear with your team. Teach them the quality you expect. Make sure they understand your expectations. And ensure that everybody knows what they should be doing.

Cat Noone revealed to me in our interview that she and her cofounder use shared Wunderlist to-do lists to track everything the small startup needs to accomplish for a launch (Figure 9-1).

FIGURE 9-1

Cat Noone uses shared Wunderlist to-do lists to track loose tasks with her team in real time.

"For our product roadmap (and our process style in general) the management is all done here," Noone said. "Compared to many others, it's very loose. Don't get me wrong, we have documents for features, an understanding of what needs to be done for it, etc. But we don't over-manage things.

"We've found that often, less process is a better process. You'll see we use hashtags to know what each task item is for or pertaining to in each folder, who is responsible for the task, etc. Wunderlist is super great for this, because no matter how many people are on a project, there should always be one individual responsible for seeing the project through from start to launch."

Katelyn Friedson, who designed mobile products at publicly traded Care.com, used a combination of JIRA user stories and shared Google Docs. The JIRA ticket is the piece that can be tracked by all parties involved on its status (Figure 9-2), and the ticket has an embedded link to the Google Doc with exactly how the feature should work (Figure 9-3).

FIGURE 9-2

Katelyn Friedson used a combination of JIRA and Google Docs when launching products at Care.com.

FIGURE 9-3

Friedson uses the
linked Google Doc to
dive deeply into key
user flows.

"I've used JIRA for writing user stories (usually each [JIRA item] can be a paragraph or a few bullets long) which has been best for tracking," Friedson said. "But I've also used a Google Doc in combination with JIRA, which I like best. It gives you real-time collaboration so that if something in your original requirements goes stale, you can update it and make a comment. But it also allows you and your dev team to track various tasks a user can complete/things they can do."

Ruby Anaya, who's built products for WeWork and Yahoo!, carries around an interesting document with her at all times: a 10-page deck for her product, updated and at the ready.

"Whether you work at a big company like Yahoo! or a tiny startup, you need to be always ready to defend and own your ideas," she said in our interview. "Keep evolving on your deck as you learn more about the space or your target market."

But what about preparing your team for what's to come? Predicting press questions, honing sales pitches, getting assets and collateral in place? Finalizing landing-page pitch copy or product pricing? Tweaking the product's launch video?

All of this rests on you—even if marketing or sales or engineering has their opinions, they're going to be looking to you for guidance.

"I think you just have to have the energy to get in there and fix [things] yourself," said Graham Jenkin in our interview. He builds products at AngelList, an online platform for startups to raise money and recruit talent. "It just takes time, it takes energy, but if you want the product to be at the level of quality that you feel is appropriate, then you have to put in that time. It's just hard work. I don't think there's any way around it."

So once it's out, and once you've worked off the celebration—which, you *definitely* should do, by the way—what do you track? Consider? Analyze?

Timoni West and Kyle Bragger—who created products for Foursquare, Flickr, and Elepath—independently identified their secret to a successful launch: monitoring customer support.

Whether it's you answering the emails post-launch, or your expert team, or a combination of the two, make sure you're at least monitoring the channels.

Yes, it's unglamorous and time-consuming. But it's the fastest, most direct conduit into the minds of your customers after you ship. And put yourself in their shoes: how cool would it be to talk with the person that made the feature or product they're using?

Even better, customer support traffic can identify what's not working and what's confusing. It identifies both technical and product problems.

"Customer support, by the way, is *the most important* job at any company," says Timoni West. "I've seen so many tiny apps—ones you think would be out of business—surviving and thriving because their customer base knows they can depend on customer support. On the flip side, if I tweet at a company with a complaint and get ignored, I know they saw it and have chosen to ignore me: bad news."

Bragger agrees:

> As a user I like nothing more than hearing, "Hey, I'm so and so, I actually worked on this feature. Tell me about what's going on." I think it's obvious that there's more of a connection and more an overt level of care when it's the person who created the thing. At least, I want to make sure that something I built is working. So I think it's super healthy when people who built the stuff have to support it. It seems almost natural.

There's a catch, though—you're going to experience the heat. We're talking about human beings, after all.

At Care.com, Friedson monitored customer feedback forums, App Store ratings and reviews, call center activity, and more. She learned quickly that one has to "resist the urge to panic or rapidly change things in response," she said in our interview.

> *Passions flare in the beginning. But if you ride out this initial 24- to 48-hour period, things will usually settle down. Most people respond before they've really dug in and used whatever you've added (or gotten along with what you've removed). So sit back, take it all in, and don't make a move until some time has passed. Then you'll be able to offer a more reasoned response. Also, remember that negative reactions are almost always louder and more passionate than positive ones. In fact, you may only hear negative voices even when the majority of your base is happy about a change. Make sure you don't foolishly backpedal on necessary, but controversial, decisions.*

What fascinates me about this trait is that it supports one of my core beliefs about products: they start and end with observation of your audience. Customer support posts and emails are a gold mine for this.

It's Not Over Yet

This is technology. We work in pixels and hardware. The chances of you hitting a grand slam the first time are slim, and even if you did—well, they're still pixels. They're going to evolve and change over time.

Shipping is only one step on a very long road. So keep observing your audience. Keep doing the research. Keep focusing on them, and you'll never be at a loss for what to do again. Armed with this knowledge, you won't fear whether you're doing the right thing.

A lot of people will want you to fail: competitors, enemies, also-rans. To paraphrase a quote from the AMC show *Halt and Catch Fire*, that's because you're the future. And there's nothing scarier than that

Wow. You've read this far? That means that by now, you've been reading my drivel for way too long. So, in the spirit of quoting TV shows, I'm going to leave you with this one from *The West Wing*:

> *What's next?*

Interview: Josh Elman

Josh Elman is an experienced product leader focused on disruptive products that change the way people interact and communicate. He's led product teams at Twitter, Facebook, LinkedIn, and Zazzle. Currently, he's a partner at venture capital firm Greylock.

Can you identify some common DNA in each of your experiences [Facebook, LinkedIn, Twitter, Zazzle] that produced such great results?

Yeah, the first thing I want to say here is, at some point who knows if it was causation or correlation. I feel super lucky. Super lucky to have gotten all the opportunities I did. And just got to see such amazing decisions. I think there were three things that really have separated all the companies I've been at, the ones that I didn't go to, or that friends went to, or that I met along the way and didn't consider going to.

The first one is, they really had a vision for how the world could be different if the company was successful. For whatever reason, it's not how can the company be successful, how can the product be successful. But really, this theory that the world could be different if this company is successful. But it was really powerful. At RealNetworks it was audio and video over the Internet. Imagine when all audio and video is delivered over IP. We're starting to live in that world. It's incredible what you can do with YouTube and Netflix and video on demand.

The second was, when I joined LinkedIn, Reid [Hoffman] said, "if we can connect all the professionals with the people that they know, you'll change the way you get a job and information on people because it'll all be indexed in a way that it's very hard to find person-to-person right now." When I joined Zazzle, it was the same thing. It was, can you imagine a world where anything we want to buy we can just order on demand and it gets made within 24 hours for us? And I can just keep going. Facebook and Twitter are probably more obvious now in retrospect.

But those were all these big missions and they had a vision for how the world would be different. And all these companies didn't just have a vision for how the world would be different, they had a stepwise way in which we were going to tiptoe our way there. Realizing that you weren't going to get that world different overnight by just making your product and getting everyone to do it, but that it was going to take a little while.

And [each company] had lots of milestones and believed in [their vision]. At LinkedIn, we knew the only way we could have all these jobs be different was if we got the network connected. At Zazzle, we knew the only way we're going to get everybody buying and selling this way is if we start by getting a couple big brands and convince people that products like stamps, which you could never imagine ordering custom, you could order custom. So Zazzle invested a lot in real postage stamps that were custom. Each one of these is, do these little small things that add up to the big thing.

The third piece is all the products were simple and the products were not perfect. People often try to get perfection, but products that connect people are always a little bit messy, and you're better off doing the best you can to get a few people in on it. And evolve it over time instead of, "it must be the product that matches this big vision or I'm not going to do it."

So I think those three: having this vision of how the world looks different, understanding just the first baby steps that you need to make so that if you get that right then you get the right to do your next ones and the next ones, and then the third being keeping it simple and getting it out and learning, and accepting it's a little bit messy, were a huge impact. That's very different than Apple, but by all means Apple runs as a very different company than the rest of us, and those startups shouldn't compare themselves to Apple today because that's just impossible.

So I like how you publicly say that you know how to balance the tradeoffs of "getting it perfect versus getting it out the door." Are there any principles there that you've kept in mind over the years? I know it's very contextual.

I haven't thought of that phrase in a while. I think it's on my LinkedIn or something. That's great. The tradeoffs are fundamentally understanding the problem that you want to solve at this time, with this feature, for this set of users. And really helping the team get to the point where we can decide whether what we're going to deliver will actually help our users get the problem they face done.

It's not [solving] the bigger problems we all want to solve with the product to make it perfect, but if we get this out, will this actually help solve the things that we want to get done now? And that's the fundamental challenge and opportunity here. I think a lot of people miss that. A lot of people try to get everything they want to get done, done, and not just—is this good enough to solve the problem? Because if it is, let's get it out.

Where does the identification of an opportunity start?

I think it starts anywhere within a company. But if you end up with a team that has resources, the thing that a product development team can do that other teams in the company can't do is actually build features and ship them to users. A marketing team can't do that. They don't have engineers. They can do a lot of interesting things with money and campaigns and design and everything else, but they can't build a product and ship it to your users. And so that's what a productive development team is for. You call it opportunity, I call it a problem. You basically say, our company would be better if we had more people spending money, more people using the product every day— whatever the big company goal is—more people talking about the product this way instead of that way.

Whatever the company goal is—and then you go, OK, give them what we have now; what's the reason why we don't have more of that? Or what is the problem that more users would like solved that if we solved it, we'd make more money or get more usage, or whatever? And then it's simply a matter of, what are the solutions to that problem that the team owns? Not the product manager and not the marketing person, but actually the whole team collectively owns. What are the solutions to the problems we've iden- tified? Problem identification ends up being somewhat company-driven, so I don't want to call it top-down, but at the end of the day the product man- ager, the GM, the CEO really owns the "this is the problem that I think it's really important that we go solve."

Then the product team's job is to go, "what's the best solution for the prob- lem?" And collectively they need to come up with it. I use this phrase talking about product management—I have a blog post I need to do on it*—that the phrase for the product manager is, *help your team shift to the right product for your users*. It's *help* your team, not *guide* your team, define what your team does, write this package.

Help your team however you can. Ship, because you've got to ship it. If you don't ship it, you're not actually doing your job as product manager.

---

* *https://medium.com/@joshelman/a-product-managers-job-63c09a43d0ec*

The *right product* means you've identified the right problem and you're actually solving it in a way that you can measure and show that you're helping it. And *to your users* means you understand your users and you've it scoped enough that you know who you're building it for and what you're going to solve. And you're actually going to measure that you've solved it. And so I use that phrase because at the end of the day, once you guys have identified the problem, the team's job is to go figure out what the right solutions are collectively and ship it.

How do your keep your team focused on the right thing?

Well, look, the first thing is you have to trust your team. I think that sounds obvious, but it's much harder in practice. I think a lot of structures and processes are built on the fact that there isn't innate trust. So that's one issue. The second issue—once you do [trust your team], then, it's really, get your team's help in how to solve the problem. The team knows what they can build. The team knows how it can be developed. The designers know what kinds of things are designable and natural in the product and what kinds of things are not. All of this matters.

So what I used to do was—well, if we know their problem, and there wasn't really a consensus for what the problem was—but I tried to do an open brainstorm with the team on what thing we were going to go build. How are we going to try to best address this? What's the number one thing we can do to convert more users to be active? Or to get more users in the system? And I had ideas from my experience, and lots of people had ideas from their intuition. And so we'd debate it and vote. And I'd trust the team to vote. And if the team voted that this thing seemed like the best way to go solve the problem, you've got to trust the collective—it's the group that's going to go build it anyway. And then you go build it together.

And look, not everyone's going to agree, but if everybody sees a public, open vote and debate, and you have to be open and honest about that, then you have a chance to actually say, "OK, we all picked this. Are we aligned? Now let's go crank on it." And then your job is to help your team actually deliver on that thing that we all decided on, but you've already gotten some kind of consensus. So I really think the debate and vote prioritized together is a really important thing.

How did you manage the process of the product getting built? How do you make sure the product feels right?

Ultimately, great designers and great engineers are going to have that *feel* just as much as I will. So my job is to be a champion. The key thing that I focus on is the story. Making sure we had a consistent name—every little feature we did I'd try to give some name. Whether it was like, "Email Retention Letter" or "Welcome Back Letter" or "New User Flow 3." It can be dumb names like that or it can be really catchy like, "WTF" or "Who to Follow," which we built at Twitter—that's our user suggestions. We always try to come up with a scope that defines the feature and then a story.

And sometimes it's written down. It should have been written down more— I often did it more *ad hoc*—but it's like, "Hey! This is the story of why we're building this feature, what we expect users to be able to do differently when it's there, and the impact we expect to have on their usage of the product and the overall business." And you tell that story enough that you hold the feature that gets built to that story. Sometimes you build it in a way that it doesn't actually feel right to the story. Sometimes you build it in a way where everybody's like, "Oh, now I understand the story, or that doesn't feel like the right story." But you're trying to always hold yourself to that. I think a lot of people miss how important story is to everything we're doing. Because once I can tell the story of what I want to do with the product, everything else will spin out from there.

What makes you step back and makes you think that you're building the wrong thing?

I think number one is when it can't be succinctly described. Or you tell it to other people and they completely don't get it and they tell it back some other crazy way. I think those are really the two that concern me. I think that's what's most important. You either can't describe it or you describe it, and people just go, "Meh." But even on that, if you really believe it's right, I'm OK with that as long as they aren't completely misunderstanding it.

Because that just means you need to describe it better. The third one is the team starts building it and everybody's like, "This sucks." You trust the resonance of the team. But sometimes you've got to fight through that because people are just bogged down because it's harder than they thought or whatever. But if you still think it's right, you still think it's right.

So when a product's about to launch, about to ship, is it the product team who is writing the marketing copy, the materials? Are they talking to a product marketer about this stuff? How do you make sure the product is well publicized in the right way?

It all comes back to that story. If you've written a good story and people in the company understand the story, why it matters, etc., then you have a shot at it being the right story that goes out to the market. If you haven't done a good job setting up that story, then you're screwed.

This interview has been edited for length, and you're missing out on thousands of words of insights. To read the interview in its entirety, go to http:// scotthurff.com/dppl/interviews.

Interview: Cat Noone

Cat Noone is an experienced product designer. She's currently building Iris, an app that notifies loved ones if you're in an emergency.

How do you define and decide what you're building? Who's involved in this process?

Myself, cofounder, and our users. They play the biggest role in what gets built next. We have a very base-level product roadmap that we want to achieve, things that need to be built, and others we take from our users that we didn't think of before.

How do you identify and solve problems?

From the very beginning, we spent a lot of time educating and submerging ourselves in the world of writers and self-publishing. You need to be an expert in your field, no matter what it is. If it's messaging, you need to know the ins and outs of communication, for productivity, how people tick—personally and professionally.

What does this discussion (or series of discussions) look like?

For us, it's usually as soon as something pops into our head. We have a list in Wunderlist for "Future Ideas" where we put everything as soon as we think of it and then it's discussed. Either right then and there, or at a later period of time when we have our meeting(s).

We discuss all of the different pros and cons it will play on our users, the platform, and company. Sometimes one of us is really psyched about something, but after discussing it, we realize something we didn't before, and it's obvious that it cannot and should not be built because it will waste time and/or resources.

What's the takeaway from this meeting—a document? A plan? A calendar? How do you communicate this?

There's almost always documentation of sorts on it and we plug it into our product roadmap document. We document when, approximately, each feature is due to be released. This is discussed right then and there upon the decision that we will move forward with a feature. We find where it fits best in the roadmap and go from there. Obviously, this is not set in stone, as things change and have to shift, but we're on track for the most part. [Because things change], we definitely don't plug anything into the calendar. The only thing that has due dates on it is GitHub, because you have to pick one for a milestone and Wunderlist just to keep us on track with deadlines.

Do you create anything from this meeting to use as a foundation to prevent design creep, keep focused, etc.?

We do our best to stay on track and keep focused on what our users are talking to us about and what is necessary from a product and business standpoint. What it comes down to is this: if it's not on the roadmap, but something a lot of people are asking for, we have a discussion about whether it can and should wait. Or, if we should shift resources to that feature for a moment in time.

What sort of competitive analysis do you and others perform? When researching competition, what are you looking to absorb? Product flows? UI conventions? What's done right or wrong?

It's a pretty big cocktail of everything possible that we can absorb. What we look at first and foremost is user experience. How easy is it to use this product and achieve the goal compared to our product? We look at everything from their experience and visual design to their monetization strategy.

Ultimately, in the end, it's all packaged into the user experience and we try to see where we compare to them on that front.

Do you use forums, app reviews, or customer "watering holes" to analyze the pain points and/or potential opportunities of customers? If so, what does that research look like?

We seek inspiration from a variety of companies, honestly. Whoever is kicking ass when providing a fantastic user experience. Oftentimes, it's not even a company in our space. We look and see how other companies are handling support, monetization, communication, marketing, and more. It all plays a role and you limit yourself a lot if you limit where you seek inspiration. There's a lot to learn from all spaces that can be applied to your own.

What tools or skills are you actively trying to learn related to building products?

When I have the time, I'm making a big effort to learn how to become more proficient in code and also with the use of tools like Origami, Framer.js, and more for prototyping. You can save a lot of development time if the iteration of prototypes is laid out well from the beginning.

It's always great to have people on a team that can hop into another person's place in case of an emergency, which is why I'm a big proponent of having designers who can work cross-platform instead of focusing solely on one.

How do you stay creatively inspired?

I was asked this question in a *Smashing Magazine* interview and thoroughly surprised myself when I realized how little creativity comes from the digital world. I make it a point to step away from the computer often for the creative inspiration, and it also helps with avoiding burnout so you kill two birds with one stone. Don't get me wrong, I'm definitely inspired by many designers out there and love checking out their work, but I turn to traveling—exploring the art, food, and lifestyle of different cultures—along with the everyday things to really "wow" me and get my creative juices flowing.

[*Appendix*]

Further Reading

There were many more citations and examples I would have loved to quote from, but, alas, there are simply too many good books about products and creativity. Here's a list of further reading that'll keep you creative and, ultimately, curious.

The Elements of User Onboarding (*https://www.useronboard.com/training/*) by Samuel Hulick

> The best (and only) book I've read about how to increase user adoption.

Masters of Doom (*http://amzn.to/1JlB5QO*) by David Kushner

> The story of John Carmack and John Romero, the "Lennon and McCartney of video games." It's the story of ID software and the creation of *Wolfenstein*, *Doom*, and *Quake*.

Good to Great (*http://amzn.to/1IVAVfM*) by Jim Collins

> The classic study of how companies build for long-term success. While some of the methods have been criticized over the years, it's a good thought exercise.

The Making of Star Wars: The Definitive Story Behind the Original Film (*http://amzn.to/1K1giAV*) by J.W. Rinzler

> One of the best explorations of the creative process I've ever seen. And, if you're a *Star Wars* fan, this is a must-own. You'll see how Lucas evolved the story that most of us can recite in our sleep, and how Ralph McQuarrie's conceptual art influenced the story (and vice versa).

The Art of Star Wars, Episode IV: A New Hope (*http://amzn.to/1IVE0fV*) by Carol Titleman

> Explore the concept art for the original *Star Wars* from Ralph McQuarrie, arguably one of the greatest conceptual artists of all time. See how the art influenced the story, and how designs evolved over time.

Droidmaker: George Lucas and the Digital Revolution (*http://amzn. to/1IVB5nn*) by Michael Rubin

> Did you know that George Lucas made computer, digital video editing, and digital sound history? Did you know that George Lucas created Pixar and sold it to Steve Jobs? There's tons of great insider info in this book, and advice on how you can turn research into the practicalities of product.

The Humane Interface (*http://amzn.to/1IVBiqD*) by Jef Raskin

> A classic from the creator of the Macintosh project at Apple.

Cadence & Slang (*http://amzn.com/0615341713*) by Nick Disabato

> An excellent primer on the intricacies of interaction design.

Rumsfeld's Rules (*http://amzn.to/1K1fDPP*) by Donald Rumsfeld

> This controversial yet highly accomplished figure has seen the halls of Congress, the Department of Defense, the White House, and two *Fortune* 500 companies as CEO. Take a look at his worldview and his work ethic through the rules he created over the years. They began as index cards in a shoebox, and circulated through Washington, DC, after they were typed up. Read by presidents, business executives, and diplomats all over the world.

Jony Ive: The Genius Behind Apple's Greatest Products (*http://amzn. to/1K1fOuu*) by Leander Kahney

> It's about Jony Ive. Enough said.

Inside Apple: How America's Most Admired—and Secretive Company—Really Works (*http://amzn.to/1IVC72O*) by Adam Lashinsky

> I take everything with a grain of salt about how "Apple really works," but there are some gems in here.

Becoming Steve Jobs: The Evolution of a Reckless Upstart into a Visionary Leader (*http://amzn.to/1K1g10O*) by Brent Schlender

> Better than the Walter Isaacson book.

Something Really New: Three Simple Steps to Creating Truly Innovative Products (*http://amzn.to/1K1g2lx*) by Denis J. Hauptly

What's a product *really* used for? Blew my mind the first time I read it.

Wabi-Sabi: for Artists, Designers, Poets & Philosophers (*http://amzn. to/1K1g6lk*) by Leonard Koren

Rumored to be a beloved tome inside Apple's walls. There's nothing like it—teaching that the antithesis of what designers think is beauty is actually beauty. Nothing is perfect.

Less and More: The Design Ethos of Dieter Rams (*http://amzn.to/1K-1gd0b*) by Klaus Klemp

I believe it's out of print, but you can still snag some copies from third-party sellers. This is a book that has an insane amount of detail about how Dieter Rams worked and approached product challenges.

Designing Visual Interfaces (*http://amzn.to/1IVCVop*) by Kevin Mullet and Darrel Sano

A classic. One of the best books on the principles of visual design. Out of print, but you can find some copies here and there.

Creating Customer Evangelists: How Loyal Customers Become a Volunteer Sales Force (*http://amzn.to/1IVDwX0*) by Jackie Huba and Ben McConnell

How to make customers so happy that they sell your product for you. A legendary book.

The Hero with a Thousand Faces (*http://amzn.to/1JlCbMs*) by Joseph Campbell

The ultimate study in comparative mythology, and a lesson in storytelling. A huge hit since its release in 1949, inspiring storytellers around the world since then. A must for those of us creating experiences.

Flow: The Psychology of Optimal Experience (*http://amzn.to/1IVDMW2*) by Mihaly Csikszentmihalyi

The famous definition of the "optimal experience" and what's required for humans to enter a unique state of consciousness. Product flow = flow.

Julius Shulman: Modernism Rediscovered (*http://amzn.to/1TLlMRb*) by Pierluigi Serraino

He's one of the greatest photographers of architectural design from the '50s and '60s of the mid-century buildings that we'll forever recognize. Go back in time to the height of California Modernism.

[Index]

[*About the Author*]

Scott Hurff is a product designer and author. He started his first company while in college, and became the youngest entrepreneur-in-residence at Kodiak Venture Partners in Boston. Scott has led product design for products used by millions of users in a variety of areas, including video sharing, entertainment, and consumer mobile apps.

Scott teaches designers how to bring their designs to life and writes about what makes products great at *scotthurff.com*. His work has appeared in a variety of publications, including Die Zeit, Quartz, Gizmodo, Business Insider, and Gamasutra.

Have it your way.

Get even more for your money.

Join the O'Reilly Community, and register the O'Reilly books you own. It's free, and you'll get:

- $4.99 ebook upgrade offer
- 40% upgrade offer on O'Reilly print books
- Membership discounts on books and events
- Free lifetime updates to ebooks and videos
- Multiple ebook formats, DRM FREE
- Participation in the O'Reilly community
- Newsletters
- Account management
- 100% Satisfaction Guarantee

Signing up is easy:

1. Go to: oreilly.com/go/register
2. Create an O'Reilly login.
3. Provide your address.
4. Register your books.

Note: English-language books only

To order books online:
oreilly.com/store

For questions about products or an order:
orders@oreilly.com

To sign up to get topic-specific email announcements and/or news about upcoming books, conferences, special offers, and new technologies:
elists@oreilly.com

For technical questions about book content:
booktech@oreilly.com

To submit new book proposals to our editors:
proposals@oreilly.com

O'Reilly books are available in multiple DRM-free ebook formats. For more information:
oreilly.com/ebooks

CPSIA information can be obtained at www.ICGtesting.com
Printed in the USA
BVOW10s1704160116

433122BV00001B/1/P

9 781491 923672